Implementing and Developing Cloud Computing Applications

Implementing and Developing Cloud Computing Applications

DAVID E.Y. SARNA

CRC Press
Taylor & Francis Group
Boca Raton   London   New York

CRC Press is an imprint of the
Taylor & Francis Group, an **informa** business

AN AUERBACH BOOK

Auerbach Publications
Taylor & Francis Group
6000 Broken Sound Parkway NW, Suite 300
Boca Raton, FL 33487-2742

© 2011 by Taylor and Francis Group, LLC
Auerbach Publications is an imprint of Taylor & Francis Group, an Informa business

No claim to original U.S. Government works

Printed in the United States of America on acid-free paper
10 9 8 7 6 5 4 3 2 1

International Standard Book Number: 978-1-4398-3082-6 (Hardback)

Library of Congress Cataloging-in-Publication Data

Sarna, David E. Y.
    Implementing and developing cloud computing applications / by David E.Y. Sarna.
        p. cm.
    Summary: "Major enterprises and small start-ups are beginning to embrace cloud computing for the scalability and reliability that cloud vendors can provide. This book demonstrates how to implement robust and highly scalable cloud computing applications. Filled with comparative charts and decision trees to help navigate the many implementation alternatives, the author describes the major available commercial offerings and guides readers in choosing the best combination of platform, tools, and services for a small, growing start-up or an established enterprise. Aimed at software developers and their managers, the text details cloud development environments, lifecycles, and project management"-- Provided by publisher.
    Includes bibliographical references and index.
    ISBN 978-1-4398-3082-6 (hardback)
    1. Cloud computing. 2. Business--Data processing. I. Title.

QA76.585.S37 2010
006.7'8--dc22   2010037120

Visit the Taylor & Francis Web site at
http://www.taylorandfrancis.com

and the Auerbach Web site at
http://www.auerbach-publications.com

Contents

Dedication

For my loving wife, Dr. Rachel C. Sarna
All that is Mine and Yours is Hers
B. Talmud Nedarim 50

Contents

Preface

I was first exposed to what would become the Internet way back in 1969, while I was still an undergraduate at Brandeis University working on ARPANet, the forerunner to the present Internet, which operated at the then blazing speed of 2,400 bps, ultimately increased to 50 Kbps (see http://www.computerhistory.org/internet_history/). I have been privileged to enjoy a front-row seat watching the technology speed up, evolve and mature over the past 45 years.

Without hesitation, I make this bold statement: Cloud computing will have a greater effect on our lives than the PC revolution and the dot-com revolution combined.

This book details how to go beyond the theory and build "industrial-strength" robust and highly scalable cloud computing applications for the enterprise. We discuss

- Whose platforms are available today
- What tools facilitate development
- How to fit the different pieces together
- How much it costs

We look at actual case studies, and examine costs, technologies, and problems that were overcome.

In this book, I'm assuming that I'm singing with the choir and that the choir knows the tune, if not quite all the lyrics. It's not my objective to convince you to develop cloud-based applications. You're already convinced. Another book in this series, Cloud Computing: Implementation, Management, and Security (paperback) by J W Rittinghouse, Hypersecurity LLC, provides a somewhat more technical (e.g., nuts and bolts) understanding of what cloud computing really means.)

I aim to help you select the best tools, to follow the best practices, and to avoid pitfalls so you can build effective and appropriate cloud applications.

Cloud Computing and Web 3.0 are disruptive technologies, and the technology is changing, developing, and improving with breathtaking speed. My blog eyeonthecloud.com keeps up with daily news and developments and is a useful supplement to this book.

Author's Acknowledgements

I have many people to thank.

My agent, Carole Jelen McClendon of Waterside Agency, who believed in me, and introduced me to my editor, Theron Shreve. Theron has been a pleasure to know and a privilege to work with, and I learned much from him. He made many, many contributions to this book. Darice L. Moore carefully and meticulously copy-edited the manuscript. My long-time friend Ivan Gelb contributed greatly to the chapter on cloud economics and capacity planning and made many helpful contributions throughout. My friend Eli Schor and Yishai Pinchover, both of Cav Systems read the manuscript and made many helpful suggestions.

A book like this could not be written without the assistance and cooperation of many vendors, from A (Amazon) to Z (Zend). Thanks are due to all the vendors for fact-checking, and for their courtesy in allowing the reuse of copyrighted material from their respective Web sites, including illustration credits, as noted.

In the vendor community, special thanks are due to Darcy Hansen and Craig Sowell, Director, Cloud Marketing and Communications, IBM; Helen Phung and Matt C. Douglass, Practice Fusion; Gordon Evans and Ariel Kelman, Salesforce.com; Jerry Huang, Gladinet; Vicki Morris, Candice Heidebrecht, and Pete Malcolm, Abiquo; Jim Kerr and Brian Daly, Unisys; Phil Libin, Evernote; Betsy Zikakis, Rightscale; Lars Leckie, Hummer Winblad; Junaid Saiyed, Elastra; Bob Gordon, and Andy Kicklighter, Senior Technical Marketing Manager – Cloud at Nimsoft, CA Technologies; and Paul Martiz, Tod Nielsen, and Aaron T. Feigin, VMware.

My children, Ariel, Leora, and Shira, helped in many ways, and are a source of never-ending joy. Last and most dear is my wife of 35 years, the love of my life, Dr. Rachel C. Sarna, without whose constant support, encouragement, and competence very little would get accomplished in my house.

Executive Summary

Cloud Computing is a True Paradigm Shift

Cloud computing is a major paradigm shift. Most of us are already using cloud computing in our daily lives for personal use, and now enterprises are rapidly moving key applications to the clouds for agility (speed of implementation and speed of deployment), improved customer experience, scalability, and cost control.

From Do It Yourself to Public Cloud—A Continuum

Cloud computing is a natural development to meet needs that have been evident for more than forty years. *Virtualization* is the key technology that enables cloud computing. Remote hosting has developed from simply renting infrastructure to providing and maintaining standardized virtual servers that can be scaled up and down as demand fluctuates. Private (often on-premise) clouds can provide increased utilization compared with deploying, installing, and maintaining traditional farms of servers deployed on a task-per-server basis. Public clouds offer increased efficiency, but are perceived as being less secure. Newer hybrid solutions, such as IBM Cloudburst, Eucalyptus, and Windows AppFabric provide a consistent development experience for easy migration, redundancy, and scalability.

Cloud Computing: Is It Old Mainframe Bess in a New Dress?

Cloud computing is very much in vogue. Many vendors are simply relabeling their offerings to pretend they are cloud applications, but they are not the real McCoy.

The vision of a computer utility goes back to the 1960s, to John Marthey, Fernando Corbató, and Fred Guenberger. The rapid development of the personal computer pushed aside interest in its development, which in any event required ubiquitous, high-speed Internet access to become a reality.

Many vendors offer managed platforms as a service. Universal standards are emerging, but there is not yet a universal standard as vendors fight for competitive advantage.

Commercial software developers and well as enterprise developers are building robust, multitenant software-as-a-service applications to run efficiently on these platforms, and usage is anticipated to explode over the next few years.

Moving Into and Around the Clouds and Efforts at Standardization

Most enterprise IT organizations have either implemented or are studying cloud projects. The two most commonly expressed fears are:

- How do we keep our data safe?
- How do we prevent being locked in to a single vendor?
- How do we move legacy applications to the cloud?

Portability of data and applications is crucial. Several versions of Linux have been optimized for the clouds. Linux, Apache, and the programming languages C++, Python, and Java, as well as PHP, have been widely adopted and are supported by many vendors. Leading tools like Eucalyptus and RightScale have also been adopted by many vendors, enhance portability, and prevent lock-in, as does the use of "wrappers" like Zend. VPN-Cubed IPsec supports hybrid clouds across multiple vendors.

The Simple Cloud API project empowers developers to use one interface to interact with a variety of cloud application services, enabling them to more easily access new technologies from cloud vendors.

Tools like Abiquo and 3Tera's AppLogic facilitate cloud management across vendors, hypervisor independence, and the support of thousands of virtual machines. Elastra's CloudServer facilitates provisioning and enforcement of policy rules.

Serious efforts are underway in the vendor community to promote portability within the cloud as well as emerging standards for high-speed interclouding and Open PaaS. The Distributed Management Task Force, Inc., (DMTF) is working to develop universal cloud service portability through the work of the Open Cloud Standards Incubator (OCSI).

Cloud Economics and Capacity Management

The goal of capacity planning is to ensure that you always have sufficient but not excessive resources to meet customers' needs in a timely fashion In this chapter, we look at the economics of cloud computing, and the tools of capacity management needed to ensure adequate performance without overpaying.

Queueing theory explains how overutilization of resources causes poor response times and erratic performance. Key Volume Indicators (KVIs) are a technique for relating computer metrics to units of forecastable work.

We discuss tools for evidence-based decision making, including measuring workloads, forecasting changes, modeling the expected workloads on different physical and virtual configurations to meet business needs at optimal cost, and validating the models for accuracy and robustness.

We discuss questions to ask cloud vendors about elasticity (scalability), and how to work through make versus buy decisions.

Demystifying the Cloud: A Case Study Using Amazon's Cloud Services (AWS)

Amazon began providing Amazon Web Services in 2005, and the early adopters did their best to treat it as a black art, known only to the cognoscenti.

Amazon's Web Services is the oldest and most mature of the public cloud service providers. An easy way to get started with AWS is to use Gladinet to create a Z disk that appears local but connects to the cloud. S3Fox Organizer is a free tool for moving static content from our own computers to the cloud. A custom instance of a virtual server on EC2 can be easily created and configured just the way we want it. Amazon's CloudWatch is useful for monitoring EC2 instances and Elastic Load Balancers in real time or by using Auto Scaling to dynamically add or remove Amazon EC2instances based on Amazon CloudWatch metrics. Nimsoft's Nimsoft Monitoring Solution (NMS) for AWS is one tool for monitoring and controlling Amazon-hosted cloud solutions.

Virtualization: Open Source and VMware

Virtualization is the main ingredient of cloud computing. While it's an old idea, it is modern and fast, and low-cost, mass-produced hardware has made virtualization cost-effective. Many powerful hypervisors, including Xen, KVM, and QEMU, are open source. VMware is the commercial leader, but is based on open source. Citrix is a form of virtual desktop, but today it often rides on VMware. Amazon uses a modified version of Xen. Monitoring is essential to managing the performance of virtual systems. Microsoft has its own patented approach in Microsoft Azure. EMC's VPLEX is an important new technology for moving blocks of storage across the cloud. Interesting partnerships have been announced among VMware, Google, Salesforce.com, Eucalyptus, and Amazon that will help grow the entire industry and prevent lock-in to a single vendor.

Securing the Cloud: Reliability, Availability, and Security

Reliability, Availability, and Security (RAS) are the three greatest concerns about migrating to the cloud. *Reliability* is often covered by a service level agreement (SLA). *Availability* addresses not only whether sufficient resources are available but also how long provisioning of new resources can take and how quickly they can be deprovisioned as needs scale back down. The main goal of *Security* is to limit access only to those approved, to let those with approved see and/or modify only the data they are entitled to see and no other data, and to ensure that no one can requisition resources beyond their budget.

However, many commercial service providers have better tools and facilities for ensuring RAS than do their clients. ISO 27001 and SAS 70 are two recognized standards designed for independently ensuring that third parties handling data have sufficient controls in place. These standards have been adapted for cloud security. The Cloud Security Alliance has been developing cloud-specific standards that will further improve on such standards. CloudAudit is developing an open, extensible, and secure interface that allows cloud computing providers to expose Audit, Assertion, Assessment, and Assurance (A6) information for cloud infrastructure (IaaS), platform (PaaS), and application (SaaS) services to authorized clients.

Scale and Reuse: Standing on the Shoulders of Giants

There are two principle attributes of cloud computing: scalability and code reuse. Service-Oriented Architecture (SOA) is a flexible set of design principles used during the phases of systems development and integration. SOA separates functions into distinct units, or services, comprised of unassociated, loosely coupled units of functionality that have no calls to each other embedded in them. Developers make them accessible over a network in order to allow users to combine and reuse them in the production of applications. SOA, Web 2.0, and SOA 2.0 promote code reuse in a cloud environment. Calls to cloud-provided services, such as Google's AJAX APIs, also let you implement rich, dynamic Web sites entirely in JavaScript and HTML.

Windows Azure

Microsoft Azure represents a major evolution both of operating systems and of Microsoft's overall strategy. While written entirely from the ground up, it benefits from a long, mostly distinguished, and expensive pedigree. It seems to be the first-to-market component of Midori, the descendant of Cairo, Microsoft's two-decades-ago planned, never released object-oriented distributed operating system. Midori's strong emphasis on concurrency issues, a willingness to break compatibility, and the idea of using a hypervisor "as a kind of Meta-OS" fits Microsoft's long-term strategy.

Azure is a great place to develop and host .Net applications, an adequate place to build and host LAMP applications, and a very good place for hosting applications developed in a mixed environment.

Google in the Cloud

Google is believed to manage one of the two or three largest server farms in the world. Recently, it has begun making its infrastructure available to others for a fee. Its widely used offerings, in addition to search, include Google Apps for Business, Google Maps, Google Finance, and Google Voice. More recently, it has introduced Google App Engine, and in its own unique way, it is now a general cloud services provider.

Google is aiming to be an enterprise cloud vendor. Its approach to development in the cloud may be summarized as:

- Stand on our tall shoulders (Use Google's extensive code base)
- Develop your applications in Java, PHP, or Python
- Use the GQL datastore as an alternative to SQL
- Let Google worry about resource allocation, load balancing, and scalability

GWT, Google App Engine and Google Apps Script offer clear evidence of Google's big push to bring enterprise development to the cloud. Google

App Engine should prove to be a worthy competitor to Amazon Web Services, one of App Engine's major competitors for hosting environments.

Enterprise Cloud Vendors

Traditional enterprise vendors all have cloud strategies.

IBM was a very early proponent of both virtualization and cloud computing. IBM Smart Business cloud solutions support clouds built behind the enterprise firewall, or the IBM cloud. IBM's public cloud offering is still new, while its private cloud offerings are, for the cloud, very mature.

IBM has partnered with Red Hat, SOASTA, RightScale, and others. HP has partnered with Microsoft; Oracle bought Sun outright and partners with Amazon AWS.

Hewlett Packard is primarily selling cloud solutions to the enterprise, and the enterprise is typically hosting the solutions in private clouds. Its SaaS offerings are still specialized and limited. HP's BSM 9.0. addresses hybrid delivery models and management of the "consumerization of IT," i.e., people who use non-company-owned devices on a company network. HP, Intel, and cloud software maker Enomaly have partnered to offer a full end-to-end IaaS platform for cloud service providers. HP and Microsoft are investing $250 million to significantly simplify cloud technology environments for businesses of all sizes.

Oracle has reclassified its clusters as private clouds while slowly moving into the "enterprise private cloud." Oracle customers can now use their existing Oracle licenses or acquire new licenses to deploy Oracle software on Amazon's EC2. Oracle has also announced its intention to license others as well. The newly introduced Oracle Secure Backup Cloud module makes it possible to move database backups to the Amazon Simple Storage Service (S3) for offsite storage. Its VeriScale architecture (part of Oracle's acquisition of Sun) optimizes load balancing by implementing the networking logic locally in the service instance's containers and treating the networking logic as part of the application.

CA Technologies (formerly Computer Associates) acquired 3Tera. Its AppLogic offers an innovative solution for building cloud services and deploying complex enterprise-class applications to public and private clouds using an intuitive graphical user interface (GUI). CA has extended its partnership with NetApp, integrating CA's virtualization, automation, and service assurance offerings with NetApp's storage management solutions. In addition, CA is planning SaaS offerings for most of its IT management solutions. It also partners with a Carnegie Mellon and a host of resellers.

Unisys places strong emphasis on security; this has carried over to its cloud offerings. Unisys Stealth security solution, an innovative, patent-pending data protection technology initially designed for government applications, is now available to commercial clients. Unisys has also partnered with VMware on the software side and with its parent, EMC, on the hardware side, among others.

Cloud Service Providers

Large cloud service providers include Rackspace, GoGrid, and Joyent (a newer entry), as well as robust cloud offerings from AT&T. EngineYard is a specialized provider of cloud services for Ruby on Rails developers. Other interesting SaaS vendors include NetSuite, Intuit, and Intacct, as well as cross-platform vendors like 3Tera, Appistry, Elastra, RightScale, BMS, and Nasuni.

Practice Fusion Case Study

Practice Fusion has demonstrated that cloud computing enables it to offer sophisticated applications to a wide audience at extremely low cost, while respecting HIPAA privacy and security mandates. Physicians are armed with good and complete data at the point of care; this is a significant paradigm shift from traditional paper-centric processes. A cloud-based environment prepares providers by focusing on the condition rather than by asking repeated questions around past medical history of the patient because they couldn't find it in a traditional paper chart or noninteroperable environment.

Support and Reference Materials

Charts and tables review the basic definitions of cloud computing, its characteristics, delivery models, and deployment models. Commonly cited benefits are listed, and the main concerns articulated. Pathways are identified for mitigating the risks. We also specifically articulate security concerns and pathways for mitigating security risks. Questionnaires are provided to ask internally and to vendors regarding:

- When to migrate to the cloud
- How to avoid lock-in
- What security is available
- What migrating to the cloud will cost

About the Author

David E. Y. Sarna

David E. Y. Sarna is a technologist, serial entrepreneur, and author of the popular blogs EyeOnTheCloud.com and GoogleGazer.com. Mr. Sarna is a Certified Systems Professional, a Certified Computer Programmer and Certified Data Processing Auditor. He is the co-author, with George Febish, of PC Magazine Windows Rapid Application Development (published by Ziff-Davis Press) which went into three printings and was translated into several languages; he has also written five other books and more than 120 articles published in professional magazines. His longtime column "Paradigm Shift" was the most popular feature in Datamation for many years. Mr. Sarna holds several patents in the fields of bar code and kiosk technologies. He has been honored by the Computer Measurement Group, Inc., by IBM, and by Microsoft Corporation, where he was a founding Regional Director of the Microsoft Developers Network. He has lectured widely and has appeared on television many times, including multiple national appearances on the Fox Network, CNN, and MSNBC.

Mr. Sarna is the founder and managing director of Hendon, Stamford Hill & Co., Inc. (HSH), strategy consulting (www.hshco.com). He has more than 35 years of experience as a merchant banker, management consultant and as an executive of high-technology companies. Prior to founding HSH, Mr. Sarna served for many years on the Advisory Board of Hudson Venture Partners, a well-known New York venture capitalist.

He has served as a board member, director and executive officer of the Ramaz School, and on the Board of Yavneh Academy, both prestigious not-for-profit schools.

Mr. Sarna was founder, chairman, chief executive officer, and a director of ObjectSoft Corporation, a publicly traded company which he founded in 1990. In 1988, Mr. Sarna founded Image Business Systems Corporation (IBS), a software company specializing in document image processing; the company was founded as a spin-off of International Systems Services Corp. (ISS), which Mr. Sarna co-founded in 1981. IBS developed ImageSystem, the first large-scale client-server software for document image processing; it was marketed by IBM. Warburg Pincus and IBM were major investors in IBS, which went public and was listed on the NASDAQ.

At ISS, he architected ISS Three, a computer capacity planning and expert systems tool which ISS successfully marketed and ultimately sold successfully to UCCEL Corp., now part of Computer Associates. ISS itself was successfully sold to a public company.

From 1976 to 1981, Mr. Sarna was employed at Price Waterhouse & Co. as a management consultant, beginning as a senior consultant and rising to the position of senior manager. At the start of his career, Mr. Sarna worked for Honeywell, Inc. and a hardware engineer from 1969 to 1970, and for IBM Corp. from 1970 to 1976 in the large systems division of IBM World Trade Corp. in engineering and sales capacities.

Mr. Sarna holds a B.A. degree cum laude with honors from Brandeis University and did his graduate work in Computer Science at the Technion-Israel Institute of Technology.

Ivan Gelb collaborated with Mr. Sarna on matters related to cloud economics and capacity planning. He is past president and a director of Computer Measurement Group. He is also President of Gelb Information Systems Corporation (GIS), a consulting firm that provides management and technical consulting services in the United States and internationally. His extensive information technology (IT) background includes determination of optimum hardware and software requirements for mainframe and client-server systems; effectiveness evaluation of computer systems and related organizations; data communications systems design and implementation; computer systems end-to-end availability management, performance management and capacity planning; development of software packages; and proprietary measurement data analysis techniques.

During his more than 30 years of experience, Mr. Gelb performed technical and management services for more than 100 organizations such as JP Morgan, Merrill Lynch, PepsiCo, the FBI, the State of California, the New Jersey State Office of Information Technology, and the New York City Board of Education. He is a speaker at various technical conferences, writes articles and serves as editor for a number of trade publications.

Chapter 1

Cloud Computing is a True Paradigm Shift

Figure 1.1   Cumulus clouds; photograph taken at Swifts Creek, in the Great Alps
of East Gippsland, Victoria, Australia. Image by Fir0002/Flagstaffotos.
Licensed under Gnu Free Documentation License (GFDL).

Chapter Overview

In this introductory chapter, we look at what cloud computing really is, why
it's generating such excitement, and who are the major players. We make the
point that most of us are already using cloud computing in our daily lives
for personal use and show how enterprises are moving key applications to
the clouds for improved customer experience, scalability, and cost control.

1.1   Introduction

A **cloud**, of course, is a visible mass of droplets or frozen crystals floating in
the atmosphere above the surface of the Earth or another planetary body. A
cloud is also a visible mass attracted by gravity. Lately, cloud computing has
been exerting a strong gravitational pull all of its own—one that has been
attracting a mass of money.

The big players in cloud computing are Google, Amazon, and, of late,
Microsoft and IBM. Maybe Oracle/Sun, maybe HP will join them. Rackspace, GoGrid, and AT&T want in too.

Google has built the world's largest cloud computing infrastructure. Amazon has not only built the world's largest marketplace, but also is a prime mover in the cloud computing revolution, hosting a myriad of other businesses on its Cloud Services infrastructure. With the recently gone-live Microsoft Azure, Microsoft has entered the cloud-computing business as well, simplifying migration for all Windows applications. Salesforce, VMware, Oracle (Sun), IBM, Adobe, and RackSpace among others, have all tied their futures to cloud computing. (Rackspace and Oracle are mostly into "private clouds").

Specialized vendors such as Intuit (maker of Quickbooks) and "command and control" vendors such as CA Technologies (formerly Computer Associates) also have cloud-based offerings.

As cloud computing matures, it is being embraced not only by small start-ups, but also by major enterprises (albeit more slowly); they appreciate the scalability and reliability that cloud computing can provide.

1.2   What is Cloud Computing?

At its simplest, cloud computing is the dynamic delivery of information technology resources and capabilities as a service over the Internet. Cloud computing is a style of computing in which dynamically scalable and often virtualized resources are provided as a service over the Internet. It generally incorporates infrastructure as a service (IaaS), platform as a service (PaaS), and software as a service (SaaS).

According to Gartner Group[1], the attributes of cloud computing are:

- Service-based
- Scalable and elastic
- Shared
- Metered by use
- Use of Internet technologies

The most frequently cited benefits of cloud computing are:

- It is agile, with ease and speed of deployment
- Its cost is use-based, and will likely be reduced
- In-house IT costs are reduced
- Capital investment is reduced

---

1.   www.gartner.com/technology/initiatives/cloud-computing.jsp.

- The latest technology is always delivered
- The use of standard technology is encouraged and facilitated

As applications migrate to the Internet "cloud," as Internet access becomes ubiquitous, and as low-cost, ultra-lightweight devices (such as the new Apple iPad tablet) and inexpensive, handheld devices built on Google's Chrome Operating System or on Google's Android all provide access to what is increasingly the ubiquitous Internet, the number and types of tasks taking advantage of the new technology will increase by several orders of magnitude, going far beyond the comparatively modest list of things that we use computers and the Internet for today.

Figure 1.2   Kelpie in agility competition. (Photo by Amos T. Fairchild, licensed under GFDL)

While a plethora of introductory books related to cloud computing have been published describing how to use specific Google- or Amazon-provided services (a search for "Cloud Computing" on Amazon.com lists more than 927 results), there are few implementation-centered books that focus on the enterprise, the major vendors, the services they provide, how to choose among them, and the supporting vendors, or on how to build real, working applications quickly and economically.

Having seen it all for more than 45 years, I retain a healthy skepticism of the supposedly new and unique. But I remain curious and excited about the truly innovative. Cloud computing is the real deal. It marks a true paradigm shift, whose effects will eventually dwarf those of the dot.com revolution.

1.3   We're Using Cloud Computing Already

Like the fellow who wrote prose but didn't know it, you and I are using cloud computing more than we realize. I use it and benefit from it every day, and probably you do too. Consider my little business. Like more than a million other businesses, I use the paid version of Google Apps (cloud-based, with an annual fee of $50 per user), so e-mail addressed to my hshco.com domain is hosted by Google, and spam filtering, archiving, and e-discovery are provided by Postini, owned by Google since 2007. Google Apps also maintains my contact list and calendar, which are all accessible from my desktop, synchronized over the cloud to my laptop and Black-Berry, and accessible from anyone else's computer equipped with a Web browser an Internet connection, and the right credentials. I can access and allow others to collaborate on my documents anywhere through Google Docs, recently enlarged to accept files of up to 1 GB, and terabytes of storage can be rented for a modest annual cost.

1.3.1   Electronic Faxing

I use RingCentral's cloud-based Rcfax.com (www.rcfax.com) to virtually (electronically) send and receive faxes. Incoming faxes are sent to a telephone number supplied by RingCentral and are routed to my e-mail address as PDF attachments; outgoing messages are sent via e-mail to their service and delivered to fax machines around the world. Google Apps and RCFax, SaaS providers both, interact flawlessly without either one having to do anything special—or even know about each other.

1.3.2   Voice in the Cloud

If you call my published phone number, (201) 490-9623, the call is handled by the cloud-based Google Voice. I can accept the call from any telephone number linked to my Google Voice account (it will try them all, in the priority I specify). It I can't pick up, you can leave me a message, which I can access through my e-mail, as an SMS message on my BlackBerry, or from any Internet browser. I can also get a (still imperfect, but usually understandable) transcript of the message delivered in the same ways.

1.3.3   Commerce in the Cloud

Some of my books are available for sale as downloadable e-books through my Web site (hosted under the covers by Google). It is interfaced with the cloud-based PayLoadz.com (www.payloadz.com) to receive and fulfill orders, which are paid for either using Google Checkout (http://checkout.google.com/sell/), E-bay's PayPal.com (www.paypal.com), or Amazon Payments (https://payments.amazon.com/sdui/sdui/index.htm), cloud-based services all.

The several sites interact seamlessly. For example, you can choose to pay via Google Checkout, via PayPal, or via Amazon's checkout system. My Web site will hand off seamlessly to Payloadz, which calls the payment service that you selected. After you've paid, you will again be handed off seamlessly to the part of PayLoadz that fulfills the order. You never left my site, and I didn't have to code all that functionality myself—a key characteristic we'll return to again and again.

1.3.4   Distributed Hosting in the Cloud

A portion of my Web site requires FTP (file transfer) and database services that Google's hosting doesn't offer (at least as of this writing). That development subdomain is seamlessly hosted by Godaddy.com. I could just as easily have used Amazon, Rackspace, or any one of hundreds of alternatives.

1.3.5   Accounting and Online Banking in the Cloud

Accounting for my little business is done using the cloud-based version of Quickbooks (http://oe.quickbooks.com/) which interfaces with the online banking system I use at CapitalOne bank (www.capitalone.com) Rather than Quickbooks, I could just as well have used NetSuite Small Business (www.netsuite.com) or several other fine cloud-based alternatives, some of which are discussed in Chapter 13. In turn, the bank's Web-based bill-paying application is handled by a separate cloud-based vendor that interfaces with the cloud-based Automated Clearing House (ACH) system for issuing the electronic checks to pay my bills. Similarly, Intuit has a subsidiary, Intuit Financial Services (formerly Digital Insight), that provides outsourced online statements, check imaging, bill payment and similar services for numerous banks (http://ifs.intuit.com/), a full SaaS application.

Most of my income is also received electronically as direct deposit ACH payments (see http://en.wikipedia.org/wiki/Automated_Clearing_House).

When I need to ship an order, PayPal's MultiOrder Shipping interfaces with a Pitney Bowes application that prints a prepaid label, obtains a tracking number from USPS, and notifies PayPal so it can charge my account. (That's three major vendors, all interoperating seamlessly with cloud applications).

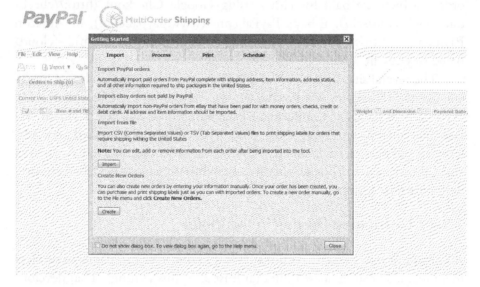

Figure 1.3   PayPal's MultiOrder Shipping interface.

If I complete an online purchase and go to the merchant's site to track delivery, I'm usually handed off to UPS, Federal Express, or the USPS, each of which operates tracking systems in the cloud.

There are many other interesting cloud services that I use but don't have space to mention, and even more that I don't [yet] use.

The important message here is that cloud computing can be used not only for enterprise-to-individual interaction, but also for enterprise-to-enterprise interaction.

1.4   New in the Cloud

Matthew Glotzbach (Director, Product Management, Google Enterprise) listed 10 things that you could do in the clouds in 2009 that you couldn't do the year before. Not surprisingly, he mostly talked about Google-related things, so his list is not complete. Still, Matthew's list is a reminder of how far we've come in a short space of time.

1. Having access to everything on the go—through an iPhone an Android-based phone like Google's Nexus One, a BlackBerry, or Apple's new iPad.

2. Being able to search through all my e-mail quickly from any device using Gmail or Google Apps (see http://mail.google.com/support/bin/answer.py?hl=en&answer=7190).

3. Chatting with customers and partners—in any language. Matthew gave a very cool live demo of inline translation of chat; my Web site, eyeonthecloud.com, implements a translate button provided by Google. Last I looked, it translates the site into 52 languages on request. You can do use it too; just copy this code snippet into your Web page:

```
<div id="google_translate_element"></div><script>
function googleTranslateElementInit() {
 new google.translate.TranslateElement({
 pageLanguage: 'en'
 }, 'google_translate_element');
}
</script><script src="http://translate.google.com/
translate_a/
element.js?cb=googleTranslateElementInit"></script>
```

4. Easy collaboration with Google products Sites and Docs. (Lee Lefavre provides a great explanation of document sharing at http://www.masternewmedia.org/online_collaboration/document-collaboration/Google-Docs-explained-in-simple-words-by-Lee-Lefever-20070919.htm). Online collaboration has been a goal for years; it's now coming of age.

5. Organizing travel using TripIt, a personal travel assistant (www.tripit.com/).

6. Easily collecting data from co-workers and customers using Google forms (see http://docs.google.com/support/bin/topic.py?topic=15166).

7. Building a scalable business application on the cloud platform with Force.com (see www.salesforce.com/platform or http://developer.force.com/appengine) to create Web and business applications that span both salesforce.com and Google's cloud computing platforms and take advantage of the key features of both.

8. Using online-templates for documents, spreadsheets, and presentations.

9. Running fast, secure, and stable Web apps (Chrome; see http://googleblog.blogspot.com/2008/09/fresh-take-on-browser.html).

10. Securely sharing video in apps with Youtube for Google apps (see www.google.com/intl/en/press/pressrel/20080902_video_in_apps.html).

1.5 Other Cloud Applications

Walt Mossberg, author of the Personal Technology column of the Wall Street Journal (and a fellow Brandeis Alum), turned me on to Evernote, a clever, cloud-based tool for capturing all your thoughts, ideas, and inspirations in a single place (www.evernote.com/) and accessing your notes, clipped Internet pages, images, music or whatever over the Web, from a BlackBerry, and so on. I used it extensively in writing this book.

1.6 What about the Enterprise?

The discussion up to now has focused on the individual user (even if that user is getting services from the enterprise). But what about the enterprise?

Quest Diagnostics (www.questdiagnostics.com), a leading testing laboratory, wanted to facilitate interaction with its customers. It has a cloud-based system where you can schedule appointments. You can also receive your test results online if the following are all true:

- Your physician is using a Quest Diagnostics computer system.
- Your physician agrees to release your results.
- You have a linked account with a health management service such as Google Health™, Keas™, Microsoft®, HealthVault™, or MyCare360™(all cloud-based).

While the bureaucracy is a bit intimidating, and not all physicians are familiar with the process for dispensing the required pins for access

(HIPAA privacy rules[2] are very strict), the service itself works very well and actually interfaces with multiple other cloud applications (as noted); this begins to demonstrate the power of cloud computing.

Providing a comprehensive cloud-based electronic health record application serving medical practitioners as well as their patients is what Practice-Fusion does. It's so interesting that we devote a chapter to a case study of this application (Chapter 12).

1.7 More to Come

We've only begun to scratch the surface of what can be done with cloud-based computing today; the most important and paradigm-changing solutions are still either a gleam in someone's eye or a sketch on his or her drawing board.

The best is yet to come, and hopefully, you will be the one to build the killer applications. The focus of this book is to guide you towards developing robust, scalable, cloud-based applications quickly and economically.

Summary

Cloud computing is here and now. Most of us use it daily in our private lives, often without our being aware of it. However, major enterprises are also moving applications to the cloud for scalability, cost savings, and speed of development and deployment.

---

2. Health Insurance Portability and Accountability Act (HIPAA) of 1996 (P.L.104-191). See www.hhs.gov/ocr/privacy for the rules.

Chapter 2

From Do It Yourself to Public Cloud—A Continuum

Chapter Objectives

- Place cloud computing in its historical perspective
- Define cloud computing
- Introduce virtualization, which is the key enabling technology for cloud computing
- Discuss various levels of remote hosting
- Review the advantages of cloud computing in general
- Compare private and public clouds, as well as newer hybrid solutions
- Introduce Eucalyptus and Windows AppFabric for a consistent development experience, for easy migration, and to improve portability

2.1 A Brief History

To appreciate what are perhaps the key issues in cloud computing, we need to have a little sense of history and evolution of computers and operating systems. While you may not initially see why this history lesson is relevant or important, please bear with me for a few paragraphs while we run through a highly compressed history of those aspects computing most relevant to cloud computing.

2.2 Virtualization

As early as the mid-1960s, something was going on that would later prove to be fundamental to the development of cloud computing. The IBM S/360-67, supporting up to four processors, was announced in 1965. It had some unique instructions to support dynamic address translation (DAT) to enable efficient paging. While it was released with an operating system

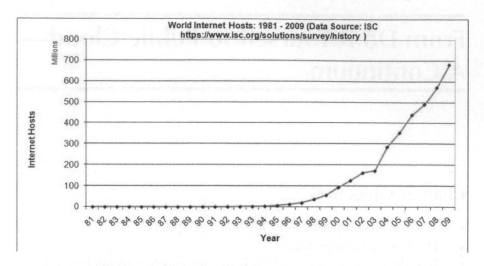

Figure 2.1   Growth of Internet hosts, 1981–2009.

called TSS to support time sharing (slowly and expensively), the real break-through occurred in IBM's Cambridge Scientific Center, closely aligned with nearby Massachusetts Institute of Technology, where CP (control program) was developed to support virtualization.

Figure 2.2   IBM 360 Model 67.

CP provided each user with a *simulated* (virtual) standalone System/ 360 computer, able to run any S/360 software that ran on the bare machine. This gave each user what was, in effect, a private computer system. Its latest grandson, z/VM, now called a *hypervisor* in common with standard industry usage, is still in active use on zSeries, System z9, and System z10 computers. z/VM can be used to support thousands of Linux virtual machines using a process known as virtualization. Its most recent release, V6.1 (at this writing), debuted in October 2009. According to IDC[1], Linux on Power and Linux on System z customers achieved on average a 6.3 month payback on their initial investment, including the initial system purchase.

Virtualization is a key technology in cloud computing, and we discuss it in detail in Chapter 7.

2.3   Remote Hosting

Figure 2.3   Hosted server room.

"Farms" of racked individual personal computers and, later on, blade servers (where up to 128 computers can be crammed into a single 42U rack) became a commonplace sight in larger- and medium-sized organizations,

---

1.   *Adding Business Value with Cross-Platform Solutions: Linux Running on IBM Servers* ftp://ftp.software.ibm.com/linux/pdfs/IDC-adding_business-value_with_cross-platform_solutions-Linux_on_IBM_Systems.pdf.

and even in smaller enterprises. Smaller organizations immediately saw the value in outsourcing the care and feeding of these servers to experts, and the rack-hosting industry was born, a further development of the co-location industry that had been primarily developed for the telecommunication and ISP industries and essentially rented space with power, cooling, and connectivity. More recently, medium- and larger-sized organizations have seen the merit of outsourced hosting.

2.4   Hosting Services

Figure 2.4   Viglen Intel Blade servers (licensed under Creative Commons 2.0 License)

Hosting services provide, in order of ascending cost:

- *Co-location services*, which only provide physical facilities, Internet connection, uninterruptible power, and climate control; the client provides and owns the equipment and is responsible for system administration.
- *Virtual private servers*, in which virtualization technology is employed to allow multiple logical servers to share a single physical server owned, supplied, and maintained by the hosting service. Virtual firewalls ensure security.

- *Dedicated hosting services*, also called managed hosting services, in which the service provider owns and manages the machine, leasing full control to the client. Management of the server typically includes monitoring (to ensure the server continues to work effectively), backup services, installation of security patches, and various levels of technical support, and may include a physical firewall.

Traditional hosting does not provide software beyond systems software.

2.5   Cloud Computing Defined

The National Institute for Standards and Technology (NIST), Information Technology Laboratory offers this definition[2] of Cloud Computing. It's as good as any.

> *Cloud computing is a model for enabling convenient, on-demand network access to a shared pool of configurable computing resources (e.g., networks, servers, storage, applications, and services) that can be rapidly provisioned and released with minimal management effort or service provider interaction. The cloud model of computing promotes availability.*

2.5.1   Essential Characteristics

On-demand self-service. A consumer armed with an appropriate delegation of rights (permission) can unilaterally provision computing capabilities, such as server time and network storage, as needed and automatically, without requiring human interaction with each service's provider.

Broad network access. Capabilities are available over the network and accessed through standard mechanisms that promote use by heterogeneous thin or thick client platforms (e.g., mobile phones, laptops, and PDAs).

Resource pooling. The provider's computing resources are pooled to serve multiple consumers using a multi-tenant model, with different physical and virtual resources dynamically assigned and reassigned according to consumer demand. There is a sense of location independence in that the customer generally has no control or knowledge over the exact location of the provided resources but may be able to specify location at a higher level of abstraction (e.g., country, state, or datacenter). Examples of separately

---

2.   http://csrc.nist.gov/groups/SNS/cloud-computing/cloud-def-v15.doc.

allocable resources include storage, processing, memory, network bandwidth, and virtual machines.

Rapid elasticity. Capabilities can be rapidly and elastically provisioned, in some cases automatically, to scale out quickly and then rapidly released to scale in quickly. To the consumer, the capabilities available for provisioning often appear to be unlimited and can be purchased in any quantity at any time.

Measured service. Cloud systems automatically control and optimize resource use by leveraging a metering capability at some level of abstraction appropriate to the type of service (e.g., storage, processing, bandwidth, and active user accounts). Resource usage can be monitored, controlled, and reported, providing transparency for both the provider and consumer of the utilized service.

2.5.2   Cloud Service Models

The three service models defined by NIST are essentially a hierarchy:

- *Cloud Software as a Service (SaaS).* The capability provided to the consumer in this highest level is to use the *provider's applications* running on a cloud infrastructure. The applications are accessible from various client devices through a thin client interface such as a Web browser (e.g., Web-based e-mail). The consumer does not manage or control the underlying cloud infrastructure, including network, servers, operating systems, storage, or even individual application capabilities, with the possible exception of limited user-specific application configuration settings.
- *Cloud Platform as a Service (PaaS).* The capability provided to the consumer in this intermediate level is to deploy onto the cloud infrastructure *consumer-created or acquired applications* developed using programming languages and tools supported by the provider. The consumer does not manage or control the underlying cloud infrastructure, including network, servers, operating systems, or storage, but has control over the deployed applications and possibly application hosting environment configurations.
- *Cloud Infrastructure as a Service (IaaS).* The capability provided to the consumer is to provision processing, storage, networks, and other fundamental computing resources where the consumer is able to deploy and run arbitrary software, which can include operating systems and applications. The consumer does not manage or

control the underlying cloud infrastructure but has control over operating systems, storage, deployed applications, and possibly limited control of select networking components (e.g., host firewalls).

2.5.3   Deployment Models

Four models of cloud deployment are recognized by NIST.

- *Private cloud.* The cloud infrastructure is operated solely for an organization. It may be managed by the organization or a third party and may exist on premise or off premise.
- *Community cloud.* The cloud infrastructure is shared by several organizations and supports a specific community that has shared concerns (e.g., mission, security requirements, policy, and compliance considerations). It may be managed by the organizations or a third party and may exist on premise or off premise.
- *Public cloud.* The cloud infrastructure is made available to the general public or a large industry group and is owned by an organization selling cloud services.
- *Hybrid cloud.* The cloud infrastructure is a composition of two or more clouds (private, community, or public) that remain unique entities but are bound together by standardized or proprietary technology that enables data and application portability (e.g., cloud bursting for load-balancing between clouds).

2.5.4   Cloud Software

Cloud software takes full advantage of the cloud paradigm by being service oriented with a focus on statelessness, low coupling, modularity, and semantic interoperability.

2.5.5   Advantages of Cloud Computing

Cloud computing offers a number of advantages when compared with remote- or self-hosting:

- *Agility*—A customer can rapidly and inexpensively reprovision technological infrastructure resources.
- *Cost control*—Cloud services are typically priced on a utility computing basis with fine-grained usage-based options.

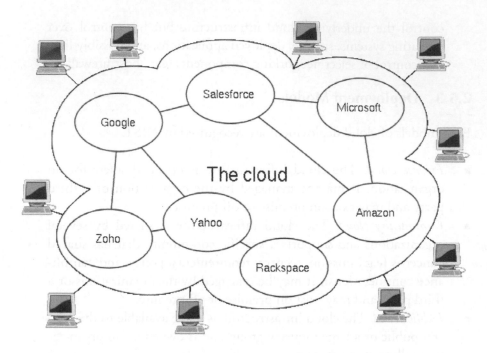

Figure 2.5   Cloud computing logical diagram.

- *Reduced level of IT skills*—Fewer and less sophisticated IT skills are required for implementation.

2.6   The Divisive Issue of Multitenancy

Multitenancy is a characteristic of SaaS, and sometimes PaaS, where numerous customers run the same application, sharing the same equipment and software, but each accesses only his or her data. Perhaps the best known example is the Google Apps Premier Edition, a SaaS service (www.google.com/apps/intl/en/business/index.html). More than two million unique enterprises, each operating under its own domain name, share the same Google infrastructure and cloud, which altogether supports tens of millions of individual users.

Some argue that multitenancy is the *conditio sine qua non* (a mandatory condition) for "true" cloud computing; certainly, it promises the greatest cost savings. Of course, the cost savings can be offset by the difficulty of scaling an application developed to support a single user to securely support many, as well as the problems of scaling from a single instance to many instances (a bigger, faster server can only take you so far) as the demand grows. In addition, the actual development of a multitenancy system is somewhat more complex, and the testing necessary for security needs to be more stringent.

On the other hand, multitenancy simplifies the release management process. In a traditional release management process, packages containing code and database changes have to be distributed to individual client desktop and/or server machines and individually installed. With browser-accessed applications using the multitenant model, the package typically only needs to be installed on a single server and is automatically propagated to other server instances. This greatly simplifies the release management process. (In essence, this is the great-grandchild of service bureaus that handle applications such as payroll on behalf of many different customers).

2.7   Advantages of Cloud Hosting Over Remote Hosting

Cloud service providers offer a number of advantages over and above those provided by remote hosting Some vendors, such as Rackspace, offer both, so a look at their offerings makes clear the incremental benefits of cloud hosting:

- *Scalability* (also called elasticity), the ability to provision one or more servers quickly and to scale up or down quickly
- *Pre-configured operating system images*, such as a variety of popular Linux distributions: Ubuntu, Debian, Novell (SUSE), Gentoo, Centos, Fedora, Arch, and Red Hat Enterprise Linux and various version of Windows-based servers.
- *Virtual servers or physical servers* that can be sized to different plans through a control panel, all the way up to 15.5 GB of RAM; servers can be configured with one to four processors and with one to four cores per processor, and disk drives are usually arranged in a fault-tolerant RAID configuration
- *Dedicated IP addresses* for cloud servers
- *Communication* among servers in the same cloud (co-located), effectuated at high-speed and free of communications charges
- *Replication and/or distribution* over various geographical areas
- *Persistence* provided by a separate cloud storage facility, as storage in a *virtual* cloud server is not persistent when the server instance is shut down

2.8   The Battle Over Public and Private Clouds

Figure 2.6   Boy drawing water from a well.

"Ever since offshoring got hot in the 90s, large companies have been moving toward a model of IT in which the IT services appear to come from a single IT department but are actually an integrated mix of cloud, virtualization and networking services, often provided by external companies," says Chris Wolf, analyst at The Burton Group.[3]

Supposedly, the big battle today is the conflict between public and private clouds. The issue has produced more heat than light. Consider these well-known facts:

- In olden times (and in some places, even today) , if you wanted water, you dug a well and then drew water. Tap water and indoor plumbing only became available in the late 19th century, and became common only in the mid-20th.
- Before the 20th century, if you wanted clothes, you needed to have them made to measure ("bespoke tailoring" in the British argot).

3.   http://www.burtongroup.com.

Ready-to-wear clothing, prior to the Civil War, was mostly for outerwear and undergarments. It took the Civil War to give the impetus to building factories that could quickly and efficiently meet the growing clothing demands of the military.

- Electricity use began with on-site generators. In 1895 at Niagara Falls, George Westinghouse opened the first major power plant using alternating current, making it possible to serve many customers and to transport electricity over considerable distances.

In each case, what was once local, time-consuming, and expensive became available to all, in quantity, and inexpensively, perhaps with some sacrifice in customizability.

So it has been with data centers.

Until the microcomputer revolution, all data centers were "bespoke"— that is, made to measure and custom designed. The concept of centrally managed data centers (empires) was justified by the need for control, standardization, and security.

Figure 2.7   A typical data center.

There has always been tension between *users,* who craved freedom and competitive advantage through agility, innovation, and their own *data silos,* and the *command and control* mentality of centralized administration.

2.9   Then Came the Internet

Lots of data became available from outside the enterprise, and it needed to be integrated with enterprise data for best effect. Conflict mounted, as the concept that "information wants to be free" (a mantra attributed to Peter Samson, a legendary member of the Tech Model Railroad Club at MIT,[4] conflicted with information's value and the competitive advantages that could be conveyed to its owner.

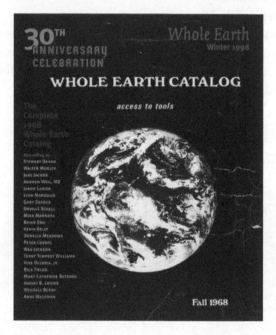

Figure 2.8   The Whole Earth Catalog, 1968 edition.

As Stewart Brand, (founder of the Whole Earth Catalog*) wrote:*[5]

In fall 1984, at the first Hackers' Conference, I said in one discussion session: "On the one hand, information wants to be expensive, because it's so valuable. The right information in the right place just changes

---

4.   http://tmrc.mit.edu.
5.   http://web.me.com/stewartbrand/SB_homepage/Home.html.

your life. On the other hand, information wants to be free, because the cost of getting it out is getting lower and lower all the time. So you have these two fighting against each other. "

If you're still with me, you're probably asking yourself, "What in heaven's name have plumbing, bespoke tailoring, and data silos got to do with cloud computing?"

The answer is that the debate within cloud computing over public versus private clouds is but a manifestation of the same old conflict between freedom and control. On the Internet, the debaters are sharpening their knives. Phil Wainewright has suggested that "Private clouds will be discredited by year end [2010]," a statement he later amended: "Year-end 2011 or mid-2012 would have been a lot safer but hey, I wanted to be provocative." (http://blogs.zdnet.com/SAAS/?p=973).

Randy L. Blas, CEO of private-cloud strategic consulting firm Cloudscaling[6] (http://cloudscaling.com) has a lot of hands-on experience, and he disagrees. He defines a private clouds as an "unshared, single tenant, self-service compute, storage, and network infrastructure." He says that private clouds come in three flavors, "virtual, external, or internal."

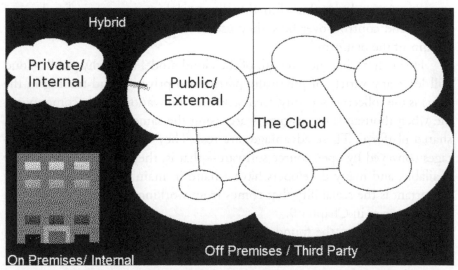

Figure 2.9   Cloud types.

---

6.   Their *Infrastructure-as-a-Service Builder's Guide* can be downloaded at http://cloudscaling.com/wp-content/uploads/2009/12/iaas-building-guide-v1.pdf.

A *virtual cloud* is a logical slice of a cloud infrastructure (see Chapter 7 for further discussion of virtualization). Blas posits that a [real] private cloud operates within a public cloud but uses virtual private networking to give individual enterprises the ability to cordon off a portion of the public cloud under their own delegated control and management. He says has no problem with them.

"On the other hand," he says, "you can make your [own] infrastructure as multitenant as you like; it's not cloud if it's confined within a closed, single-enterprise environment."

Many disagree with this view and see private clouds operating behind an enterprise's firewall as not only completely legitimate, but as the only "safe" alternative in today's environment.

An *external private cloud*, in Blas' view, refers to cloud infrastructure hosted by third-party providers. "But a lot of it is going to be as alluring as lipstick daubed on a pig, because behind the scenes the hosting providers will be doing a lot of covert physical partitioning to cut corners (actually, some of them will openly tout that partitioning as a selling point)."

For Blas, "A public cloud is one that's concurrently shared by thousands of discrete customers, all of whom access precisely the same (though continuously enhanced) baseline functionality and have complete freedom of action (and control) over how they use that functionality within the constraints of the platform."

He predicts that the strength of the cloud model (and why public cloud will leave any variety of physically partitioned private cloud trailing in the dust) is the collective scrutiny, feedback, and innovation that becomes possible when thousands of customers are using the same, constantly evolving, shared platform. These advantages are real. They are similar to the advantages conveyed by open source software—that is, they are readily and freely available, and many developers have a hand in maintaining them. Equally important is the scalability that comes from working with large numbers, a topic we cover in Chapter 9.

Sam Johnston, the founder and CTO of Australian Online Solutions, has been working in cloud computing since 2007. He wrote in his blog:[7]

It's no secret that I don't very much like this whole private cloud or internal cloud concept[8] on the basis that while advanced virtualization

---

7.   http://samj.net/2009/03/cloud-computing-types-public-cloud.html.
8.   http://samj.net/2008/07/future-of-cloud-computing-army-of.html and http://samj.net/2008/08/case-against-private-clouds.html.

technologies are valuable to businesses they are a severe short sell of what cloud computing is ultimately capable of. The electricity grid took over from the on-site generators very quickly, and I expect cloud computing to do the same with respect to private servers, racks and datacenters. Provided, that is, that the concept is not co-opted by threatened vendors pushing solutions that they claim are "just like cloud computing, only better." The potential for cheap, commoditized computing resources far outweighs the benefits of in-house installations, which carry few of the benefits that make cloud computing so interesting (e.g., no capital expenditures, minimal support requirements, accessible anywhere any-time, peak load engineering is handled by the cloud vendor, costs are shared, etc.).

Many data center managers have a vested interest in keeping their empires going, so we can expect them to put up a fight before ceding control over a considerable portion of their empires to outsiders. The change is inevitable nonetheless.

2.10   The Argument for Private Clouds

Some argue forcefully that multitenancy is inherently less secure (never mind that PayPal processes billions of dollars securely that way, or that Google Apps and Gmail process billions of e-mails securely, too). As Sam noted, this is a view most often espoused by those seeking to protect their turf. As an alternative, they offer up so-called "private clouds," which still offer some of the advantages of public clouds. Private clouds use dedicated servers, but the servers exist as part of a larger server farm, so the number of dedicated servers can be [somewhat] scaled and re-allocated on demand. Large financial institutions with huge self-maintained server farms are typically the loudest advocates of this approach, in the interest of security.

2.11   Hybrid Solutions

Hybrid clouds are seen as a way to resolve the debate of "public versus private" clouds.

2.11.1   Hybrid Cloud—Not Really

Randy Blas points out that the term *hybrid* usually means combining two things to make a new one. For example, hybrid cars have a single kind of

new engine and power train that use either gas or electricity. It's neither a
gas engine, nor an electric engine; it's a new kind of engine—a hybrid
engine. A hybrid flower is a new flower that is a cross-breed of two flowers;
it is the genetic descendent of both parents but is like neither of them. It is a
new kind of flower that is a combination of both.

In cloud computing, hybrid solution often means simply private and
public clouds bound together by standardized or proprietary technology
that enables more or less seamless data and application portability. (This is
the definition proposed by the NIST, cited earlier.) Cloud bursting, cloud
bridging, or federating clouds may be better terms to use, as the NIST itself
acknowledges, but it seems that the term *hybrid cloud* has stuck; therefore,
we adopt it.

2.11.2   The Hybrid Cloud Model

The hybrid cloud model is a technique advocated by many IT professionals in larger organizations. Moving some less sensitive or less critical applications, such as HR, CRM, and collaboration, to the cloud (where larger
vendors such as Salesforce.com have built successful followings) delivers
strong business value, while applications involving sensitive and proprietary information can remain either on premises or in private clouds until
security, compliance, and governance issues in the cloud are unambigu-
ously resolved.

Another possibility is to use the public clouds for overflow capacity.
The hybrid model is customarily accomplished by a virtual private connection (VPN) between the public and private clouds, in which the data travel-
ing over the VPN is generally not visible to, or is encapsulated from, the
underlying network traffic. This is done with strong encryption. Internet
Protocol Security (IPsec)[9] is a commonly used protocol suite for securing
Internet Protocol (IP) communications by authenticating and encrypting
each IP packet of a datastream.

2.12   Cloud Computing for Development

Additionally, development is very wasteful of physical resources, and testing
volumes are low. According to IBM,[10] the average enterprise devotes up to
50 percent of its entire technology infrastructure to development and test,
but typically up to 90 percent of that remains idle. Cloud computing, by

---

9.   http://technet.microsoft.com/en-us/network/bb531150.aspx (accessed June 25, 2010).
10.   www.marketwatch.com/story/ibm-extends-development-and-test-to-the-ibm-cloud-2010-03-16.

using virtual resources, reduces this waste. Even when the developed application will run on dedicated servers, it is attractive to be able to carry out development using cloud computing.

In all events, developers want and need a single, consistent, experience, whether they are developing for an internal private cloud, a walled off portion of a public cloud, or a public cloud.

2.13   Eucalyptus—Open Source Software Supporting Hybrid Solutions

A popular way of integrating public and private clouds is using Eucalyptus (www.eucalyptus.com). Eucalyptus is an open source software platform that implements IaaS-style cloud computing using the Linux-based infrastructure found in many modern data centers. While it can be deployed solely for private clouds, because it is interface-compatible with Amazon's AWS (see Chapter 6), it is possible to move workloads between AWS and the data center without code modification.

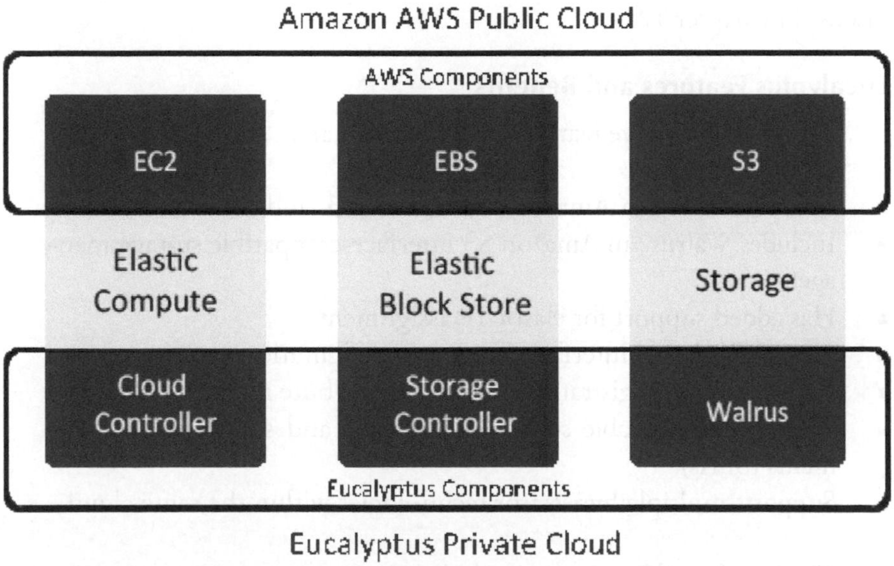

Amazon AWS Public Cloud

Figure 2.10   Eucalyptus for hybrid public and private clouds.

Many other cloud vendors support Eucalyptus, so today, it is the most portable option available. Eucalyptus also works with most of the currently available Linux distributions, including Ubuntu, Red Hat Enterprise Linux (RHEL), CentOS, SUSE Linux Enterprise Server (SLES), openSUSE, Debian, and Fedora. Importantly, Eucalyptus can use a variety of virtualization technologies, including VMware, Xen, and KVM, to implement the cloud abstractions it supports. Eucalyptus's Walrus is an S3-compatible implementation of cloud storage. It is well-described in *The Eucalyptus Open-source Cloud-computing System.*[11] We discuss Eucalyptus and Eucalyptus Enterprise in Chapters 7 and 8, and refer to it again in Chapter 12.

The Ubuntu Enterprise Cloud (UEC) is powered by Eucalyptus and brings an Amazon EC2-like infrastructure inside the firewall.[12] It appears that the recently announced Nimbula, which supports private versions of EC2, is similar.

Ubuntu UEC is open source, with commercial support available from Canonical Ltd., a company founded (and funded) by South African entrepreneur Mark Shuttleworth (formerly the official maintainer of Debian, a version of Linux, and founder of Thawte Consulting) for the promotion of free software projects. Canonical is registered in the Isle of Man (part of the Channel Islands), a favorable tax jurisdiction, and employs staff around the world, as well as in its main offices in London. Ubuntu JeOS is an efficient variant of Ubuntu configured specifically for virtual appliances, which we discuss in Chapter 12.

Eucalyptus Features and Benefits

The most attractive features of Eucalyptus are:

- Is compatible with Amazon AWS (EC2, S3, and EBS)
- Includes Walrus, an Amazon S3 interface-compatible storage manager
- Has added support for elastic IP assignment
- Has a Web-based interface for cloud configuration
- Provides image registration and image attribute manipulation
- Provides configurable scheduling policies and service level agreements (SLAs)
- Supports multiple hypervisor technologies within the same cloud

The benefits of Eucalyptus include:

---

11.   Daniel Nurmi, Rich Wolski, Chris Grzegorczyk, Graziano Obertelli, Sunil Soman, Lamia Youseff and Dmitrii Zagorodnov, *The Eucalyptus Open-source Cloud-computing System.* The paper can be downloaded at http://open.eucalyptus.com/documents/ccgrid2009.pdf.

12.   See http://www.ubuntu.com/system/files/UbuntuEnterpriseCloudWP-Architecture-20090820.pdf.

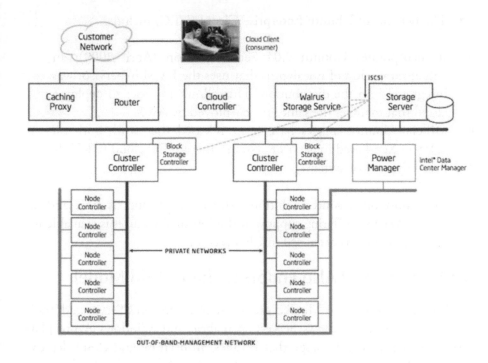

Figure 2.11   Eucalyptus reference cloud.

- The ability to build a private cloud that can "cloud-burst" into Amazon AWS
- Easy deployment on all types of legacy hardware and software
- Leveraging of the development strength of a worldwide user community
- Compatibility with multiple distributions of Linux, including support for the commercial Linux distributions, Red Hat Enterprise Linux (RHEL) and SUSE Linux Enterprise Server (SLES)

Eucalyptus Enterprise Edition 2.0 was built on the core Eucalyptus open source platform, with additional functionality designed to optimize the building and deploying of massively scalable, high performance private clouds in the enterprise. The latest release adds support for Windows Server 2003 and 2008 and Windows 7 virtual machines. (Previously, only Linux images were supported). Other changes include new accounting and user group management capabilities, allowing administrators to easily define groups of users and allocate different levels of access based on a group's needs.

The benefits of Ubuntu Enterprise Cloud (UEC) include:

- It incorporates Ubuntu 9.04 Server Edition (April 2009); an enhanced version of Eucalyptus that uses the KVM hypervisor was integrated into the distribution. This allows any user to deploy a cloud that matches the same API employed by AWS.
- Official Ubuntu images have been released that work both on AWS (a Xen-based hypervisor system) and a UEC cloud (a KVM-based hypervisor system)

Like most open source solutions, the basic product is free, and an "Enterprise Version" offering support and additional features is available for a charge. Eucalyptus is discussed in Chapters 4 and 7.

2.14   Microsoft Also Endorses the Hybrid Model

In November 2009, Bob Muglia, president of Microsoft's Server and Tools business, unveiled Windows Server AppFabric and Windows Azure platform AppFabric, a technology that bridges on-premise and cloud deployment and management scenarios for the Microsoft development environment.

Windows Server AppFabric delivers a set of capabilities for hosting services (RESTful or SOAP-based), workflows, and application-level monitoring (based upon efforts formerly code-named "Dublin"). This technology provides developers with a prebuilt infrastructure that improves the scalability and manageability of composite applications. As a result, much of the complexity related to infrastructure is already taken care of.

AppFabric is complemented by Windows Azure, which will help developers build composite applications that span both on-premise and cloud environments. The Service Bus and Access Control services (previously called .NET Services) provide capabilities for secure connectivity between loosely coupled services and applications, enabling them to navigate firewalls or network boundaries. Microsoft Azure is discussed in more detail in Chapter 10.

Summary

Cloud computing is a natural development toward meeting needs that have been evident for more than 40 years. *Virtualization* is the key technology enabling cloud computing. Remote hosting has developed from simply renting infrastructure to providing and maintaining standardized virtual servers that can be scaled up and down as demand fluctuates. Private (often on-premise) clouds can provide increased utilization compared with deploying, installing, and maintaining traditional task-per-server farms of servers. Public clouds offer increased efficiency, and are perceived as being less secure. Newer hybrid solutions, such as IBM Cloudburst, Eucalyptus, and Windows AppFabric provide a consistent development experience for easy migration, redundancy, and scalability.

I expect that over time, as usage of public clouds increases and security is demonstrated to be at least as robust as with private clouds and on-premise solutions, the economic advantages of public clouds, with suitable privacy and security safeguards, will win out, just as few organizations maintain private telephone systems for security reasons anymore.

Chapter 3

Cloud Computing: Is It Old Mainframe Bess in a New Dress?

Chapter Overview

This chapter addresses these key questions:

- What marketplace forces are at work to obfuscate and confuse what's real, what's new, and what is just recharacterized?
- What was the original vision of the computer utility, and what factors delayed its development?
- Is cloud computing a new concept, or is it a natural progression from tried and true concepts?
- How is cloud computing different from remote hosting?
- What is the difference between PaaS and SaaS?

3.1   Déjà Vu?

In the late 1960s, the first generalized database management systems (DBMSs) started to emerge (IBM's IMS, Cullinane's IDMS, Software AG's Adabase, etc.). These systems replaced old-fashioned indexed-sequential files (ISAM), a data organization method with fixed length records, limited indexing capabilities, and limited possibility of inserting records without performance deterioration. Vendors lacking a DBMS felt that they were at a competitive disadvantage. What did the hapless "have-nots" do? They tinkered slightly with their products and rechristened them as DBMS.

To paraphrase Yogi Berra, the baseball giant, is it déjà vu all over again? Is anyone who is running a hosted service of any description tinkering with it slightly and renaming it as an SaaS service, claimed to be delivered as a cloud application?

Many vendors do invent a new name, put out a press release, crank up the hype and tell stockbrokers that they've got a cloud computing application.

To quote a young Chicago White Sox fan outside a Chicago grand jury hearing related to the Black Sox scandal who said to Shoeless Joe Jackson, "Say it ain't so, Joe."[1]

3.2   Not Remote Hosting

As we discussed in Chapter 2, cloud computing is *not* any old Internet application running on a rack server someplace. Rather, it's a technology designed to securely handle many different clients at once (multitenancy), and to scale (in both directions) in minutes, not months. It requires a different mindset and a different approach to writing code. And right now, let's be honest about it, the tools aren't all there yet.

Remember when most Web sites were developed entirely by coding in HTML? It was difficult, tedious work, and the sites were mostly static "brochureware." It took a few years, but now "any dummy" (meaning me) can create decent-looking, updatable, interactive sites. E-commerce can be added with a few clicks. Tools for cloud development are maturing quickly, but they aren't all there yet.

3.3   Cloud Computing is Maturing Quickly

Cloud computing today is roughly at the stage that the World Wide Web was 15 years ago, but it's maturing at an even more rapid pace.

"Cloud computing is all the rage," wrote InfoWeek in April 2008. Indeed it is. "Some analysts and vendors," they say, "define cloud computing narrowly as an updated version of utility computing: basically virtual servers available over the Internet. Others go very broad, arguing that "anything you consume outside the firewall is 'in the cloud,' including conventional outsourcing," Naturally, those who don't have a real cloud computing offering (the "have nots"), but still want to be considered *chic* go with the InfoWeek's broader definition.

---

1.   Another version of the story:
   "When Jackson left criminal court building in custody of a sheriff after telling his story to the grand jury, he found several hundred youngsters, aged from 6 to 16, awaiting a glimpse of their idol. One urchin stepped up to the outfielder, and, grabbing his coat sleeve, said:
   "It ain't true, is it, Joe?"
   "Yes, kid, I'm afraid it is," Jackson replied. The boys opened a path for the ball player and stood in silence until he passed out of sight.
   "Well, I'd never have thought it," sighed the lad.
   "It Ain't True, Is It, Joe?' Youngster Asks," Minnesota Daily Star, September 29, 1920, pg. 5.

I prefer to define cloud computing as highly scalable, secure, reliable, distributed services, available on a "pay-as-you-go" basis, what I like to call "rent-a-cloud."

Cloud Computing is Not a New Concept

The notion of cloud computing is certainly not new. In his 2003 biography, Dr. Jack B. Dennis, Emeritus Professor of Computer Science and Engineering at MIT (and MIT Class of '53), a pioneer in the development of computer science wrote:

> *In 1960, Professor John McCarthy, now at Stanford University and known for his contributions to artificial intelligence, led the "Long Range Computer Study Group" (LRCSG) which proposed objectives for MIT's future computer systems. I had the privilege of participating in the work of the LRCSG, which led to Project MAC and the MULTICS computer and operating system, under the organizational leadership of Prof. Robert Fano and the technical guidance of Prof. Fernando Corbató.*

Figure 3.1   Fernando J. Corbató (photo by Jason Dorfman, Creative Commons Attribution and ShareAlike licence).

Corbató is known for *Corbató's Law.* which states:

The number of lines of code a programmer can write in a fixed period of time is the same, independent of the language used.

Essentially, it holds that a programmer's productivity is directly proportional to the productivity and economy of his tools.

3.4   Vision of Computer Utility

In 1960, Professor Fano had a vision of computer utility, the concept of the computer system as a repository for the knowledge of a community, its data, and its procedures in a form that could be readily shared and that could be built upon to create ever more powerful procedures, services, and active knowledge by building on what was already in place. Professor Corbató's goal was to provide the kind of central computer installation and operating system that could make this vision a reality. With funding from DARPA, the Defense Advanced Research Projects Agency, the system he developed became known as MULTICS.

For those who, unlike me, are still under sixty and therefore are probably not old enough to remember, MULTICS (an acronym for Multiplexed Information and Computing Service) was an extremely influential early time-sharing operating system, started in 1964. It went live at MIT in 1969 and proved that (mainframe-based) computing could serve many people in remote locations at the same time. It set creative minds to thinking about a generally available computer utility, connected to your house through a cable. MULTICS remained operational right up to the dot.com era. Believe it or not, the last MULTICS system was not shut down until October 31, 2000. (See www.multicians.org for more information.)

Multics inspired far-reaching thoughts. I still have my original copy of Professor Fred Gruenberger's influential book, *Computers and Communications; Toward a Computer Utility* (Prentice-Hall, 1968), which I read when it first appeared. It was based in part on "The Computers of Tomorrow," a May 1964 article in *Atlantic Monthly* by Martin Greenberger, another influential computer scientist. Back then, I was an undergraduate, during an era characterized by pot-smoking, bra-burning, and anti-Vietnam War protests, and nearly all computing was still based on mainframes and batch processing. Punch cards were the norm for both programming and for data entry. Despite the prevailing limitations, Gruenberger looked at MULTICS and its teletype data entry terminals and saw far into the future. He imagined a

Figure 3.2   Honeywell H6180 MULTICS computer.

"computing utility" that would operate much like an electrical utility, letting you draw as much or as little as you need, while paying only for consumption—what you use.

What he articulated in detail didn't exist, except in his imagination. The technology wasn't there. But now it does;we know it as cloud computing.

In 1969, Leonard Kleinrock, an expert in queuing theory and one of the chief scientists of the original Advanced Research Projects Agency Network (ARPANET) project which seeded the Internet, said: "As of now, computer networks are still in their infancy, but as they grow up and become sophisticated, we will probably see the spread of 'computer utilities' which, like present electric and telephone utilities, will service individual homes and offices across the country."[2]

To appreciate the depth of this vision, let's remember where things really were in those days.

Nearly all computing was still done with batch processing. Punched cards were the primary means of input. Time sharing was still in its infancy. As a 19-year old, back when Lyndon Johnson was still president, I read an article in *Business Week* which reported that all you needed to do to attract

---

2.   L. Kleinrock. A Vision for the Internet. ST Journal of Research, 2(1):4-5, Nov. 2005.

venture capital funding was to stroll down Sand Hill Road in Menlo Park, California (then, as now, home to some of the most prominent and success- ful venture capitalists) and shout "time-sharing." Venture money would be poured on you. The idea back then was that we all needed slices of comput- ing "on-demand," but only for short bursts of activity.

Figure 3.3   Model 33 Teletype, including paper tape reader and printer (photo by Allison W, on display at The National Museum of Computing, licensed under the Creative Commons Attribution-Share Alike 3.0 Unported License).

Back then the Teletype Model 33 was the "terminal" of choice; its printing speed was limited to about 10 characters per second. It could send data at a maximum rate of 300 bps and often used an acoustic coupler to connect it to a telephone handset. Later, faster models supported 30–120 characters per second. Like Bill Gates, I gained my first computing experience on the Model 33.[3]

Of course, the slow speed limited the use of time-sharing to applications requiring limited data entry and output. Payroll and sales data entry from branch offices, sales force management, light accounting, and modeling were the prime applications.

Ultimately, however, the PC revolution put the kibosh on timesharing, for not as a modest, one-time investment users were no longer tethered to a money-guzzling mainframe via the maddeningly slow lines of communication of that era—all the while being charged for it by the minute.

But while time-sharing died a slow and painful death, the concept behind timesharing, "hosted applications," had enduring merit. As the world recognized that personal computers were not always appropriate or powerful enough, client/server applications became the next big thing, running locally what could be processed on a personal computer, and using the back-end servers for the heavy lifting. This was followed by three-tier solutions.[4] In 2004 (in the infancy of cloud computing), when the world first started talking about "hosted applications," Laurie Sullivan noted in *Information Week*,[5]

> *"Hosted enterprise applications are nothing new. They first emerged as time-sharing apps in the 1960s, when companies rented hardware and software computing resources because they lacked the money and expertise to run applications internally. Among those to first offer such services were IBM and General Electric. The strategy eventually morphed into the [ASP] application-service-provider model in the late 1990s. The business model for both approaches failed, giving rise to the next iteration of hosted applications. The hosted, on-demand model is the third wave," says Jim Shepherd, a senior VP at AMR Research. "The difference is this time, heavy hitters like IBM and Oracle are pushing the*

---

3.   Bill Gates interview, National Museum Of American History, Smithsonian Institution http://americanhistory.si.edu/collections/comphist/gates.htm (accessed June 25, 2010).

4.   Typical of the era was Sarna, David E. Y. and George J. Febish. "Building three tier client-server business solutions," white paper, Object Soft. Corp., Englewood, NJ, 1995. (www-rcf.usc.edu/~anthonyb/ITP250/docs_pdf/Building3Tier.doc)

5.   Laurie Sullivan, "History 101: Hosted Apps, From Time-Sharing To On-Demand," Information Week, June 21, 2004, accessed June 10, 2010. www.informationweek.com/news/global-cio/outsourcing/showArticle.jhtml?articleID=22100717.

concept, so there's no question as to whether it will survive. . . . The
question now is, how big will it become?"

The answer?
Very big indeed.

Utility computing, *InfoWeek* wrote years later, "is a [type of cloud computing that provides a] way to increase capacity or add capabilities on the fly without investing in new infrastructure, training new personnel, or licensing new software. Cloud computing encompasses any subscription-based or pay-per-use service that, in real time over the Internet, extends IT's existing capabilities."

That sure sounds like Gruenberger's computer utility to me.

3.5   Desktop Virtualization

The first widespread use of virtualization was on the desktop. Companies tired of maintaining armies of technicians to tweak, fix, and upgrade desktop PCs. Operating system migrations, PC replacements, operational PC costs, and PC security concerns had become major and unaffordable costs. Managers wanted a standardized environment. Even better, they wanted an environment that can physically sit in a closet or a room full of servers.

The two main vendors to jump on this bandwagon were Citrix and VMware. As the workforce became more mobile, the importance of remotely accessing a virtual desktop increased. Today's desktop is really an end-user environment defined by a profile consisting of applications, documents, and configuration data. As end users rely more and more on mobile devices such as laptops, smart phones, and removable storage drives, they need desktop environments that they can access anytime, anywhere. With the traditional "monolithic" desktop, the applications, operating system, and user data are all tied to a specific piece of hardware. Virtualization breaks the bonds between these elements into isolated layers, enabling IT staff to change, update, and deploy each component independently for greater business agility and improved response time. End users also benefit from virtualization because they get the same rich desktop experience, but with the added ability to access that computing environment from multitude of devices and access points in the office, at home, or on the road.

Virtual desktops are also superior to terminal services because they eliminate the headaches associated with application sharing and application compatibility. Instead of having to share a limited subset of applications that are compatible with terminal services, each end user gets a complete, standardized, and fully customizable desktop computing environment—a virtual machine. Each virtual desktop is completely isolated from other virtual machines, and IT administrators can provision and manage OS and application software just as they would with a traditional PC

Use of virtual desktops began about the turn of the millennium (2000) and are still a big deal. According to a June 2010 Morgan Stanley report,[6] half of the CIOs surveyed plan to use desktop virtualization within twelve months, which the firm believes could double the reach of client virtualization. Morgan sees the VDI (virtual desktop infrastructure) market growing to a $1.5 billion opportunity by 2014. This would represent a 67 percent compound annual growth rate. Not surprisingly, VMware and Citrix are expected to remain the dominant vendors behind that trend.

3.6   PaaS: Platform as a Service

The PaaS form of rent-a-cloud is available commercially from Amazon.com (see www.amazon.com/gp/browse.html?node=201590011), Google (see http://code.google.com/appengine), Sun (zembly.com for creating and hosting social applications, and Network.com for pay-as-you-go computing), Microsoft (with Azure; see http://www.microsoft.com/azure/windowsazure.mspx), IBM with IBM Cloud (http://www-03.ibm.com/press/us/en/pressrelease/22613.wss), GoGrid, Joyent, Rackspace, VMware (through its partners), and others; these now also offer storage and virtual servers that IT can access on demand. These vendors are offering PaaS (Platform as a Service).

Are they getting traction?

In InfoWeeks's view,

Early enterprise adopters mainly use utility computing for supplemental, non-mission-critical needs, but one day, they may replace parts of the datacenter.

However, you and I know better. Many smaller, fast-growing high-tech outfits run their entire businesses from the "cloud" of one (or more) of these major vendors, and by all reports, reliability exceeds that of most IT shops by a large margin.

---

6.   http://www.readwriteweb.com/cloud/2010/06/what-the-cio-says.php?utm_source=Read-WriteCloud&utm_medium=rwchomepage&utm_campaign=ReadWriteCloud_posts&utm_content=What%20the%20Bankers%20Say%20About%20the%20Cloud#more.

3.7 SaaS Applications

Software as a Service (SaaS) is a type of cloud computing that delivers a single application through the browser to many, (potentially thousands or tens of thousands) of customers using a multitenant architecture. On the customer side, it means no upfront investment in servers or software licensing; on the provider side, with just one app to maintain; costs are low compared to conventional hosting. APIs are also increasingly available in the cloud; they enable developers to exploit functionality of others over the Internet, rather than developing, hosting, and delivering it themselves, a topic we discuss in Chapter 9. Table 3.1 shows some cloud service providers and the services that they offer:

Table 3.1   Cloud service providers and their offerings (a partial list).

Product	Services	Link
Strike Iron	Address verification, sales tax calculation, SMS and e-mail alerts	www.strikeiron.com
Xignite	Financial data feeds	www.xignite.com/
Google Maps	Embedded maps	http://goo.gl/uD1N
Google Voice	Place calls, send SMS, download voicemails/ recorded messages	http://goo.gl/xcWl
Salesforce.com	Sales management, service management	www.salesforce.com/
Force.com	Cloud development platform	www.salesforce.com/platform/
Yahoo BOSS	Open search Web services platform.	http://goo.gl/6pTx
Bloomberg	Financial data	http://goo.gl/8as1
USPS	Address information, tracking	http://goo.gl/ckNg
NetSuite	Financials, CRM, inventory, and e-commerce	www.netsuite.com
RightNow Technologies	Customer experience across the Web, social networks, and contact center	www.rightnow.com/

These providers range from those offering discrete services made to interface seamlessly with your applications—such as Strike Iron,[7] Xignite[8] (a provider of on-demand financial market data), Google Maps,[9] and Google Voice—to the full development platform offered by Salesforce.com's Force.com and the range of APIs offered by Yahoo BOSS,[10] Google, Bloomberg LP, and even the U.S. Postal Service.[11] Many online banking and conventional credit card processing services are also headed in this direction.

SaaS is now solidly coming into its own and is now increasingly being renamed "On Demand" software, which is certainly more euphonious.

3.8   Force.com and Standing on Tall Shoulders

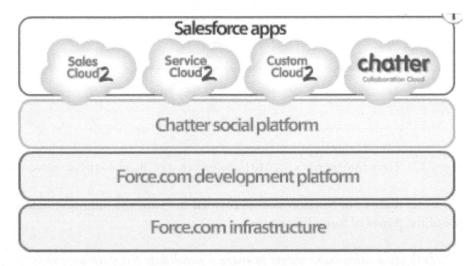

Figure 3.4   Force.com overview (©2010 by Salesforce.com. Reprinted by permission).

Some of the same types of applications that originally fueled the time-sharing boom in the late 1960s and early 1970s are now leading the explosive growth of cloud computing, but with some important differences.

Salesforce.com is perhaps the most advanced and successful of all SaaS cloud vendors; it provides the most widely used sales management service. Salesforce.com is successful not just because it has thoroughly integrated its

7.   www.strikeiron.com.
8.   www.xignite.com.
9.   maps.google.com and http://code.google.com/apis/maps.
10.   http://developer.yahoo.com/search/boss.
11.   http://www.usps.com/webtools/webtoolsapirequestform.htm.

applications with those of Google (others are doing that also), but because it has followed Google's lead in making its applications available at the API-level with Force.com, greatly reducing the time and cost of developing new and unique applications that go far beyond Salesforce.com's roots in customer relationship management. (Their free downloadable book on creating on-demand applications is highly recommended. Register at no charge at http://wiki.apexdevnet.com/events/book/registration.php to download).

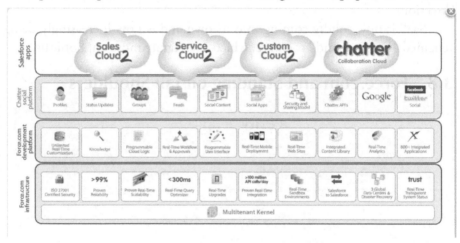

Figure 3.5   Force.com overview (©2010 by Salesforce.com. Reprinted by permission).

Ariel Kelman of Salesforce.com provided me with the following example of the power of using Force.com.

Let's say a salesperson wants to share a candidate list with an outside recruiter but not give the recruiter full access to the application. The salesperson can e-mail the recruiter a Google spreadsheet from Google Docs.

As the salesperson makes changes in Force.com through the Google Data APIs, it will update the candidate list on the spreadsheet. So, the recruiter can see those changes and interact with those changes.

"We can read and write information between our database and Google Docs," Kelman confirmed, and continued:

What we're trying to do is make it easier for developers to build applications that run in the cloud, and as all of these cloud computing platforms proliferate, the more that vendors can do to allow developers to have access to the different computing platforms, the easier it becomes.

In effect, it's no different than what Microsoft did when it partnered with SAP and Business Objects in business intelligence . . . back in the day to bolster its on-premises software functionality.

Another example of using Force.com to quickly develop an application is ServoTerra, which has built and deployed an asset planning application and B2B trading exchange built entirely on the Force.com platform and the new Force.com *Sites* capability. ServoTerra (www.servoterra.com) provides IT asset disposal solutions, including SaaS asset life cycle planning, virtual consignment, and environmental compliance tracking, enabling companies to achieve a 35 percent higher return on average than other models. Significantly, ServoTerra teamed with Appirio (www.appirio.com), a cloud solution provider and leader in Force.com development; they designed, developed, and deployed a hardware asset planning application and B2B marketplace solution in less than 12 weeks. Obviously, Force.com provided them with tall shoulders to stand on.

We discuss the partnership between VMware and Salesforce.com in Chapter 7.

Standing on tall shoulders is such an important topic that we discuss it in detail in Chapter 9, *Scale and Reuse: Standing on the Shoulders of Giants*.

3.9   Other Popular SaaS Applications

SaaS is also commonly deployed for HR applications (which are subject to whimsical government edicts and hence lend themselves to specialized solution-providers). They are also used in ERP applications from vendors such as Workday.[12] More recently, SaaS applications such as Google Apps (which we discuss in Chapter 11), and Zoho Office[13] have been gaining in popularity as collaboration and "access anywhere" tools. Newer on-demand software providers with promising futures include Concur,[14] which focuses on travel and expense management; Ultimate Software,[15] an established vendor focusing on HR, payroll, and talent management; SuccessFactors (www.successfactors.com), another experienced vendor of performance and talent management solutions; and DemandTec (www.demandtec.com), offering

---

12.   www.workday.com.
13.   www.zoho.com.
14.   www.concur.com.
15.   www.ultimatesoftware.com.

integrated merchandising and marketing solutions. The reason for these vendors' success is that the software was (re)written specifically to function as hosted applications, and it's all high maintenance and complex, encouraging the notion of "letting George do it." Slide Rocket[16] has an SaaS application for creating stunning presentations; it has recently integrated this application with Google Apps. A number of other SaaS vendors are briefly discussed in Chapter 13.

3.10   The Holy Grail of Computing

The type of cloud-based offerings epitomized by Google and Force.com get us ever closer-tantalizingly closer-to the holy grail of computing: building blocks of robust, reliable, and updatable software, all hosted in the Internet cloud, allowing all of us to stand on the tall shoulders of others while quickly creating totally unique, high-volume, industrial-strength applications that were heretofore the exclusive province of exceedingly well to do big businesses (the Goldman Sachs "money is no object" kind).

Throughout history, and certainly since the Industrial Revolution, the democratization that brings formerly one-of-a-kind expensive widgets (custom-tailored suits, custom-built carriages, custom-built automobiles, hand-assembled mainframe computers, or whatnot) within reach of everyone also creates new jobs and improves the standard of living around the globe.

3.11   SaaS 2.0

Bill McNee of Saugatuck Technology has coined the term SaaS 2.0.[17] His company has published a study, *SaaS 2.0: Software-as-a-Service as Next-Gen Business Platform*, in which he argues that SaaS is at a fundamental "tipping point" between the current generation of software functionality delivered as a cost-effective service—the familiar SaaS he dubs "SaaS 1.0"—and the emerging generation of blended software, infrastructure, and business services arrayed across multiple usage and delivery platforms and business models, which he dubs "SaaS 2.0."

Saugatuck's research indicates that SaaS adoption has begun a pronounced acceleration, particularly among small to mid-sized businesses (SMBs). This acceleration coincides with the emergence of the SaaS value proposition that Saugatuck refers to as SaaS 2.0. "The bottom line?" he asks. "SaaS 2.0 is about changing business and enabling new

---

16.   www.sliderocket.com.
17.   See http://sandhill.com/opinion/editorial.php?id=80.

Figure 3.6   The Holy Grail: Saint Graal de la légende du Roi Arthur et des Cheva-
liers de la Table Ronde. (Illustration by Arthur Rackham.)

business." For users and for software and services vendors, success will lie in
the balance achieved by using and managing SaaS 2.0, predicts McNee.

Figure 3.7 illustrates this confluence of SaaS adoption and evolution
and reflects Saugatuck's evolution of this model as published in *An Endless
Cycle of Innovation: Saugatuck SaaS Scenarios Through 2014*, published
August 27, 2009.

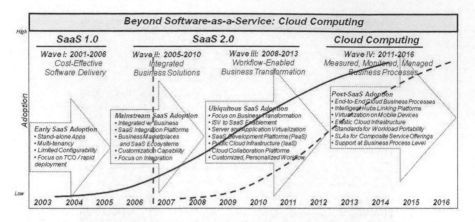

Figure 3.7   Software as a Service (Source: Saugatuck Technology).

Summary

Cloud computing is "in," and many vendors are simply relabeling their offerings to pretend they are cloud applications, but these are not the real McCoy. Caveat emptor (let the buyer beware).

The vision of a computer utility goes back to the 1960s, to John Marthey, Fernando Corbató, and Fred Gruenberger. The rapid development of the personal computer pushed aside interest in its development, which in any event required ubiquitous, high-speed Internet access to become a reality. Many vendors offer managed platforms as a service. Universal standards are emerging, but there is not yet a universal standard, as vendors fight for competitive advantage. Commercial software developers and well as enterprise developers are building robust, multitenant SaaS applications to run efficiently on these platforms, and usage is anticipated to explode over the next few years.

Chapter 4

Moving Into and Around the Clouds and Efforts at Standardization

Most enterprise IT organizations have either implemented or are studying cloud projects. The three most commonly expressed fears are:

- How to keep our data safe
- How to prevent being locked in to a single vendor
- How do we move legacy applications to the cloud

Security is discussed in Chapter 8. Vendor lock-in is addressed in this chapter. Moving to the cloud is addressed here and in Chapters 5 and 10. In Chapter 6, we discuss moving a simple application to the Amazon cloud.

In this chapter, we first explore the issues generally but systematically; then we look at various vendor offering designed to mitigate these valid concerns. Finally, we look at the various "open cloud" efforts towards standardization.

4.1 Portable Software

In the beginning, the hardware vendor owned it all (a single vendor provided all equipment and all software). Not long after mainframes came into general use in enterprises, portability became recognized as an important goal. As faster computers became available, customers wanted to upgrade. They were stymied because the newer machines were incompatible. Workarounds were developed. For example, IBM pioneered the use of microcode on its System/360 models to enable them to run 1401 applications. Such emulators were often used to allow so-called legacy applications to run (albeit with significant overhead) on newer machines. According to a comment by Tom Bell on one blog, *Good Morning Silicon Valley*,[1] programs

---

1. http://blogs.siliconvalley.com/gmsv/2009/10/mainframe-memory-the-ibm-1401-turns-50.html (accessed June 17, 2010).

written for the IBM 1401 (announced October 5, 1959 and withdrawn February 8, 1971[2]) continued to function well into the 1990s.

The virtue of portability, always important, became obvious to everyone once the IBM PC (Model 5150) entered the marketplace on August 12, 1981. With its open architecture, it and its successors were an instant and enduring hit, with one billion shipped by the end of 2008, and 135 million during the first half of 2010, according to Worldometers, which tracks computer shipments in real time.[3] Brandon LeBlanc of Microsoft says that 150 million licenses for Windows 7 were sold between November 2009 and June 2010.[4] Cheap multisourced components, the related DOS operating system, and frequent improvements in processors and other components that still retained op-code-level compatibility sparked the personal computer revolution.

In September 1991, Linus Torvalds released Linux version .01, and it became open source under the GNU Public License (GPL) in February 1992. Linux jumpstarted the open source revolution. Open source versions of Linux and all of the Internet-oriented software built on top of it, such as Apache (see below), MySQL, and PHP/PERL/Python (collectively the LAMP architecture) and the myriad of ISPs offering hosting services built on that architecture amply demonstrate the benefits of openness.

4.2   Openness, Linux, and Apache

The first version of the Apache Web server software running under Linux was created by Robert McCool in 1992, and since April 1996, Apache has been the most popular HTTP server software in use. As of June 2010, fifty-four percent of the 111 million http servers used Apache;[5] they accounted for 66.8 percent of those carrying the bulk of the traffic.[6]

Apache Tomcat, sometimes called Jakarta Tomcat or simply Tomcat, is an open source servlet container maintained by the Apache Software Foundation (ASF).[7] Tomcat implements the Java servlet. A servlet is a Java class that conforms to the Java servlet API, and the JavaServer Pages (JSP) specifications

---

2.   www-03.ibm.com/ibm/history/exhibits/mainframe/mainframe_PP1401.html (accessed June 17, 2010).
3.   www.worldometers.info/computers/.
4.   Blogging Windows, windowsteamblog.com/windows/b/bloggingwindows/archive/2010/06/23/150-million-licenses-of-windows-7-sold-windows-live-betas-announced.aspx (accessed June 25, 2010).
5.   Netcraft June 2010 Web Server Survey news.netcraft.com/archives/2010/06/16/june-2010-web-server-survey.html (accessed June18, 2010).
6.   Ibid.
7.   www.apache.org.

from Sun Microsystems (now part of Oracle).[8] SpringSource tc Server is an enterprise version of Apache Tomcat; it's now owned by VMware. We discuss it in Chapter 7.

4.3   Closed Architectures

In contrast to open source, those who were locked into closed architectures such as DEC Alpha, a series of 64-bit RISC processors made by Digital Equipment Corp. (DEC), ultimately were forced to recode, as DEC was pushed into a merger with Compaq in 1998, and Compaq was itself acquired by HP in 2002; the underlying RISC processor was phased out. The fear of being locked in is real and well-founded.

Vendors are well-aware of the tradeoffs between locking customers into a closed architecture and losing customers who refuse to be locked in. As a result, even classically closed architectures such as Windows have become much more open, bowing to a survival instinct.

A consortium of vendors is working hard to prevent lock-in in the cloud; we discuss their efforts later in this chapter.

4.4   Legacy Applications and Migration to the Cloud

While some might disagree, I define legacy applications as those not written to support a standards-based, Internet-based, and Web-based architecture. With this broad definition, I am obviously sweeping in all "native" personal computer applications, including such stalwarts as Microsoft Office (at least prior to Office 2010).

Sooner or later, enterprises will want to rewrite or replace their legacy applications with those written using a modern architecture, migrate them to the cloud, and manage and control them remotely. In the meantime, the second and third goals can be accomplished using Citrix or VMware's desktop virtualization tools, which we discuss in Chapter 7. Also, in Chapter 6, we discuss tools such as Gladinet for moving data to the cloud, even when the application remains on the desktop and the data needs to be accessed by the legacy desktop application. In Chapter 13, we discuss Nasuni and other vendors whose products reduce or eliminate the potential for data lock-in.

---

8.   JSP was released in 1999 as Sun's answer to ASP and PHP. JSP was designed to address the perception that the Java programming environment didn't provide developers with enough support for the Web. A servlet is a protocol for how a Java class may respond to HTTP requests and provides a "pure Java" HTTP Web server environment on which Java code can be run.

4.5   Preventing Vendor Lock-In as You Migrate to the Cloud

"Insanity is when you keep doing the same things expecting different results," wrote Rita Mae Brown.[9] In a similar vein, in *The Life of Reason*, George Santanyana (1863–1952) famously wrote, "Those who cannot remember the past are condemned to repeat it."[10] While IT has been battling lock-in since the earliest days of computing, not too much attention has been paid to this problem as IT rushes to madly to embrace the cloud.

4.5.1   What to do?

To prevent being locked in to a single vendor, you need to ensure that the architecture you have selected can run on multiple clouds, and that the data can be easily migrated from Cloud A to Cloud B.

While that sounds trite and simple, it's still true. And in theory, it's not hard. But as usual, God (or the Devil; take your pick) is in the details.

Totally new development without any use of legacy code is the easy case, but it is not so common; we all carry around the accumulated baggage of the past. However, should you be fortunate enough to have this luxury, I would suggest developing on Eucalyptus (see the later section on this platform) or OpenStack,[11] a new open source effort led by Rackspace and NASA[12], and using one or more of the most favored languages for cloud development, namely C++, Java, or Python, or PHP for less-demanding applications. This approach gives you the greatest choice of providers, including those discussed in Chapters 3, 5, and 8 through 11. Eucalyptus runs under VMware, is compatible with AWS, supports Windows Virtual Machines (in Eucalyptus Enterprise Edition 2.0), and is supported by many, if not most, of the cloud service vendors. In addition to Linux images, Eucalyptus EE 2.0 customers can now deploy images running on Windows Server 2003 and 2008 and Windows 7, along with an installed application stack in a Eucalyptus private cloud environment.

---

9.   Rita Mae Brown cited it as her own in *Sudden Death*, 1983, p. 68. It has also been variously attributed to an old Chinese proverb, Benjamin Franklin, and Albert Einstein.

10.   George Santanyana, *The Life of Reason*. Project Gutenberg eBook, www.gutenberg.org/files/15000/15000-h/15000-h.htm (accessed June 18, 2010).

11.   See Sean Michael Kerner, "Rackspace, NASA Partner on OpenStack Cloud Computing Install," Internet.com, July 19, 2010. Available at www.serverwatch.com/news/article.php/3893726/Rackspace-NASA-Partner-on-OpenStack-Cloud-Computing-Install.htm (accessed July 20, 2010).

12.   www.microsoft.com/visualstudio/en-us/visual-studio-2010-launch.

OpenStack, currently built with the Ubuntu Linux distribution and using the KVM virtualization hypervisor, is compatible with Amazon's AWS and is expected to run directly on Linux as well as be compatible with VMware, Xen or Hyper-V. However, if, like most enterprises, you need to deal with an accumulation of legacy applications, then it is obviously important to understand what the accumulated inventory of platforms and languages consists of, and to determine whether source code is available or has been partially or totally lost (this happens much more than one might imagine).

Next, you need to determine whether to use this as the opportunity to recode or to just make the existing applications work in cloud. If you are recoding, then the previous advice holds. If not, vendor choices for migrating applications to the cloud will be dictated (and limited) by several constraints:

- Does the vendor support the operating system(s) and programming languages that you require?
- Which database management systems are required? Is there a vendor-maintained "image" that supports your DBMS?
- How much memory and processing power is required? Does the vendor provide sufficiently powerful machines, and is there room to grow?
- Do you choose a private, public, or hybrid cloud? What impels your decision?
- Do the management tools you have in place support management in the cloud? Are there upgrades available? If not, you need to select one or more of the tools described in this book.
- How rapidly do your needs change, and can your vendor provision and deprovision fast enough?
- Does the vendor's service level agreement (SLA) meet your needs?
- Is your auditor satisfied with the vendor's documentation of its compliance with SAS 70 and ISO 27001? Is SysTrust certification available?

4.5.2   More Questions

As RightScale.com states on its Web site:

All clouds are not created equal, and all clouds do not create equal lock-in. Consider the following questions regarding the portability of your current application from one environment or cloud to another. They provide a way to measure the degree to which you may risk lock-in with a given cloud choice.

- *Application—Do you own the application that manages your data, or do you need another tool to move your data or application?*
- *Web services—Does your application make use of third-party web services that you would have to find or build alternatives?*
- *Development and run-time environment—Does your application run in a proprietary run-time environment and/or is it coded in a proprietary development environment? Would you need to retrain programmers and rewrite your application to move to a different cloud?*
- *Programming language—Does your application make use of a proprietary language, or language version? Would you need to look for new programmers to rewrite your application to move?*
- *Data model—Is your data stored in a proprietary or hard-to-reproduce data model or storage system? Can you continue to use the same type of database or data storage organization if you moved, or do you need to transform all your data (and the code accessing it)?*
- *Data—Can you actually bring your data with you, and if so, in what form? Can you get everything exported raw, or only in certain slices or views?*
- *Log files and analytics—Do you own your history and/or metrics, and can you move it to a new cloud, or do you need to start from scratch?*
- *Operating system and system software—Do your system administrators control the operating system platform, the versions of libraries, and the tools, so you can move the know-how and operational procedures from one cloud to another?*

Source: http://www.rightscale.com/products/advantages/avoiding-lock-in.php. Adapted by permission.

4.5.3   Comparing Costs

As this book is written, if we use a normalized example of a virtual 8 GB RAM system with 320 GB of disk running Windows Server Enterprise 64-Bit operating system, operating continuously for a month, the charges from four large vendors are as shown in Table 4.1.

Table 4.1   Vendor prices.

Vendor	Month	Hourly	What is Provided
Rackspace Cloud	$ 417	$0.58	8 GB RAM 320 GB Disk included in base
Amazon—AWS	$ 394	$0.48	7.5 GB RAM, Incl. 320 GB S3 Storage
Terremark—vCloud	$ 607	$0.722	Incl. 8 GB RAM and 4 CPU + 320 GB Disk
SoftLayer—CloudLayer	$ 435	$0.50	Incl. Windows Server + 350 GB Disk

Bandwidth charges can vary significantly (and are excluded), as can surcharges for heavy processor (CPU) usage and for extra disk space. A more detailed discussion of economics and performance is provided in Chapter 5.

Linux platforms are less expensive, as no licensing fees are due to Microsoft.

4.6   Narrowing the Choices

To narrow the choices, we need to understand the development tools needed and the resources required. Then we look at the specialized tools to support your enterprise in the cloud.

4.7   Scripting Languages

Much enterprise development is not done with traditional compiled programming languages, but with scripting languages. To start, it is helpful to distinguish scripting languages from compiled languages, as illustrated in Table 4.2.

Table 4.2 Where scripts are located and executed.

Method	Where script code is located	Where script code is executed
CGI*	In files in the CGI-BIN directory on the server.	On the server.
PHP, ColdFusion, ASP	Embedded in the HTML document.	On the server.
Javascript	Embedded in the HTML document.	On the user's PC, by browser.
Java**	In files on server.	On user's computer, by browser.

* Perl and CGI are NOT the same. CGI programs, or scripts, can be written in a variety of computer languages, including C. CGI is the process by which scripts are run. However, Perl is the most commonly used language for writing CGI scripts.
** Java is a compiled language.

Microsoft Visual Studio and Other Development Environments

Today, most new (full-bodied) applications are developed for the enterprise either using Microsoft's .Net architecture with Visual Studio or in the C++, Java or Python languages using other tools. Simpler projects or parts of projects may be coded in PHP or PERL (CGI scripts), and run in a J2EE container, if necessary, so they can integrate well with Java; they may also be coded in JavaScript. Some developers are fanatical about C# and Ruby. Considerable in-house development is done with cascading style sheets (CSSs) and ASP.Net, a Web framework. ASP.Net applications need to be hosted on a Windows hosting provider; there are many.

Programs developing with .Net tools will (after recompilation) run most directly in the Microsoft Azure cloud platform. They also will run in the cloud on a Windows virtual server.

C++ produced with Microsoft tools is, of course, compatible with that produced by other C++ compilers.

Visual Studio is probably the most popular enterprise development tool. The latest version, Visual Studio 2010 is a single development environment for Windows, Web, Cloud, Office and Sharepoint development. Built-in languages include C/C++ (using Visual C++), VB.NET (using Visual Basic .NET), C# (via Visual C#), and F#. Support for other languages such as M, Python, and Ruby, among others, is available via language services installed separately. It also supports XML/XSLT, HTML/

XHTML, JavaScript, and CSS. Visual Studio 2010 is packaged in a range of editions for different needs.[13]

4.8   Cloud Software

In the following sections, we discuss Eucalyptus, three flavors of cloud-optimized versions of Linux, VPN-Cubed IPsec to support hybrid architectures, Cohesive FT to wrap code in containers for better portability and management, Zend and Abique for vendor independence, RightScale and 3Tera for vendor independent frameworks, Elastra to automate scalability, and Cloud Brokers for interoperability.

We conclude the chapter with a discussion of initiatives for cloud portability and interclouding.

Eucalyptus Enterprise Edition

We discussed Eucalyptus briefly in Chapter 2 and Eucalyptus Enterprise Edition in Chapter 7. Eucalyptus is an acronym for *Elastic Utility Computing Architecture Linking Your Programs To Useful Systems*. It enables the implementation of cloud computing within a data center by providing an infrastructure as a service (IaaS) solution that is compatible with Amazon Web Services (AWS), including Amazon's Elastic Compute Cloud (EC2), Simple Storage Service (S3), and Elastic Block Store (EBS). This solution facilitates movement between AWS, AWS-compatible vendors, and in-private clouds, whether behind the firewall or managed by a third-party vendor, as we discussed in Chapter 2.

Eucalyptus is also compatible with VMware, so it works on most cloud configurations. Users can remotely connect to their Windows VMs via Remote Desktop Protocol (RDP) and use Amazon get-password semantics,[14] vSphere™, ESX™, and ESXi™. A June 16, 2010 press release from Eucalyptus stated that the company

> . . . also supports other hypervisors typically found in a data center, such as Xen® and KVM, providing customers the flexibility to configure cloud solutions that best meet their infrastructure needs. In addition, Eucalyptus EE provides an image converter that helps users develop

---

13.   See http://developer.amazonwebservices.com/connect/entry.jspa?externalID=1767 (accessed June 25, 2010).

14.   http://www.cloudlinux.com/benefits/ (accessed July 25, 2010).

VMware-enabled Eucalyptus applications that are compatible with Amazon EC2.
Source: http://www.eucalyptus.com/news/06-16-2010

4.9   Cloud-Optimized Linux

Vendors have sensed that as migration to the cloud accelerates, there is an opportunity for cloud-optimized versions of Linux. Three early entries in this category are Peppermint, CloudLinux, and Ubuntu Enterprise Cloud. We discuss them in the following sections.

4.9.1   CloudLinux

CloudLinux states that it is ". . . optimized for Web hosting, so it improves the stability of your servers, which helps to reduce churn related to downtime and outages."[15] CloudLinux is an operating system (OS) that is commercially supported and interchangeable with the most popular RPM-based distribution on the market. RPM is the baseline package format of the Linux Standard Base (LSB), which is a joint project of several Linux distributions under the organizational structure of the Linux Foundation. Its goal is to standardize the software system structure, including the file system hierarchy, used with the Linux operating system. The LSB is based on the POSIX specification, the Single UNIX Specification, and several other open standards, but extends them in certain areas.

CloudLinux is a commercially supported OS designed specifically for the service provider market. CloudServer's revenue is derived mostly from support subscriptions (currently $14 per month, per server).

Lightweight Virtual Environment (LVE) Technology

LVE is an isolation technology that increases server density, stability and reliability. LVE limits the amount of resources (CPU, I/O, and memory) available to a specific process or customer. It is a lightweight and transparent shell. LVE wraps the accounts on a shared server to give hosting providers control over CPU resources.
Source: http://cloudlinux.com/solutionsoverview.html

The advantages of LVE are outlined as follows:

---

15.   http://www.cloudlinux.com/company/news/index.php?ELEMENT_ID=382.

What Can LVE Do?

- *Give hosting providers control over CPU resources (I/O and memory limits to be released)*
- *Prevent individual accounts from slowing down or taking down a server*
- *Protect servers from unpredictable issues that drain resources for other tenants*
- *Increase density so you can host more tenants on one server*
- *Identify accounts that are over-using resources so you can address their needs*
- *Lower risk and increase efficiency on shared servers*
- *Improve server performance*

Source: http://cloudlinux.com/solutionsoverview.html

LVE Wrappers

LVE Wrappers, based on LVE technology, allow you to manage resources at the application level. For example, CloudLinux can enable you to control server resources like Mail, MySQL, and Apache within the server.

According to a CloudLinux press release, LVE Wrappers' tools "allow the administrator to control CPU usage on a server at the tenant or application level. LVE Wrappers allow the server owner to control resources for each application they run, which gives them greater flexibility and stability from the overall server infrastructure."[16] LVE Wrappers enable the server owner to:

. . . start individual applications and daemons inside LVE environments, isolating resource usage for each program. That allows greater overall stability of the server, as one application cannot affect all the other applications running on the server. This is especially useful for servers running multiple applications. For instance, a dedicated server runs a variety of software, such as mail, MySQL and Apache, often at the same time. A spike in mail traffic or a bug in the antispam filtering could affect the Web server—and cause the Web site to slow down. CloudLinux lets the administrator have better control and make sure each daemon only gets the preset amount of CPU. The administrator

---

16. http://prism.mozillalabs.com.

now has the tools to alter the amount of CPU any application can get—
on the fly.
Source: *www.cloudlinux.com/company/news/*
index.php?ELEMENT_ID=382
Cloud Linux Resources

- LVE Wrappers: www.cloudlinux.com/docs/lve_wrapper.php
- Cloud Linux Documentation: www.cloudlinux.com/docs/ index.php
- Download CloudLinux ISO Images (CD-ROM images saved in ISO-9660 format): www.cloudlinux.com/downloads/index.php

4.9.2 Peppermint

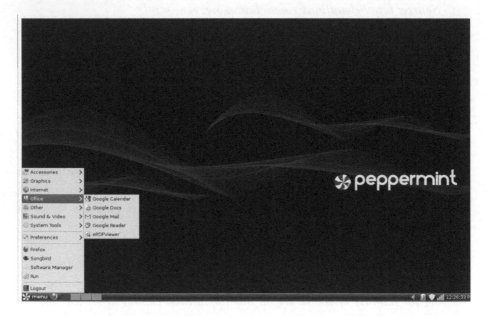

Figure 4.1   Peppermint OS desktop and menu.

Peppermint (peppermintos.com) was designed for enhanced mobility, efficiency, and ease of use. It is cloud- and Web-centric, lightweight (under 512 MB), fast, and boots quickly. It contains:

- Linux Kernel 2.6.32
- Xorg 7.5
- Openbox 3.4.10

- PCManFM 0.9.5
- LXSession 0.4.3

Its default applications are Firefox Web Browser, Drop-Box, Exaile (music management and player), Prism, X-Chat (IRC client), and Transmission (bit torrent client). Of course, you can add your own.

Prism[17] is designed to create a better environment for running your favorite Web-based applications. Much of what we used to accomplish using an application running locally on our computers is moving into the Web browser. Thanks to advances in Web technology, these apps are increasingly powerful and usable. As a result, applications like Gmail, Facebook and Google Docs are soaring in popularity.

Prism allows you to launch and operate Web- and cloud-based applications as if they were actually installed as desktop programs. When you first log into Peppermint, you can access the Main Menu on the bottom left of the desktop by clicking on the Peppermint Candy icon. If you browse to the Sound & Video section, take a glimpse of the applications listed. There are several preloaded Prism "launchers" in this menu, including Pandora, Hulu, and YouTube. By selecting any one of these, Prism will launch each service in its own application window—not in your Web browser. Peppermint is different from (but related to) Linux Mint (www.linuxmint.com), a Debian-based distribution developed by Clement Lefebvre and his team.

4.9.3   Ubuntu's Cloud Strategy

Ubuntu (http://cloud.ubuntu.com/) adopted the following approach (as outlined by Simon Wardley of the Linux distribution's commercial sponsor, Canonical):

- *make the cloud simple.*
- *focus on one layer of the computing stack (infrastructure) to begin with.*
- *help drive standardization (a key requirements of this shift towards a service world) by adopted public de-facto standards.*
- *provide open source systems to avoid lock-in issues.*
- *actively work to mitigate risks and concerns over cloud by giving our users options.*

---

17.   www.eucalyptus.com

Source: http://blog.gardeviance.org/2010/03/cloud-computing-made-simple.html

Ubuntu's approach, Wardley continues,

> *. . . was based around the adoption of Amazon EC2/S3 and EBS as the public de facto standard . . . We provided images for use on Amazon EC2 (public cloud) and the technology to build your own private cloud (known as Ubuntu Enterprise Cloud) that matched the same APIs of Amazon. We also added management tools which could cross both public and private domains because of our adoption of a standard API set.*

Source: http://blog.gardeviance.org/2010/03/cloud-computing-made-simple.html

Ubuntu's partners include:

- *Eucalyptus[18] whose open source technology was adopted into the distribution as a core part of Ubuntu Enterprise Cloud (UEC). [See Chapters 2 and 7, as well as the comments earlier in this chapter.]*
- *Intel, whose Cloud Builder program[19] provides best practices on how to create a private cloud using UEC. I'd strongly recommend reading the white paper.*
- *RightScale[20] and CohesiveFT[21] [described separately in this chapter] to provide best-of-breed public management tools alongside Ubuntu's own Landscape system.*

Source: http://blog.gardeviance.org/2010/03/cloud-computing-made-simple.html

Wardley states that Ubuntu offers:

- *Simple Choices: You can have either private, public or hybrid (i.e. public + private) infrastructure clouds.*

---

18. software.intel.com/en-us/articles/intel-cloud-builder/.
19. www.rightscale.com.
20. www.coheseiveft.com.
21. www.cohesiveft.com/solutions/cloud_container/cloud_container_home/.

- *Simple Setup: If you want to build a private cloud, then Ubuntu makes the set-up ridiculously easy. You can be up and running with your own cloud in minutes. . . .*
- *Simple Management: You can use the same tools for both your private and public clouds because we've standardised around a common set of APIs.*
- *Simple Bursting: Since we provides common machine images which run on both public and private cloud offerings combined with standardised APIs, then the process of moving infrastructure and combining both private and public clouds is . . . simpler.*
- *Enterprise Help: . . . 24x7 support and a jumpstart program to get your company into the cloud are provided at a cost [similar to most open source vendors].*
- *Open source: UEC, the Ubuntu machine images and all the basic tools are open sourced. . . . The system is open source and free and so are all the security patches and version upgrades.*

Source: http://blog.gardeviance.org/2010/03/cloud-computing-made-simple.html

4.10   CohesiveFT

CohesiveFT states that it "provides customers with a cloud container approach that protects them from un-needed differentiation and vendor lock-in."[22]

CohesiveFT has been providing enterprise-grade virtualization and cloud products since 2006 (Elastic Server and VPN-Cubed). . . . Our Cloud Container process is an experience informed methodology proven to take . . . the relevant aspects of their existing physical infrastructure, and create a Cloud Container Solution to enable the rapid on-demand deployment of the cluster topology in cloud environments. CohesiveFT's founders bring enterprise technology expertise to their products and claim to be focused on delivering cloud "on-boarding solutions" for companies with a suite of three products: Elastic Server® for template based assembly of virtual servers, VPN-Cubed® for securing and controlling cloud networking, and Context-Cubed® for managing boot time configuration of virtual servers.
Source: www.cohesiveft.com/solutions/cloud_container/cloud_container_home/

---

22.   www.cohesiveft.com/vpncubed/.

4.10.1   Elastic Server

CohesiveFT offers the Elastic Server platform:

> *The Elastic Server platform is a web-based "factory" [offered by CohesiveFT] for assembling, testing, and deploying custom stacks and servers to virtual machines or clouds. These custom Elastic Servers can be comprised of open source, third-party or proprietary software components from multiple vendors, saved as templates, updated, augmented, or redeployed in minutes. Made-to-order application stacks mean faster assembly and limitless configurations. The Bring Your Own feature lets you pull in your project from GitHub or upload custom components.*

> *Source: www.cohesiveft.com/elastic/*

> *Sound security practices and compliance with data protection regulations boils down to control. If you do not encrypt you data as it moves around the internet, within each hosting facility, and inside each cloud provider's network - do not sign you companies quarterly compliance report, because you are taking unacceptable risk.*

> *In 2008, experts in the cloud computing business were expressing concern and frustration with the lack of security and control with public clouds. At that time, CohesiveFT invented VPN-Cubed, a novel solution, and began the US Patent process. CohesiveFT filed the original patent application(s) for VPN-Cubed on October 21, 2008. A copy of the full patent document for: "A System and Methods for Enabling Customer Network Control in Third-Party Computing Environments" can be found at: US Patent Office: http://tinyurl.com/VPN-Cubed.*

> *Elastic servers are assembled from bundles, which are groups of packages. You can build your own private packages and turn them into bundles.*

> *A server's bill of materials is a permanent record of the bundles used to create it, and can be used to recreate the server at any time for multiple virtualization and cloud platforms.*

> *Source: http://elasticserver.com/servers/new*

4.10.2   VPN-Cubed IPSec to Cloud for Hybrid and Cloud-to-Cloud Applications

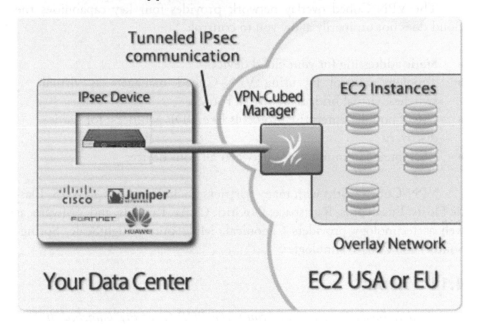

Figure 4.2   VPN-Cubed. (Courtesy CohesiveFT)

CohesiveFT describes its VPN-Cubed as "a commercial solution that enables customer control in a cloud, across multiple clouds, and between private infrastructure and the clouds."[23]

VPN-Cubed is based on open source VPN over IPsec virtual private networking software. VPN-Cubed is based on Open VPN:

> *VPNCubed provides an overlay network that allows customer control of addressing, topology, protocols, and encrypted communications for YOUR devices deployed to virtual infrastructure or cloud computing centers. When using public clouds, your corporate assets are going into 3rd party controlled infrastructure. Enterprise checks and balances require you to exhibit control over your computing infrastructure. VPN-Cubed gives you flexibility with control in third-party environments*

> *Source: http://www.cohesiveft.com/vpncubed/*

---

23.   http://vmblog.com/archive/2010/03/22/cohesiveft-s-vpn-cubed-now-available-for-ter-remark-s-vcloud-express-environment.aspx

VPN-Cubed facilitates secure hybrid connections over firewall-protected environments.

The VPN-Cubed overlay network provides four key capabilities the cloud does not ordinarily allow you to control:[24]

- Static addressing for your cloud devices
- Topology control by using VPN-Cubed managers as virtual switches, virtual bridges, or virtual routers
- Use of popular enterprise protocols like UDP Multicast for service discovery
- Encrypted communications between all your devices

VPN-Cubed works with many partners, including Amazon AWS, Elastic Hosts, Eucalyptus, Rackspace, GoGrid, Citrix, Parallels, and VMware, as well as technology providers Canonical, MuleSource, RightScale, SpringSource, and Zeus Technologies.

4.11   Zend[25]

Zend Technologies [www.zend.com], the PHP Company, launched the Simple API for Cloud Application Services project, a new open source initiative that allows developers to use common application services in the cloud, while enabling them to unlock value-added features available from individual providers. The project aims to facilitate the development of cloud applications that can access services on all major cloud platforms. Zend, IBM, Microsoft, Nirvanix, Rackspace and GoGrid are co-founding contributors to this community project.

The Simple Cloud API project empowers developers to use one interface to interact with a variety of cloud application services, enabling them to more easily access new technologies from cloud vendors. The first deliverables will include interfaces for file storage, document database, and simple queue services from platforms like Amazon Web Services, Windows Azure, Nirvanix Storage Delivery Network, and Rackspace Cloud Files. As a result, developers can deploy software applications to access

---

24.   From the Zend Technologies press release, "Zend Teams with IBM, Microsoft, Rackspace and Other Cloud Leaders on Open Source Initiative to Drive Cloud Application Development." Content used with approval from Zend.

25.   This section is partially drawn from Abiquo's Web site, http://www.abiquo.com Content used with approval from Abiquo.

services in these environments without making time-consuming and expensive changes to their source code.

"The Simple Cloud API combines the benefits of open source community processes with the active participation of the cloud vendors themselves," said Andi Gutmans, CEO of Zend. The Simple Cloud API project is designed to encourage widespread participation and contributions from the open source community, resulting in the availability of Simple Cloud API adapters for virtually all major cloud providers. Zend Cloud adapters will be available for services such as:

- *File storage services, including Windows Azure blobs, Rackspace Cloud Files, Nirvanix Storage Delivery Network, and Amazon S3*
- *Document Storage services, including Windows Azure tables and Amazon SimpleDB*
- *Simple queue services, including Amazon SQS and Windows Azure queues*

Other adapters, such as those for Rackspace Cloud Files API, will work with external libraries with no changes to application code. Microsoft is also contributing Simple Cloud API adapters, along with the official PHP client libraries for Windows Azure storage, to future versions of Zend Framework. These adapters will allow applications to take advantage of many Windows Azure features through the Simple Cloud API interface, while Microsoft's client libraries will put Windows Azure innovations, such as transaction and partial upload support, at the fingertips of cloud application developers.

IBM will also be contributing adapters for IBM's cloud service interfaces, as well as adapters to IBM's data storage products, allowing developers to easily switch between public clouds, private clouds and traditional data center environments.

An initial Simple Cloud API proposal and reference implementation is available now for community review and participation at http:// www.simplecloud.org. Developers can also evaluate the Simple API for Cloud Application Services by deploying their applications that use it on the Amazon cloud using the freely available Zend Server Community Edition Amazon Machine Image (AMI) for EC2.

Source: www.zend.com/en/company/news/press/zend-teams-with-ibm-microsoft-rackspace-and-other-cloud-leaders-on-open-source-initiative-to-drive-cloud-application-development

4.12   Abiquo[26]

Abiquo is a complete solution designed from the ground-up to provide next generation Cloud management. Abiquo provides features like virtual to virtual conversion; reportedly, it is easy to implement and operate and facilitates managing thousands of virtual machines, without relinquishing control of the physical infrastructure.

Authorized users and groups are empowered to manage their own virtual enterprises within allocated resource limits. New virtual machines or pre-built appliances can be deployed in seconds, dramatically improving efficiency and allowing you to regain business agility.

Source: http://www.abiquo.com/products/abiquo-overview.php

Abiquo manages all aspects of the virtualization infrastructure, including the physical cores, network and storage resources. It is vendor agnostic, supporting all of the popular hypervisors and will convert one supported hypervisor type to any other in a simple drag-and-drop operation, ending vendor lock-in. Abiquo will capture and store stateful virtual images in shared, private, and public image repositories. The repositories allow customers to view all virtual images, centrally load gold images from an enterprise's existing storage systems, and immediately deploy. As a result, enterprises no longer needed to start from scratch on the Cloud; they could leverage and deploy existing images, a major time-saver when migrating.

Source: http://www.abiquo.com/news-and-events/abiquo1.6.php

4.12.1   Abiquo's Vision

The Resource Cloud

In the Abiquo vision, the provision of physical infrastructure is completely separated from the virtual application infrastructure by a "Resource Cloud". Physical infrastructure, managed by the IT infra-

---

26.   Adapted with permission from Abiquo's website, www.abiquo.com.

structure organization, contributes resources to the Resource Cloud, while virtual enterprises (containing virtual datacenters, virtual machines and virtual appliances) consume it. Today, we might think of the resources as CPU cores, memory, storage and connectivity, but these terms will change to more universal units of resource as the market evolves.

. . . the IT infrastructure organization delegates management of the virtual enterprises. It simply creates a virtual enterprise, assigns someone to administer it, and sets limits as to the resource that may be consumed. All of this takes less than a minute. The assigned administrator could be a development lab manager, or similar, but in many cases, especially in enterprise organizations, he or she will be an IT organization professional in another area—for example the messaging group that manages operation of corporate email.

The decision as to where a virtual machine is deployed (i.e., the actual physical server it will run on) is determined entirely automatically, according to policy. In fact, neither the virtual enterprise administrator, nor any other consumer of the Resource Cloud knows either. And so long as deployment has occurred according to policy, they don't care.

Policy is however vitally important. It governs obvious rules, like "don't try to run this workload on a server that has insufficient capacity or the wrong hypervisor", [and also implements] security polic[ies such as] "this application must be network separated from that application", to "this application is so sensitive it can only run in a local datacenter." It also covers how available physical resources are to be utilized, by implementing appropriate policies such as, "spread the load across all available machines" where maximum performance is required to "load each physical machine fully before loading the next one" in a hosting environment.

Elasticity

Physical resources can be provided by a local datacenter, remote data centers owned by the organization (together a Private Cloud) or by third party providers (Public Cloud). The IT infrastructure organization has full control of the resources added to the resource cloud and, in the case of public cloud resources such as Amazon EC2, of the amount that may be consumed with each vendor. Combined with workload policy, this allows third-party resources to be consumed safely and in line with suitable security, taking advantage of standards as they evolve.

Libraries Manage Virtual Machine Images

Where permitted by role, users can capture and store virtual machine images in private, shared or even public libraries. They can combine sets of VM images into a single appliance for easy redeployment. Shared libraries allow the IT organization to define standard VM images—for example built to company antivirus, directory, and control requirements. Public VM images from reputable vendors can be downloaded for rapid deployment of complex systems, dramatically reducing implementation and evaluation times.

Benefits

[Abiquo] reduces the load on the IT infrastructure organization, by delegating responsibility for virtual enterprise management. Given that virtual enterprise users don't have direct access to physical machines, and that virtual enterprises cannot exceed allocation resources (because workload management doesn't allow it), there is no danger in this delegation. The IT infrastructure organization can then rest easy, [and] focus on meeting service levels. . .

Source: *http://www.abiquo.com/resources/vision.php*

4.12.2   Management Benefits

Using VMWare's VCloud (Cloud User API) standard, Abiquo offers a Cloud Service API enabling self-service administrators to migrate existing VMs and other resources into the resource cloud quickly and easily.

Abiquo 1.6 includes network management capabilities such as support for 802.1Q VLAN model with trunking, multiple NICs per virtual machine, multiple virtual LANS (VLANs) per virtual datacenter, named networks, fully configurable address spaces, allocation policy management based on VLAN availability, physical NIC customization, and support for DHCP relays. Earlier releases of Abiquo already provided the ability to identify, purchase, and assign public IP addresses at a targeted location, as well as the ability to centrally track all networks running in virtual enterprises. A Cloud Operator API, inspired by Sun Public Cloud (Resource Cloud API), enables an Operator to run a dynamic, scalable cloud that is configured based on automated capacity rules.

4.12.3   Other Abiquo Benefits

Hypervisor Independence
Abiquo was designed to avoid dependence on any hypervisor. Not only are all major hypervisors fully and simultaneously supported, Abiquo allows conversion of virtual machines from one hypervisor to another in any combination, completely eliminating vendor lock-in with a single drag and drop operation. Supported hypervisors include all the major hypervisors in use today:

- *VMware ESX and ESXi*
- *Microsoft Hyper-V*
- *Citrix XenServer*
- *Virtual Box*
- *Xen*
- *KVM*

Multi-tenancy with Delegated Control
Hierarchical user management and role based permissions allow delegation of management tasks according to the organization's needs. Since any user's view is limited to the hierarchy below them, Abiquo provides multi-tenancy with full isolation, whether to internal groups, or to external customers. A single Web-based management console is context sensitive to the role and permissions of the relevant user, reducing complexity and providing unparalleled ease of use.

Setting and Enforcing Resource Limits
Defined CPU, memory and storage limits for each Virtual Enterprise, including both hard (enforced) and soft (warning) levels for each ensure that no Virtual Enterprise can exceed its allocated resource limit; there is no danger of users exceeding the capabilities of the physical infrastructure.

Network and Storage Management
Storage resources from popular standards and vendors can be managed, including OpenSolaris ZFS and LVM/iSCSi, allocating them to Virtual Enterprises and allowing Enterprise Administrators to perform volume management tasks, as well as allocation to specific virtual machines. Abiquo 1.6 adds extended Logical Volume Manager (LVM) storage support on Linux-based Servers to manage iSCSI LUNs.

Source: *http://www.abiquo.com/products/abiquo-overview.php*

Abiquo partners with Red Hat, IBM, Oracle (Sun), HP, Microsoft, and VMware.

4.13   3Tera

3Tera, acquired by CA in June 2010, offers Cloudware (www.3tera.com/ Cloud-computing), an architecture providing an open framework to allow the development of a cloud computing environment that's open enough to work on nearly any Web/enterprise application. The absence of cloud computing standards have led to vendor lock-in, where each cloud vendor offers a proprietary cloud. Cloudware is a big step toward bridging clouds and creating standards that will lead to an open environment for clouds, providing customers with mix-and-match capability and freedom of movement.

3Tera presents its vision of "Utility Computing" on its Web site:

> *3Tera's AppLogic grid operating system eliminates the binding of software to hardware through self-contained software components called virtual appliances. Combined with an expansive management capability and simple graphical interface, implementing, managing and deploying applications to a cloud is fast and easy. The use of virtual appliances also makes services scalable within 3Tera AppLogic. In essence 3Tera provides the fundamental elements of a cloud solution that can be offered by a service provider or used directly by enterprises.*
>
> *When virtual appliances aren't running, they consume no processing resources and only a small amount of storage. As such, rather than using them sparingly like traditional software, virtual appliances can be packaged with every application that uses them. In essence, the virtual appliances form a disposable infrastructure on which the application relies while operating. When the application is run, the virtual infrastructure it requires is created dynamically on the grid, maintained while it runs, and disposed of when it stops.*
>
> *3Tera AppLogic enables users to build a cloud computing environment in a matter of hours, and includes the features needed to operate and manage the cloud. Users take virtual appliances and assemble them into composite services through a simple drag-and-drop interface. These services are then deployed and scaled as needed on the 3Tera AppLogic cloud as a single logical entity. The platform also provides a single point of management for the cloud, and access to advanced high availability features, resource metering, operations monitoring, and a scriptable command line interface.*

3Tera AppLogic is vendor-neutral. It uses advanced virtualization technologies to be completely compatible with existing operating systems – Windows, Linux and Unix – middleware and applications. Minimum requirements are Intel P4 or compatible AMD processor at 1GHz or better, 512MB of RAM, 80GB of ATA/SATA storage, one gigabit Ethernet interface for the backbone and another Ethernet interface for the public network.

Source: *www.3tera.com/Utility-Computing*

4.14   Elastra

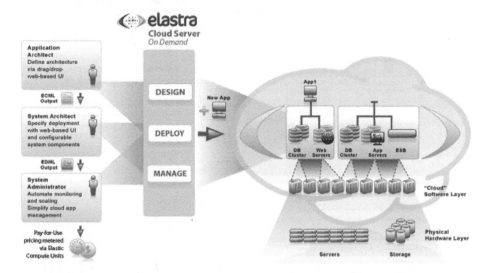

Figure 4.3   Elastra Cloud Server On Demand.

Elastra (www.elastra.com) is a company with an interesting kind of cloud-based middleware. It was founded by serial entrepreneur Kirill Sheynkman, who successfully sold companies to IBM and to BEA. Elastra is funded by Hummer Winblad Venture Partners, an experienced venture capital firm who invests almost exclusively in software and middleware and lately has been investing heavily in Software as a Service (SAAS) and in cloud computing. John Hummer sits on their board.

Elastra aims to help you easily overcome the challenges of scalability in the cloud, by making it seem almost transparent to you:

The Elastra Cloud Server gives your IT organization the ability to:

- *Rapidly model and provision application infrastructure*
- *Automate changes to the system deployment process*
- *Efficiently utilize internal, external, and virtualized IT resources on demand*
- *Enforce IT policy rules*

Source: *www.elastra.com/products/elastra-enterprise-cloud-server*

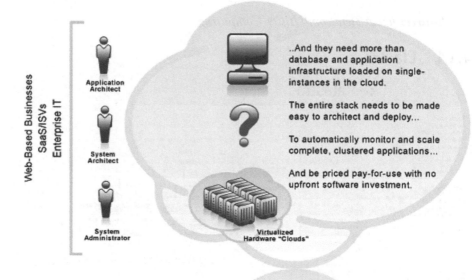

Figure 4.4   Controlling virtualized servers in the cloud. (Courtesy Elastra)

Elastra has three design goals for an end-to-end cloud design approach:

- *Separated Applications from Infrastructure, through modeling the application in terms of its architecture and infrastructure requirements without tying the application to a specific set of underlying infrastructure*
- *Enabling Computer-Assisted Modeling and Control Automation, provided by a set of control agents and user-guided by graphical design tools. This could help IT architects and operators determine design constraints on the application, match the design to the underlying infrastructure, and enable goal-driven*

automation to deploy, scale, or recover their IT systems on demand.

- *Explicit Collaboration To Enact Changes, through models that codify, relate, and analyze the constraints and preferences that are appropriate to stakeholders across enterprise IT—from architects and developers, through operators, administrators, and managers.*

Source: *www.elastra.com/technology/reference-architecture-introduction*

Elastra has defined a set of modeling languages and a reference architecture and has built an implementation that integrates both existing and emerging IT automation and management servers. This work is based on a set of eight characteristics desirable for an information system that addresses cloud application design and operations problems holistically. These characteristics are listed in Elastra's Reference Architecture introduction, available at www.elastra.com/technology/reference-architecture-introduction (accessed July 20, 2010).

Elastra for Amazon Web Services[27]

Model Open Source Infrastructure
Use the design workbench to quickly and easily create a variety of reusable application infrastructure designs. Create anything from an Apache web farm to a J2EE stack, or just a design with a single piece of software.

Deploy to Amazon Web Services
Automate the deployment of models with a click of a button. Quickly generate end-to-end, executable, model-driven deployment plans that streamline provisioning of EC2 resources and open source components such as Apache, JBoss, Tomcat and MySQL.

Source: *www.elastra.com/products/elastra-for-aws*

4.15 RightScale

RightScale (www.rightscale.com) has focused on creating a transparent platform that embraces open standards, giving you the tools to avoid lock-in.

---

27. This section adapted from http://www.rightscale.com/products/advantages/servertemplates-vs-machine-images.php. Content used with approval from RightScale.

The RightScale Cloud Management Platform lets you choose freely from a variety of programming languages, development environments, data stores, and software stacks. You choose the components and at any time you can make changes, add additional components, or move it all back into your own data center.

Your freedom to choose extends to the cloud provider or infrastructure as a service (IaaS) layer as well. You can select the best cloud infrastructure for your application, migrate to a new one, or split deployments across multiple clouds—public or private—all from within RightScale's single management environment. With new cloud providers emerging all the time, you'll be able to select the best cloud for your specific application requirements, security or SLA mandates, geographic locations, usage patterns, or pricing to maximize performance, flexibility, and return on investment.

This portability is offered without sacrificing the automation you need to be productive. Other solutions delivered by PaaS vendors have automated their environments at the expense of portability. While these vendors provide well-established and robust offerings, they often lock you in to proprietary programming languages, data stores, or black-box environments. Such PaaS platforms largely eliminate your freedom to develop using the best tools for your application, maintain a tight grip on your data, and restrict your visibility into all levels of execution of your application.

RightScale sets itself apart through Cloud-Ready ServerTemplates. This is a unique approach to managing complete deployments—comprising multiple servers and the connections between them—across one or more clouds. Within such deployments, each server can be preconfigured and controlled using a cloud-ready ServerTemplate. A ServerTemplate starts with a RightImage, a simple base machine image (similar to Amazon's AMI) that normally contains only the operating system, and then adds RightScripts, scripts that define the role and behavior of that particular server. RightScripts may run during the boot, operational, and shutdown phases of the server's lifecycle.

One key advantage of ServerTemplates lies in their ability to deploy cloud-ready servers. These servers know how to operate in the cloud—i.e., how to obtain an IP address, how to access and manage storage, how to submit monitoring data, and how to collaborate with other servers in a cloud deployment. Another advantage lies in their innovation beyond the "machine image" model, allowing you to more flexibly and quickly modify server configurations.

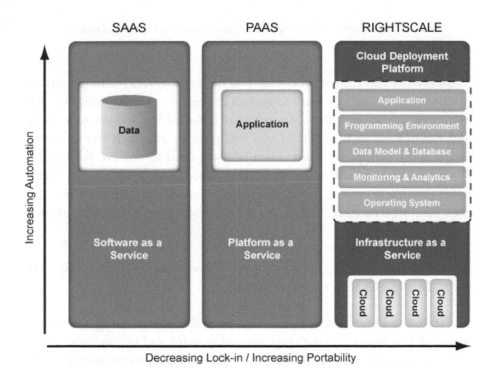

Figure 4.5   RightScale for vendor independence. (Courtesy RightScale Inc.)

ServerTemplates versus Machine Images[28]

ServerTemplates speed the configuration and simplify the management of servers in your deployments by innovating beyond the "machine image" model. With machine images, configuration information is forced into a static machine image on disk into which scripts, executables, and variables are hard-coded and frozen. ServerTemplates store their components outside the machine image in a modular fashion. You don't need to launch a server to change it—just make the change to the ServerTemplate or to one of the components—and the next time a server launches, the change will be included automatically. And because these scripts are stored separately from the template, they can be shared across multiple templates. Update a script and, if you like, it will be updated for all templates that use it.

---

28.   http://www.readwriteweb.com/enterprise/2010/05/google-cloud-service-points-
to.php?utm_source=feedburner&utm_medium=feed&utm_campaign=Feed:+read-
writeweb+(ReadWriteWeb) (accessed June 25, 2010).

Source: *www.rightscale.com/products/advantages/servertemplates-vs-machine-images.php*

Consider this scenario: Let's say you have ten servers running based on machine images and you want to make a change to the syslog script of each. With machine images, the syslog script is included in each machine image and running on each server, so you will need to edit each live (running) image one at a time, by hand. Then you will need to retrieve the saved or "bundled" images held in the data store, launch a server with that image, make the change manually, resave the image, place the disk file ("bundle") back into the data store, and decommission the server. That's a lot of manual labor!

COST = Time to Change Image × Live Images + Time to Retrieve, Launch, Change × Stored Images

If you deploy those same servers with RightScale using ServerTemplates, all you have to do is change the syslog script and relaunch the appropriate servers. The new syslog will click into the boot process automatically. To have already-running servers reflect the new syslog script, the systems administrator simply needs to tell RightScale which servers to update and the change will be automatically propagated. That's a huge step forward in time-saving automation.

4.16   Today is Like 1973

Vint Cerf, a founder of the Internet back in the day and now a Google employee, says the situation today reminds him of the e-mail delivery situation in 1973. There aren't yet universal standards for moving data around. Vendors need to work cooperatively so customers can easily move information between services. Until that happens, enterprises will exercise caution about moving vital data to the cloud. Cloud computing today is similar to the earliest days of snail mail delivery, when a nationwide network did not yet exist to reliably and expeditiously move letters from one location to another. From the need to deliver mail came *peering*, in the form of reciprocal agreements and flat rates. Mail began to be charged by weight. Address standards emerged. Standardized envelope sizes and stamps allowed for better handling and portability; the emergence of trains and steamships provided an improvement in infrastructure.

Today, Alex Williams, an editor for ReadWriteWeb says, "we need cloud peering in the form of reciprocal agreements and flat rates. Compatibility means open APIs and formats. Portability is about standard virtual machines and images. And better infrastructure is needed to reduce intercloud latency."[29]

It's not tremendously complicated, and we are moving rapidly in the right direction. "Peering agreements can be relatively simple," Williams says. Peering should be simplified, as most data centers are clustered in specific geographic regions. Tom Hughes-Croucher (Yahoo! Developer Network) and Carlos Bueno (Yahoo! Mail) point to the effects on carriers when SMS messages could freely flow between the networks. SMS message volume increased anywhere from 250 percent to 900 percent in the span of a short six months.[30]

As Hughes-Croucher says, lock-in is not just about APIs and data formats. "It's a BIG mistake to think that lock-in has gone away because we have open-source software. There are some kinds of problems that you can't program your way out of."

Vendors are listening.

4.17 Interclouding, Standards, and VMware's Focus on Open PaaS

Google started The Data Liberation Front[31] at the urging of Vint Cerf. This is an engineering team at Google whose singular goal is to make it easier for users to move their data in and out of Google products. Google says,

> We do this because we believe that you should be able to export any data that you create in (or import into) a product. We help and consult other engineering teams within Google on how to "liberate" their products. This is our mission statement:

> Users should be able to control the data they store in any of Google's products. Our team's goal is to make it easier to move data in and out.

Source: *www.dataliberation.org/*

29. The Cloud's Hidden Lock-In: Network Latency, http://assets.en.oreilly.com/1/event/31/The%20Cloud_s%20Hidden%20Lockin_%20Network%20Latency%20Presentation.pdf.
30. Ibid.
31. http://www.dataliberation.org/.

The statement is a recognition that data liberation, in the end, grows the business faster and larger than forcing customers into lock-up data silos. Cloud vendors, especially Google and VMware, noted that enterprises are very concerned with the portability of their applications—something that is often a concern or blocker for public PaaS offerings. As we discuss in Chapter 8, they are also rightly concerned about reliability, availability and security.

Amazon, too, has made available AWS Import/Export,[32] which makes it easier to move data to and from Amazon S3 using portable storage devices for transport, with a maximum device capacity of 4TB. While this form of "sneaker-net" has been around since system engineers hand-carried floppy disks from one stand-alone PC to another, it's much cheaper and more reliable than trying to send very large files over the Internet.

Still, it's a stopgap measure at best. VMware's PaaS will have a significant focus on enterprise-grade qualities—providing strong controls for privacy, identity, and authorization control, allowing applications to be extensions of those in the corporate datacenter.

VMware's entries into this space focus on addressing this challenge and, with the company's partners (described earlier), creating "Open PaaS" offerings:

> *Virtualization is about separating the logical view of server assets from the physical resources upon which they run. By severing the tentacles that crept in between traditional operating systems and hardware, it enables virtual machines with hardware independence and mobility (among many other capabilities). In similar fashion, a PaaS offering can be architected in a way that clearly separates layers and avoids the restrictions seen in many of today's implementations. Furthermore, the parts of a PaaS offering that the applications depend on (e.g. libraries, messaging, data access) can be built using open development frameworks and technologies with liberal licensing programs. Ultimately this makes it easier for an ecosystem of more compatible PaaS offerings to grow, providing choice for the developers and consumers of the applications.*
> *Our initial open PaaS offerings focus on a particularly important choice . . . choice as to where you deploy and run your applications.*

---

32.   http://aws.amazon.com/importexport/.

Source: *http://blogs.vmware.com/console/2010/04/vmforce-and-vmwares-open-paas-strategy.html*

As VMware knows, offering a choice such as this requires industry-wide standards.

4.18 DMTF

Industry-wide, the standardization effort is being coordinated through The Distributed Management Task Force, Inc., (DMTF[33]) a not-for-profit organization devoted to developing management standards and promoting interoperability for enterprise and Internet environments. Winston Bumpus, VMware's director of standards architecture and DMTF president, formed the Open Cloud Standards Incubator together with others as a committee within DMTF. The Open Cloud Standards Incubator (OCSI) was to focus on ways to facilitate operations between private clouds within enterprises and other private, public, or hybrid clouds by improving the interoperability between platforms through open cloud resource management standards. The group also aimed to develop specifications to enable cloud service portability and provide management consistency across cloud and enterprise platforms. As the Web site states:

> *The DMTF Standards Incubation process enables like-minded DMTF members to work together and produce informational specifications that can later be fast-tracked through the standards development process. The incubation process is designed to foster and expedite open, collaborative, exploratory technical work that complements the DMTF mission to lead the development, adoption and promotion of interoperable management initiatives and standards.*
>
> *The current incubator leadership board currently includes AMD, CA, Cisco, Citrix, EMC, Fujitsu, HP, Hitachi, IBM, Intel, Microsoft, Novell, Rackspace, RedHat, Savvis, SunGard, Sun Microsystems, and VMware.*
>
> **Source:** *http://www.dmtf.org/about/cloud-incubator (Courtesy, Distributed Management Task Force, Inc.)*

Only Amazon is conspicuously absent.

----

33.   www.dmtf.org/about/cloud-incubator/VMAN_Cloud_Tech_Note_Digital_081909.pdf.

The DMTF works with affiliated industry organizations such as the Open Grid Forum, Cloud Security Alliance, TeleManagement Forum (TMF), Storage Networking Industry Association (SNIA), and National Institute of Standards and Technology (NIST).

OCSI Standardization Efforts

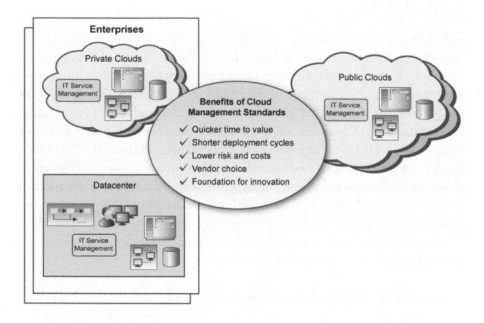

Figure 4.6   Scope and benefits of OCSI. (Courtesy Distributed Management Task Force, Inc.)

The management standards developed within DMTF deal predominantly with IaaS and help manage clouds that provide infrastructure as a service. One OCSI initiative is Virtualization MANagement (VMAN): A Building Block for Cloud Interoperability.[34] VMAN standards address packaging/distribution, deployment/installation, and management of cloud IaaS that rely on virtualized systems. Open Virtualization Format (OVF) is a DMTF standard for packaging and distributing virtual appliances. A *virtual appliance* is a prebuilt software solution, comprised of one or more virtual machines that are packaged, maintained, updated, and managed as a unit. OVF enables portability and simplifies *installation* and *deployment* of virtual appliances across multiple virtualization platforms.[35]

---

34.   www.dmtf.org/standards/published_documents/DSP0243_1.1.0.pdf.

The issues relating to interoperable clouds are discussed in OCSI's white paper.[36] This white paper describes a snapshot of the work being done in the DMTF Open Cloud Standards Incubator, including use cases and reference architecture as they relate to the interfaces between a cloud service provider and a cloud service consumer.

The main use cases being addressed are:

- How building on standards provides flexibility to do business with a new provider without excessive effort or cost.
- How multiple cloud providers may work together to meet the needs of a consumer of cloud services.
- How different consumers with different needs can enter into different contractual arrangements with a cloud provider for data storage services.

4.19   The Problem of Metering

Benjamin Franklin famously said, "The only things certain in life are death and taxes," to which Bert Murray added, "It used to be that death and taxes alone were inevitable. Now there's shipping and handling." In the cloud world, it's metering that seems to be inevitable. This began with the cloud ethos of "pay only for what you use, and don't tie up your money in infrastructure." But that ethos had some (probably unanticipated) negative consequences. Data transfers "inter-colo" (within a collocation facility) are usually fast and free.

Data transferred in to a cloud is usually not as fast, but often is still free. Data transferred out is usually metered (i.e., taxed) and also is not so fast. The delay in data getting from cloud A to cloud B is called latency. Low latency makes it feasible to use Amazon S3 with Amazon EC2, as they are co-located.

4.20   Remember the Dodo Bird

While fees for data transfer of e-mail long ago went the way of the extinct dodo bird of Mauritius, latency and metering of data transfer for intercloud transfer is still an issue. Sending a GB of data from Amazon to Rackspace

---

35.   www.dmtf.org/about/cloud-incubator/DSP_ISO101_1.0.0.pdf.
36.   Tom Hughes-Croucher and Carlos Bueno, "The Cloud's Hidden Lock-In: Network Latency." http://assets.en.oreilly.com/1/event/31/ The%20Cloud_s%20Hidden%20Lockin_%20Network%20Latency%20Presentation.pdf.

Figure 4.7   Extinct dodo bird of Mauritius (Photo by Daniel Endres, released into the public domain).

(or vice versa) is expensive. There are tolls to pay at each end, and it is time-consuming. As Carlos Bueno and Tom Hughes-Croucher point out, "If it costs more money to physically move your data than to maintain it where it is, or if it's too slow to feasibly use Service A on Cloud B, you're effectively locked-in to one vendor."[37] Expressed another way:

Latency + Metering = Lock-in

Carlos Bueno summarizes the problem this way: "The proposition is pretty stark. Stay inside one cloud and everything is fast and cheap. Stray outside and suddenly everything gets slow and expensive."[38]

What to do?

---

37.   Ibid.
38.   DMTF, "Interoperable Clouds: A White Paper from the Open Cloud Standards Incubator", available at http://www.dmtf.org/about/cloud-incubator/DSP_IS0101_1.0.0.pdf (accessed July 26, 2010).

The Treaty of Bern (1874) established the General Postal Union, today known as the Universal Postal Union, to unify disparate postal services and regulations so that international mail could be exchanged freely and cheaply. It provided for uniform letter rates between countries, equal handing of foreign and domestic mail, and for the country of origin keeping all fees (in the belief that in the long run, the volume of mail into and from a country would be approximately equal). In a similar vein, peering agreements and accounting-free, high-speed interchanges for e-mail traffic have become universal.

The cloud needs the same tonic. We need better infrastructure in the form of optimized routes between clouds; we need to be able to move our virtual machines and configurations around without special help; we need to make sure we don't get locked-in by odd APIs or data formats; and we need vendors of cloud and Web services to honor each other's traffic without metering.

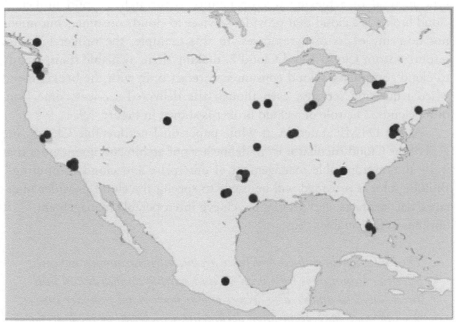

Figure 4.8   Locations of known data centers for main cloud vendors (**source:** www.cloud-peering.com).

Achieving high-speed interclouding is not as expensive as you might imagine. Cloud-peering.com contains a map (Figure 4.8) that shows the locations of six large cloud vendors: Amazon, Google, 3tera (now CA), Microsoft Azure, Rackspace, and Yahoo. The overlap is striking, but if you think about it, unremarkable. Each vendor chose its locations for the same reasons: proximity to the Internet backbone, security, low land costs, low power costs, etc. Unsurprisingly, they are clustered together in a few locations. This simple geographical fact enables ultra-high-speed data transfer at very modest cost.

Stay tuned.

While fast, free, and transparent interclouding isn't quite there yet, some solutions, such as Zend and Abiquo for vendor independence, Right-Scale and 3Tera for vendor independent frameworks, and Elastra to automate scalability, are available today. Most of these are smaller startups that are likely to be acquired by large vendors in the coming years. We discussed these earlier in this chapter and will return to them in Chapter 13.

4.21   Cloud Broker

One method of achieving interoperability is through a cloud broker. A cloud broker is a cloud that provides services to cloud consumers but might not host any of its own resources. In this example, the broker federates resources from Cloud 1 and Cloud 2, making them available transparently to cloud consumers. Cloud consumers interact only with the broker cloud when requesting services, even though the delivered services come from other clouds. The role of a cloud broker is shown in Figure 4.9.

As the DTMF stated in its white paper on Interoperable Clouds, the goal of the Cloud Incubator is "to define a set of architectural semantics that unify the interoperable management of enterprise and cloud computing." Building blocks provided will be used "to specify the cloud provider interfaces, data artifacts, and profiles to achieve interoperable management."[39] It outlines its deliverables thus:

> *The Phase 1 deliverables—reference architecture, taxonomy, use cases, priorities, submissions from vendors, and existing standards and initiatives—will be analyzed to deliver one or more cloud provider interface informational specification documents, which will be the basis for the development of future cloud standards. These documents will describe functional interfaces, protocols, operations, security, and data artifacts. These building blocks are being worked on, but have not yet been published. Phase 2 will deliver a recommendation for each standard, which will include the gaps and overlaps as well as abstract use*

---

39.   http://cloud-standards.org/wiki/index.php?title=Main_Page.

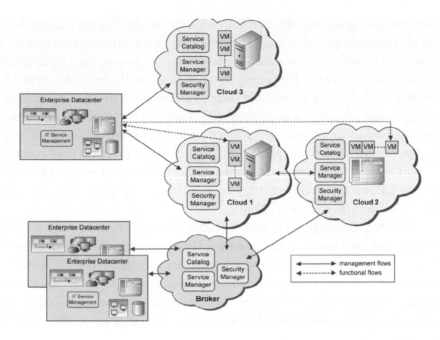

Figure 4.9   Role of a cloud broker (Courtesy DMTF).

cases (usage scenarios that describe one or more business contexts) applicable to the sub-domain of each standard.

Source: *http://www.dmtf.org/about/cloud-incubator/ DSP_IS0101_1.0.0.pdf*

The evolution of cloud standards is coordinated by cloud-standards.org, and they maintain a Wiki for that purpose.[40]

Open Cloud Consortium (OCC)[41] is a member-driven organization that supports the development of standards for cloud computing and frameworks for interoperating between clouds, develops benchmarks for cloud computing, and supports reference implementations for cloud computing.

The OCC also manages test-beds for cloud computing, such as the Open Cloud Testbed, and operates cloud computing infrastructures to support scientific research, such as the Open Science Data Cloud.

OCC seems to be an effort driven mostly by Yahoo! and its university research partners.[42] However, its concerns are industry-wide; its Working Group on Standards and Interoperability For Large Data Clouds (one of

40.   opencloudconsortium.org.
41.   http://opencloudconsortium.org/members.

four working groups at this writing) focuses on developing standards for interoperating large data clouds. For example, what are standard interfaces to storage clouds and compute clouds? What are appropriate benchmarks for large data clouds? The group is concerned with an architecture for clouds popularized by a series of Google technical reports that consists of a storage cloud providing a distributed file system. A compute cloud supporting MapReduce is a patented[43] software framework introduced by Google to support distributed computing on large data sets on clusters of computers and a data cloud supporting table services. The open source Hadoop[44] system follows this architecture. The working group uses the name *large data clouds* for these types of clouds.

One big challenge with today's PaaS offerings is that they are all fairly unique and incompatible with one another and with the way that enterprises run their applications. Once you select a PaaS offering, it is easy to become locked into their particular offering, unable to easily move your applications and data to another PaaS provider or back into your own datacenter should the need arise, which is a challenge for cloud computing as a whole.

Interclouding, DTMF and OVFS

Google's Vint Cerf says that what we need is Intercloud, a goal that Google, VMware, and several others are working to address within the DMTF[45] including the Open Virtualization Format Specification. Just as personal computers didn't really take off until there were just two standards (Apple and IBM-compatible), so too we can expect to see Interclouding, once supported by all major vendors, to greatly accelerate movement to the cloud.

---

42. http://patft.uspto.gov/netacgi/nph-Parser?Sect1=PTO1&Sect2=HIT-OFF&d=PALL&p=1&u=/netahtml/PTO/srch-num.htm&r=1&f=G&l=50&s1=7,650,331.PN.&OS=PN/7,650,331&RS=PN/7,650,331.

43. http://patft.uspto.gov/netacgi/nph-Parser?Sect1=PTO1&Sect2=HIT-OFF&d=PALL&p=1&u=/netahtml/PTO/srch-num.htm&r=1&f=G&l=50&s1=7,650,331.PN.&OS=PN/7,650,331&RS=PN/7,650,331

44. http://hadoop.apache.org

45. DMTF Document Number DSP0243, www.dmtf.org/standards/published_documents/DSP0243_1.1.0.pdf

4.22   Product Offerings

Product solutions discussed in this chapter include Zend, Abique, Right-Scale, 3Tera and, Elastra. Appistry and Nasuni are discussed in Chapter 13.

Summary

In this chapter, we saw why portability is crucial and discussed the questions you need to ask before choosing a vendor. We looked at several versions of Linux optimized for the clouds, briefly reviewed applicable development tools, and then looked at innovative tools that ensure portability. Finally, we looked at efforts underway in the vendor community to promote portability within the cloud as well as emerging standards for high-speed interclouding.

Chapter 5

Cloud Economics and Capacity Management

Overview

In this chapter,[1] we discuss the basis for queueing theory and performance and capacity analysis, look at the economics of cloud computing, introduce key volume indicators for more accurate forecasting, and present the tools of capacity management needed to ensure adequate performance without overpaying.

Choices Abound

The three legs of the cloud computing stool are

- Elasticity (scalability)
- Fee for service
- Agility and standing on tall shoulders

---

1.   This chapter was written with input from Ivan Gelb, who also prepared the related charts in Chapter 15.

The decision to deploy in the clouds is primarily influenced by each of the three legs of the stool, but other, external considerations also play a role. These include:

- Special security considerations (which may eliminate certain solutions, restrict you to a private, in-house cloud, or dictate a hybrid cloud)
- Underlying software requirements (does the vendor offer the existing [customizable] virtual image that you need; what operating system and components do you need?)
- Time to deploy initially (deploying clouds using virtual resources is typically much quicker than procuring and provisioning physical resources)

The chief advantage and chief disadvantage of cloud computing are one and the same: many choices. Cloud computing frees you from investing in infrastructure. So you aren't intending to be too committed. Rather, you are renting the infrastructure you need, on a pay-as-you-go basis. Many support tasks are offloaded to the provider and are bundled into the price charged. You can also be a victim of your own success. A sudden spurt of popularity and resulting spike in usage can bring your system to its knees.

You crossed the abyss and made the basic decision to cloud. You now face a bewildering multiplicity of vendors offering competing services with a variety of capabilities, limitations, lock-ins, and pricing models. How is anyone to make rational choices?

The goal of this chapter is to answer exactly this question.

5.1   Capacity Planning: A Play in Three Acts

The goal of capacity planning is to ensure that you always have sufficient but not excessive resources to meet customers' needs in a timely fashion. The game is acted out as a play in three acts.

The first act is to instrument (measure) what's going on. As Mark Twain said in an interview with Rudyard Kipling, "Get your facts first, and then you can distort them as much as you please."[2] The second act is to forecast the expected workloads (the demand to be placed on the system) and in the third act, you model various combinations to determine the least

---

2.   Rudyard Kipling, "An Interview with Mark Twain," p. 180, *From Sea to Sea: Letters of Travel*, 1899, Doubleday & McClure Company. http://ebooks.adelaide.edu.au/k/kipling/rudyard/seatosea/chapter37.html (accessed July 5, 2010).

costly combination for getting the job done with the response times and service levels that you require. But as Shakespeare says in Hamlet's soliloquy to Ophelia, "Aye, there's the rub."[3]

Act Three of our play is a *model*. And this model has to be *validated*, which means proven correct. Mathematical induction cannot be extrapolated infinitely. If your measurements in Act One were based on 10 transactions a minute, and your forecast in Act Two is for 500 transactions a minute, then you model based on that forecast, and your model was not validated beyond 60 transactions a minute, it's unlikely that the model will be accurate for predicting behavior at 500 transactions per minute. Capacity planning is iterative and requires that you constantly revalidate your models.

The key to success is making accurate assumptions.

Classical assumptions for analysis include:

- The sample must be representative of the population for the inference prediction (in other words, are you comparing apples to apples or cherries to grapefruits?).
- The error is assumed to be a *random variable* with a mean of zero conditional on the explanatory variables (in other words, the variations between the predicted and measured values should be a little higher or a little lower, but the average variance, ideally, is zero, and the error must be explainable).
- The predictors must be *linearly independent* (i.e., it must not be possible to express any predictor as a linear combination of the others. So, for example, varying processor speed should not affect disk speed).
- The variance of the error is constant across observations (in running the model across a variety of circumstances, the degree of accuracy should be roughly equal) .

Models that have been verified over a range of real-life conditions are said to be robust and are useful for prediction.

Capacity Mangement: An Old-New Technique

Capacity management in the clouds is an old-new story. In the early 1970s and continuing through the 1980s, capacity management—configuring just the right configuration of resources to meet response time requirements at

---

3.   William Shakespeare, *Hamlet*, Act III, scene i.

the lowest possible cost—was a hot field. Mainframe computers were complex to configure, had long lead times, and were expensive, often costing more than $1 million ($4 million, adjusted for inflation). It was vital to configure them correctly and to accurately model workloads and related resource utilizations to ensure acceptable response times.

It is no less vital when deploying in the clouds. To configure correctly, we need a basic understanding of queuing theory.

5.2 Queueing Theory

Most capacity planning is based around queueing theory, which is the mathematical study of waiting lines. Agner Krarup Erlang, a Danish engineer working for the Copenhagen Telephone Exchange, published the first paper on queueing theory in 1909. It explains (among other things) the powerful relationship between resource utilization and response time. Queueing theory was used to develop modern packet-switching networks that became the basis for developing the Internet. Important work was performed by Leonard Kleinrock in the early 1960s.

Queueing means standing in line waiting (as in Figure 5.1) for resources to become available. Aside from being the British national pastime (David can say that, as he was born one of Her Majesty's loyal subjects, by "facts of birth" as the passport says), it is the only word in the English language with five consecutive vowels (in its British spelling *queueing*, which we adopt here as this spelling was adopted by the leading journal in the field, *Queueing Systems)*. In the next few paragraphs we explain everything you need to know about queueing but didn't know you needed to ask.

5.3 Queuing and Response Time

Queues form because resources are limited and demand fluctuates. If there is only one bank teller, then we all need to queue (stand in line) waiting for the teller. Typically, more people go to the bank at lunch time than during normal working hours, but even during the peak lunch-hour timeframe, customer arrival rates are not uniform. People arrive when they feel like it. Queueing theory explains what happens when utilization of resources increases and tasks serialize (wait) for a resource to become available. That is, what happens as the teller gets busier and busier. Since requests aren't evenly spaced (people arrive at the bank haphazardly[4]), as utilization of a resource (the teller) increases, waiting times go through the

Figure 5.1   Queue of buses in Scotland (Photograph by Ian Britton, licensed under Creative Commons Attribution-Noncommercial-No Derivative Works 3.0 License from FreeFoto).

roof. The classic queue length (response time) versus utilization curve looks like the curve shown in Figure 5.2.

Now consider this:

Response Time = Waiting Time (Queueing Time) + Processing Time

and

Waiting Time = Time to Service One Request × Queue Length

For example, let us consider a resource (say, a disk drive servicing a database query) that takes, on average, 200 milliseconds per query. The response time is 200 milliseconds if no request is ahead of yours. But if there are 20

---

4.   Technically speaking, incoming traffic to computer systems (as for bank tellers) is usually modeled using a *Poisson distribution*—a discrete probability distribution that expresses the probability of a number of events occurring in a fixed period of time if these events occur with a known average rate (e.g., 100 per hour) but independently of the time since the last event—and are assumed to be subject to Erlang's queuing theory assumptions, including:
Pure-chance traffic—requests arrive and depart at random and independent events.
– *Equilibrium*—(arrivals = departures).
– *Congestion is cleared as soon as servers are free.*

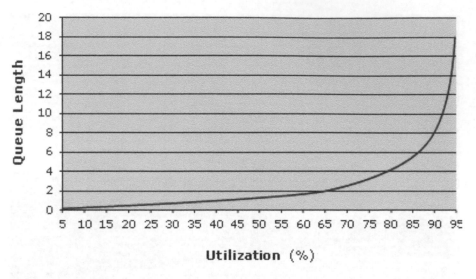

Figure 5.2 Queue length increases as utilization increases.

requests queued ahead of yours, then the average response time will be 200 times 20 or 4,000 milliseconds (4 seconds) of waiting time in addition to the 200 milliseconds needed to get the job done. And as Figure 5.2 shows, the queue grows exponentially as utilization of the resource increases, in a characteristic "hockey-stick" curve.

The magic is that doubling the number of servers has a dramatic effect on response times. In Figure 5.2, if one server is ninety-five percent busy, the queue length is eighteen milliseconds. If we add another server, and these two servers are *both* serving the same workload, each server will, on average, only be busy 47.5 percent of the time, and from Figure 5.2, the average queue length drops from eighteen milliseconds to less than two milliseconds. But the magic is not infinite, and the economic law of diminishing returns (also called diminishing marginal returns) applies. Doubling down[5] to four servers has little effect on improving response times. The servers mostly sit idle, and the resources are wasted. Notice that the "knee" of the above curve occurs between sixty-five and seventy-five percent; for utilization above the knee, response times deteriorate rapidly.

You've observed queuing theory in action while waiting in line at the post office, the bank, or the Department of Motor Vehicles for a single clerk, and then all of a sudden, another clerk is added. Waiting times drop quickly.

You may have also observed it in heavy rush-hour traffic where the road is jammed with cars (very high utilization) and the speed of travel slows to a crawl, but there is no sign of an accident.

Of course, in a computer system, there are numerous resources, and queues form for access to each of them

This explanation was a long-winded way of demonstrating the importance of getting it right. Too few resources, and response times become unacceptable; too many, and resources are wasted.

Cloud computing is a capacity planner's dream. The beauty of cloud-based resources are that you can dynamically and elastically expand and contract the resources reserved for your use, and you only pay for what you have reserved.

5.4   Historical Note on Computer Capacity Management

In the old mainframe days, IBM computers reported extensive information about themselves in a form known as RMF and SMF records. Barry Merrill's classic 1980 book[6] and his related SAS code were widely used to gather and reduce mainframe utilization data. Tools like BEST/1,[7] based on Dr. Jeff Buzen's pioneering work[8] with applying Kleinrock's analytical queuing

---

5.   *Double down* in blackjack: After receiving his first two cards and before any more are dealt to him, a player has the option to *double down*: to double his initial bet in exchange for receiving only one more card from the dealer. The hand played consists of his original two cards plus one more from the dealer. To do this he moves a second bet equal to the first into the betting box next to his original bet.
(If desired and allowed by casino rules, the player is usually allowed to "double down for less," placing an amount less than the original bet next to it in the betting box, although this is generally not a good idea, as the player should only double in favorable situations, but should then increase the bet as much as possible. Conversely, a player cannot double down for more than the value of the original bet.)

6.   Merrill, H. Barry. *Merrill's Guide to Computer Performance Evaluation Analysis of SMF/RMF data with SAS.* SAS Institute, 1980.

7.   BEST/1 Capacity Planning Tool (http://publib.boulder.ibm.com/iseries/v5r1/ic2924/index.htm?info/rzahx/rzahxplangrowbest1.htm).

8.   Buzen, J. P., et al. "BEST/1—Design of a tool for computer system capacity planning." *AFIPS Conference Proceedings*, Vol. 47. pp. 447–455.

models[9] to computer capacity analysis, allowed pretty accurate modeling, analysis, and calibration.

Then came the personal computer revolution.

In the era of exploding availability of ever more powerful and cheap personal computers, capacity planning became a largely forgotten art. Also, it wasn't as easy. The kind of self-reporting embedded into mainframe operating systems just wasn't there. Obtaining utilization data was a major chore, and modeling simply wasn't worth the effort. Computers were cheap, and if there were performance problems, you simply added resources until the problem went away.

With cloud computing, it's back-to-the-future time, folks. And capacity planning is once again a much-sought-after skill.

Keep in mind that in the cloud, for the most part, you are dealing with two levels of resources: virtual resources and physical ones. While getting into the cloud was easy, managing numerous cloud servers can be a challenge. Older folks who had capacity planning skills are being called out of retirement, dusting off their long-dormant skills and picking out the cobwebs. Folks too young to remember are reinventing the tools of yesteryear in a cloud environment.

They are much needed.

5.5   Evidence-Based Decision Making

To reserve virtual and physical resources appropriately, you need to understand resource consumption associated with different tasks. This requires *instrumentation* (adding in the self-reporting about resource consumption that was standard in mainframes but largely absent, at least until recently from PCs and even servers) as well as *"what-if"-type analysis* to predict the effect of changes in the transaction mix, transaction volume, and resources reserved.

5.6   Instrumentation (Measuring Resource Consumption)

> *In God we trust; all others must bring data.*
> —*W. Edwards Deming[10]*
> *You can't control what you can't measure.*
> —*Tom DeMarco[11]*

---

9.   Analytical models are equation-based and fast, compared to simulation models, which are more detailed but much, much more complex to build and slower to run.

10.   Quoted in Davenport, Thomas H., and Harris, Jeanne G. *Competing on Analytics: The New Science of Winning.* Harvard Business School Press, 2007.

11.   Demarco, Tom. *Controlling Software Projects: Management, Measurement, and Estimation.* Prentice Hall/Yourdon Press, 1982.

Computer performance management has usually been deemed more an art than a science. Unfortunately, this belief often causes the effort to degenerate into a tendency to "wing it." Since not all that happens in computer is intuitive, as Figure 5.2 conclusively demonstrated, the results can be catastrophic.

5.6.1 First, Get Your Business Needs Down Clearly

As they say, when the boss says, "jump," you need to ask, "how high?" Goals not clearly articulated cannot be achieved. You need to start by asking the hard questions:

- What is the response time (speed) at which services must be delivered to the user?
- What level of availability is required? (Many cloud service level agreements promise 99.99% uptime, but what does that mean to your business?) Does availability mean the server is running or that applications are performing to your specifications? Is availability measured from within the cloud's firewall or from end users' actual devices?
- What level of elasticity (scalability) do you need, and how quickly (at what velocity) must scaling be accomplished?

Elasticity = Velocity + Capacity

A requirement for a quick ramp-up during peak customer usage periods, and only during those times, requires a high degree of elasticity. How efficiently can the system scale to your needs? If you need to ramp up too early, the benefit of scalability is diminished; scale too late, and your system performance deteriorates under the increased load. The goal is "just-in-time" scalability. Will the required ramp-up be fast at all times of the day and across all geographies? And just how much capacity can you get? Will an additional hundred or 300 instances be there when you need them? How much human intervention is required to scale? Can it be accomplished automatically by setting policies?

- What are the propagation delays? Is a transaction made in your London office available minutes later for use by the Mountain View, California sales team trying to close an end-of-quarter deal? How long does it take the end user to complete a multistep workflow process, irrespective of the time of day, time of the month, or geographical location?

5.6.2 What Technologists Must Know to Manage Performance and Capacity

As noted by Philip Mucci and his colleagues:[12]

Many factors contribute to overall application performance in today's high performance cluster computing environments. These factors include the memory subsystem, network hardware and software stack, compilers and libraries, and I/O subsystem. [However], [t]he large variability in hardware and software configurations present in clusters can cause application performance to also exhibit large variability on different platforms or on the same platform over time.

The following categories of system resources are often tracked by capacity planners.

CPU Utilization: The central processing unit is always technically either busy or idle; from a Linux perspective, it appears to be in one of several statuses:

- *Idle*: in a wait state, available for work
- *User*: busy doing high-level (application-level) functions, data movement, math, etc.
- *System*: activities taking place in "protection code 0" that perform kernel functions, I/O and other hardware interaction, which users are prevented from accessing directly
- *Nice*: similar to user state, it's for interruptible jobs with low priority willing to yield the CPU to tasks with higher priority.

Analysis of the average time spent in each state (especially over time), yields evidence of the overloading of one state or another. Too much idle is an indication of excess capacity; excessive system time indicates possible thrashing (excessive paging), caused by or insufficient memory and/or a need for faster I/O or additional devices to distribute loads. Each system will have its own signature while running normally, and watching these numbers over

---

12. Philip Mucci, et al. "Automating the Large-Scale Collection and Analysis of Performance Data on Linux Clusters." *Proceedings of the 5th LCI International Conference on Linux Clusters* (LCI-04), Austin, TX. May 2004.

time allows the planner to determine what constitutes normal behavior for a system. Once a baseline is established, changes are easily detected.

Interrupts: Most I/O devices use interrupts to signal (interrupt) the CPU when there is work for it to do. For example, SCSI controllers will raise an interrupt to signal that a requested disk block has been read and is available in memory. A serial port with a mouse on it will generate an interrupt each time a button is pressed/released or when the mouse is moved. Watching the count of each interrupt can give you a rough idea of how much load the associated device is handling.

Context Switching: Input/output devices and processors are mismatched in terms of speed. This phenomenon makes computers appear to be doing multiple jobs at once by allocating slices of processor time to multiple applications. Each task is given control of the system for a certain "slice" of time, and when that time is up, the system saves the state of the running process and gives control of the system to another process, making sure that the necessary resources are available. This administrative process is called context switching. In some operating systems, the cost of this task-switching can be fairly expensive, sometimes consuming more resources than the processes being switching. Linux is very efficient in this regard, but by watching the amount of this activity, you will learn to recognize when a system exhibits excessive task-switching time.

Memory: When too many processes are running and using up available memory, the system will slow down as processes are paged or swapped out to make room for other processes to run. When the time slice is exhausted, that task may have to be written out to the paging device to make way for the next process. Memory-utilization graphs help highlight memory problems.

Paging: Page faults are said to occur when available (free) memory becomes scarce, at which the virtual memory system will seek to write pages in real memory out to the swap device, freeing up space for active processes. Today's disk drives are fast, but they haven't kept pace with the increases in processor speeds. As a result, when the level of page faults increases to such a rate that disk arm activity (which is mechanical) becomes excessive, then (as we saw in Figure 5.2) response times will slow drastically as the system spends all of its time shuttling pages in and out. This, too, is an undesirable form of thrashing. Paging in a Linux system can also be decreased by loading needed portions of an executable program into pages that are loaded on-demand, rather than being preloaded. (In many systems, this happens automatically).

Swapping: Swapping is much like paging. However, it migrates entire process images, consisting of many pages of memory, from real memory to the swapping devices, rather than page-by-page.

Disk I/O: Linux maintains statistics on the first four disks: total I/O, reads, writes, block reads, and block writes. These numbers can show uneven loading of multiple disks and show the balance of reads versus writes.

Network I/O: Network I/O can be used to diagnose problems and examine loading of the network interface(s). The statistics show traffic in and out, collisions, and errors encountered in both directions.

5.7   Managers Are from Mars, Technologists Are from Venus

Dr. John Gray famously titled his book, *Men Are from Mars, Women Are from Venus.*[13] The book offer many suggestions for improving relationships in couples by understanding the communication style and emotional needs of the opposite gender.

We face the same problem. User management asks business needs questions, and their related forecasts and projections appear to have no relationship to the technical data that capacity planners use to manage resource and performance. The managers and technologists don't speak the same language, and they speak right past each other.

The problem is made even more complex because of bottlenecks that develop within systems, which are a key to capacity management, but are irrelevant at best to users, for whom computers are just black boxes. Keep this problem in mind until we get to the section on key volume indicators.

5.8   Bottlenecks

A bottleneck is a phenomenon where the performance or capacity of an entire system is limited (gated) by a single or limited number of components or resources. The terms is based on the analogy of water being poured out of a bottle. The rate of outflow is limited by the width of the conduit of exit—that is, the bottleneck. Increase the width of the bottleneck, and you can increase the rate of which the water flows out. The sad part is, that in computer systems, one bottleneck often masks the existence of the next one down the line, so long as it remains the gating factor. Limit the capacity of one process in a chain of processes, and it reduces the capacity of the whole system. Expand the capacity of the constraining resource, and the system's processes flow freely until they are once again constrained by the next bottleneck in the chain.

---

13.   Gray, John. *Men Are from Mars, Women Are from Venus: The Classic Guide to Understanding the Opposite Sex.* Harper Paperbacks, New York, 2004.

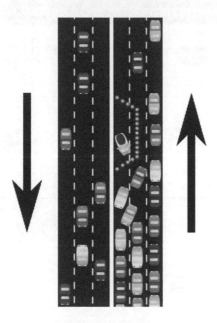

Figure 5.3   A traffic bottleneck.

What this all boils down to is that until you make the change designed to relieve the bottleneck and then re-measure, you can't be *sure* that you have resolved the problem; however, with adequate understanding, you can fairly reliably *predict* what will happen.

5.9   Getting the Facts

One popular set of tools for satisfying the demand for facts that Mark Twain called for and for obtaining measurements in the cloud is made by Nimsoft, recently acquired by CA, Inc., formerly known as Computer Associates (www.nimsoft.com). Its overall (enterprise) monitoring system, called Unified Monitoring (see Figure 5.4), allows you to view both in-house and external cloud systems.

The dashboard is interactive. The screenshot in Figure 5.5 is an overall summary. Each panel is clickable, allowing you to drill down for more information. The next screenshots drill down on specific measurement data. When coupled with measures of the work done (i.e., transactions), you have a basis for model building.

Figure 5.6 shows query response time.

Figure 5.7 shows the average number of processes in the queue.

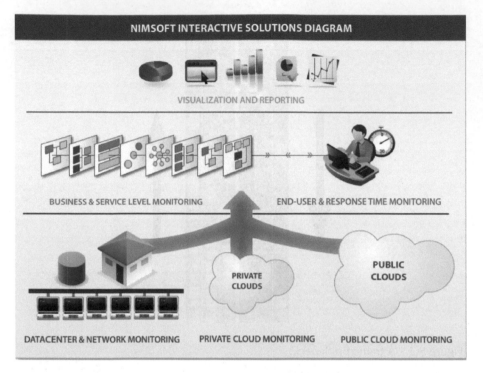

Figure 5.4   Nimsoft Unified Monitoring (Courtesy CA Technologies, Inc.)

Figure 5.8 shows the disk activity associated with a virtual server.

5.10   Strategies for Capacity Planning

Essentially, there are three strategies for capacity planning:

- *Just Too Late (JTL)*: If capacity is added after pain is caused via missed SLAs, then it is certain that some losses will be caused.
- *Just In Case (JIC)*: This approach causes higher spending without provable benefit, and is often practiced when not enough information is analyzed to really know what services and service levels the application requires.
- *Just In Time (JIT)*: This is the approach with the best economic benefits for the business.

5.11   Critical Success Factors (CSF) and Best Practices

The concept of *success factors*—identifying those few things that are imperative to get right and then focusing on them—was first developed by D.

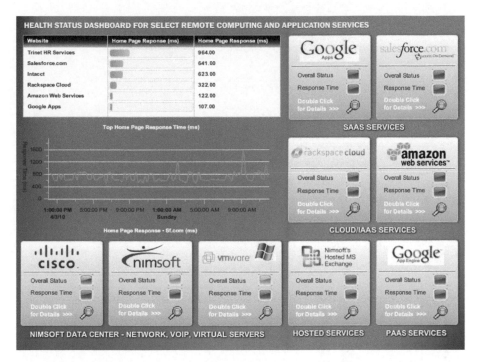

Figure 5.5   Nimsoft Unified Monitoring Dashboard (Courtesy CA Technologies)

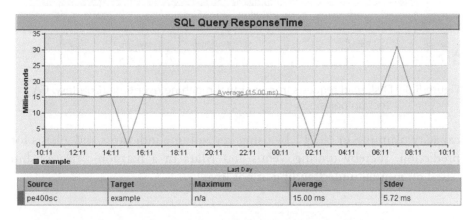

Figure 5.6   SQL response time (physical). (Courtesy CA Technologies)

Ronald Daniel of Mc Kinsey & Co. in a seminal article in 1961.[14] Dr. John F. Rockart then further developed Daniel's ideas and applied critical success factors (CSFs) to information systems in two widely quoted articles.[15] The author's modest contribution was to adapt the general concept of CSFs to

14.   Daniel, D. Ronald. "Management information crisis." Harvard Business Review, Sept/Oct 1961.

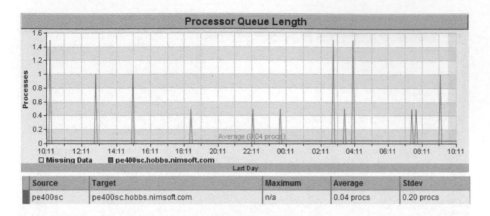

Figure 5.7   Processes in queue by time. (Courtesy CA Technologies)

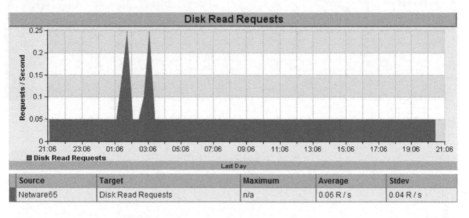

Figure 5.8   Disk read requests from a virtual machine over time.(Courtesy, CA
Technologies)

capacity planning in 1979[16] by using key volume indicators and a basis for
prediction, thereby uniting Venus and Mars in a harmonic relationship
based on mutual understanding, if not love.

15.   Rockart, John F. "*Chief executives define their own data needs.*" *Harvard Business Review*, Mar/
Apr 1979, Vol. 57 Issue 2, p81-93, 13p
and
Rockart, John F "The changing role of the information systems executive: A critical success factors perspective." *Sloan Management Review*, Fall 1982; 24, 1, Available online at http://
bit.ly/cVMGwu (accessed July 5, 2010).
16.   Sarna, David E. Y. "Forecasting computer resource utilizations using key volume indicators." Presented at AFIPS Conference and published in *AFIPS Conference Proceedings*, 1979 National
Computer Conference, June 4-7, New York, NY. AFIPS Press, Montvale, NJ, ed. Richard E. Mer-
win, 1979: 185–192. Available online at http://bit.ly/cVMGwu (accessed July 5, 2010).

First, here are some critical success factors for capacity planning in the clouds:

- Management:
  - Provide reliable business activity indicators and forecasts
  - Analyze the cost of failures and benefits of meeting SLAs
- Technical:
  - Ensure that all system components are included in the analysis
  - Maintain sufficient subject matter expertise for analysis of load test and performance analysis
  - Present results in business terms rather than by using computer jargon

5.12   Key Volume Indicators

Forecasting growth in computer utilization is the key to successful capacity planning. Three basic techniques have been used, with varying degrees of success, to forecast computer utilization:

- Divide up the total current usage by department. Ask each department to estimate next year's requirements in terms of processor (CPU-seconds) and disk operations, sometimes breaking out reads and writes separately.
- Take this year's accounting figures and adjust them for the expected changes over the next year.
- Apply a trend analysis to this year's accounting data to obtain an (overall) forecast for next year.

The author noted as far back as 1979 that these typical forecasting techniques are inadequate.

What are the disadvantages of using such techniques?

- *Ask the user*—Try forecasting asking a family to forecast its monthly requirements for dishwashing liquid! For most users, CPU-seconds or I/Os are quantities even more obscure and impossible to estimate.
- *Estimate based on last year's results*—This is the classic seat-of-the-pants approach. Some are better at it than others. Some are so bad at it that they lose their shirts.
- *Watch the trend*—This is a step in the right direction. Use of this technique presupposes that past is prologue and that next year's

usage pattern continue this year's trend. If sufficient data is used, and the trending techniques are sufficiently sophisticated, good results can sometimes be obtained, especially in mostly static environments (not typically encountered with cloud computing). However, there is no assurance that the current trend will continue.

As an example, consider the real estate market: Houses that had been appreciating in value for years started suddenly to retrench. For an example in our domain, consider that an installation may experience flat growth this year, but may experience a large workload increase when the applications currently under development go online, or when a company suddenly achieves notoriety. Simple trend analysis is never going to predict that type of growth, which is caused by "exogenous" events (something coming from outside the system, such as a mention on *The Oprah Winfrey Show*, which can cause usage to skyrocket), rather than endogenous ones related to the system's internal workings.

Key Volume Indicators to the Rescue

For many years, we have been using a concept called key volume indicators (KVIs) to overcome deficiencies in forecasting using other methods. The tools required are a usage analysis program (such as Nimsoft, discussed earlier) and a regression program, found in the Microsoft Excel Analysis Toolpak add-in or any standard statistical software package such as SAS.

The underlying principle behind this technique is that the end user, given sufficient information, understands his business best. He should be responsible for predicting his own needs. He cannot be expected to predict computer usage, but he probably can predict business-related growth with a fair degree of success (and let's face, if he can't, it's his problem). The key volume indicator is a way of relating an application's units of work to computer resource utilization. Appropriate KVIs must be chosen to prepare reliable forecasts. The key volume indicators must relate to computer usage and at the same time be business- and application-related in order to be forecastable by the users. A useful by-product of the process is the availability of unit costs for many applications, permitting comparisons among user constituencies and better cost estimates for planned applications.

Once the indicators have been identified, the user will prepare a forecast in terms of the key volume indicator units and the computer will translate these units into a forecast of computer resources. I/O operations,

CPU-seconds, or any other measure of utilization can be forecast using this technique.

5.12.1   Types of Workloads

Growth in corporate computer use will come primarily from three sources: (1) Increased workloads for existing applications, (2) environmental and geographic workload shifts, and (3) new applications. Other factors influencing use are related to changes in processing time caused by program modifications, new techniques such as a change in data base management system, or changes in run frequency.

5.12.2   Determining KVIs for an Application

Potential KVIs are selected for their forecastability, relationship to the application, and the availability of their historical data. The historical volume and computer utilization data is examined statistically in order to select potential volume indicators with the greatest correlation to computer utilization over time.

5.12.3   Monitoring and Improving Forecastability

Forecasts will improve because (1) users will be able to do a better job of forecasting KVIs than forecasting using computer-related measures, (2) the indicators will be chosen carefully and bear a known relationship to computer resource utilization, and (3) users will prepare forecasts periodically, and as they gain experience in actual usage as compared to their forecasts, their forecasts should improve.

5.12.4   Standard Costs

An additional benefit from the use of KVIs is the collection of data relating to the computer resources required per KVI unit of work. This data can be used to develop standard costs for applications, to compare standard costs with actual costs to highlight variances, and to compare cloud-based costs to traditional server architecture costs. Comparisons of the costs of similar applications among divisions can assist in identifying inefficient programs and in reducing costs.

5.12.5 Determining Whether Resources are Adequate for Projected Demand

As we noted earlier, queueing models can be used to predict the effect on response times and CPU utilization of workload changes. For a given computer configuration and workload, the model will predict the average CPU utilization, the average batch job turnaround times, and the average terminal response times to be expected due to workload changes. The model also can be used to predict the effect of volumes different from the forecasts.

5.12.6 New Applications

Usage data is not available for applications not yet installed. If a similar application is installed at another division, the key volume indicators and coefficients may be borrowed as a first approximation. If such comparable data is not available, the analyst will have to base his estimate on the time required to process the approximate number of CPU instructions and database operations per transaction. If a new application will replace an existing application, care must be taken to deduct from the total forecast all resource utilization to be displaced by the new application. After the application is placed in production, and the usage data becomes available, the procedure for existing applications should be followed.

5.12.7 Accuracy of Forecasts

What unusual conditions may arise when preparing forecasts using KVIs? The most obvious possibility is that the standard error reported by the regression program is unacceptably large. This indicates either that the KVIs selected are not, in fact, good predictors of resource utilization, or that the data are incomplete or reflect a temporary exceptional condition. This question can be resolved by inspecting the output from the regression program and noting the variance.

If the variance is large for most months, the potential KVIs were not found to correlate well with utilization, and different indicators must be selected. However, if the data generally correlate well, but correlate poorly for a few months, this would also impact the standard error of estimation. If possible, the data should be researched to determine whether there were any unusual conditions relating to processing the application system for those months where the variance is large. The non-representative data should then be disregarded and the regression program run once again, using the remaining data. This will often produce an acceptable result.

Another item of concern in some shops relates to distribution of the workload by time of day. An advantage of cloud computing is that resources can be added and subtracted to reflect varying arrival rates of transactions by time of day. However, a key point to remember is that computer capacity does not generally come in very small increments. The purpose of preparing a capacity forecast is to determine the need for additions or changes to the computer configuration. The forecasting accuracy is sufficient if it can correctly predict the need for equipment changes. One useful way to test the sensitivity of a capacity prediction to small changes in user forecasts is to bracket the projected forecasts when preparing the capacity plan. This is especially easy to accomplish where a model is employed.

5.12.8   Queueing Models

Dr. Buzen's BEST/1 capacity planning tool[17] is still available from IBM as part of the Performance Tools for iSeries licensed program.[18] A variety of other modeling tools are available.

Java Modelling Tools (JMT) is a suite of applications developed by Politecnico di Milano and released under GPL license. The project aims to offer a complete framework for performance evaluation, system tuning, capacity planning, and workload characterization studies. The current stable version of the suite encompasses six Java applications:

- JSIMgraph—Queueing network models simulator with graphical user interface
- JSIMwiz—Queueing network models simulator with wizard-based user interface
- JMVA—Mean value analysis of queueing network models
- JABA—Asymptotic analysis of queueing network models
- JWAT—Workload analysis from log and usage data
- JMCH—Markov chain simulator (didactic tool)

17.   *IBM eServer, iSeries, Best/1 Capacity Planning Tool, Version5.* IBM Publication SC41-53401-01, 2001. https://docs.google.com/viewer?url=http://publib.boulder.ibm.com/iseries/v5r1/ic2924/books/c4153411.pdf (accessed July 5, 2010).
18.   http://publib.boulder.ibm.com/iseries/v5r1/ic2924/index.htm?info/rzahx/rzahxperftools-desc.htm (accessed July 5, 2010).

The entire suite of tools can be downloaded without charge from http://jmt.sourceforge.net/Download.html. A low-cost Excel-based queueing model called, appropriately enough, Queuing Model Excel 30 is available at http://www.bizpeponline.com/QueuingModel.html or http://www.toggle.com/lv/group/view/kl78420/Queuing_Model_Excel.htm.

A list of available modeling tools is maintained at http://web2.uwindsor.ca/math/hlynka/qsoft.html.

5.12.9   Make or Buy a Cloud

It's not sufficient to merely produce a validated model of a configuration validated to meet the projected requirements. The next questions inevitably are: make or buy; internal cloud versus external; public versus public. The major issues affecting these decisions come in two flavors: tangible and intangible. Tangible considerations have a quantifiable dollar cost and value of service. Intangible costs and benefits are harder to quantify but should never be ignored, because they are often points of project failure.

As we have seen, folks move to external clouds for many reasons, but two stand out:

- Agility
- Reduced cost

Sometimes, one comes at the expense of the other. Two very basic facts must be always remembered. First, if all the critical service attributes and the IT resources inventory are identical, then the cost of a service purchased from a provider will always be higher than the in-house estimate, based on the simple fact that the provider is (trying) to operate for a profit, while in-house costs are frequently underestimated and don't include all costs. Based on our experience with multiple customers, a provider's charges, like for like, are typically about 20 percent higher than the in-house service. A second fact of life is that economies of scale are very much alive and well in the IT world. The cost per unit of IT resource decreases as the quantity increases. It follows, then, that the cost per server for a 500-server complex (all costs included) is about double the cost of an identical configuration of 5,000 or more servers. Purchasers of cloud computing services need to establish at what point the outsourced cloud service is more cost effective, based purely on economic considerations. Large cloud vendors are good at cost containment and spread many of the overhead and fixed costs over a large quantity of devices, so for a modest-sized installation of <500 servers, they are often cheaper even when their profit margins are factored in.

Capacity planners now have a new mission, in addition to their traditional responsibilities:

- Determination of make versus buy, with all costs considered
- Planning and maintaining an adequate but not excessive supply of all IT resources to ensure the cost-effective delivery of services and adequate redundancy, as required by business activity goals and plans, while minimizing outages caused by capacity shortages

A step-by step work program is provided in Chapter 15.

Summary

Cloud computing, generally based on a pay-as-you-go charging algorithm, presents new challenges and new opportunities for cost savings. Capacity planning, a nearly lost art, was revived by the migration to cloud computing. It starts with an understanding of the users' projections and requirements, including service levels. Key volume indicators (KVIs) are a technique for relating user-forecastable units of work to computer resource requirements. Queueing models are used to determine bottlenecks and to find the lowest priced configuration delivering adequate response times.

Chapter 6

Demystifying the Cloud: A Case Study Using Amazon's Cloud Services (AWS)

When I tell people, even many computer-literate people, that I work in cloud computing, the most common response is, "What's that?" Many who do know seem to deliberately want to add mystery as cloud cover.

This is not a new phenomenon. The Mishnah (a Jewish code of law redacted around 70 CE) has a "hall of infamy," whose members had skills that they refused to teach.[1] It reminds me of the beginning of the World Wide Web (completed by Tim Berners-Lee in 1990) and Marc Andreessen's development of the Mosaic browser in 1992 (an invention that made the Web what it is today). Up until 2002, Web development was seen as an obscure (and highly compensated) black art. Now of course, anyone can click his or her way through even sophisticated Web page creation using a plethora of freely available, and often free, tools.

So it is with cloud computing. Amazon began providing Amazon Web Services in 2006 with the launch of the Amazon Simple Storage Service (Amazon S3), and the early adopters did their best to treat it as a black art, known only to the cognoscenti.

It has gotten much easier, and the goal of this chapter is to demonstrate that like the fellow who wrote prose and didn't know it, you know much more about cloud computing than you think, and you can easily move an application from a local personal computer or server up into the cloud with a minimum of muss and fuss.

---

1. Mishnah, Tractate Yoma, Chap. 3, Mishna 12, http://www.mechon-mamre.org/b/h/h25.htm (accessed June 27, 2010).

6.1   Why Amazon?

Figure 6.1   Levi Strauss.

They're *all* up in the clouds—a multiplicity of cloud vendors. Amazon, Google, HP, IBM, CA and Oracle (Sun) are in. Intel, Microsoft and Yahoo are all muscling their way in too.

So while the air itself is thinner up in the clouds, airspace in the Internet cloud is definitely getting more congested. As cloud computing races towards becoming mainstream (if it's not already), more and more folks want to become the Levi's of cloud computing.

Levi Strauss & Co. profited from the California Gold Rush when Levi Strauss moved to San Francisco in 1853 to make his fortune, not by panning for gold, but by selling supplies to the throngs of miners who arrived daily in the big city to outfit themselves before heading off to the gold fields. Following his model, a host of vendors are supplying cloud computing infrastructure to all the would-be enterprises and entrepreneurial prospectors staking claims for their piece of this new land grab. The big guys are all buying in heavily at the high-stakes poker tables. For example, in January 2010, Microsoft and HP announced that they were teaming up in a $250 million project to develop hardware and software products that are designed to work together smoothly in their customers' data centers and in cloud computing facilities. Microsoft's CEO, Steve Ballmer, told a group that he is betting the farm on cloud computing. "The real thing to do today is to capture, what are the dimensions of the thing [cloud computing] that literally, I will tell you, we're betting our company on, and I think pretty much everybody in the technology industry is betting their companies on," Ballmer said during an appearance at the University of Washington.

This is not a product-specific or offering-specific book, and not a cookbook either. Products are updated very rapidly, and even more so in cloud computing, where the software sits on vendor-managed servers and can be (and is) updated all the time without any effort on your part.

However, concepts must be grounded in reality. Amazon today, according to "State of the Cloud," hosts over half of the top 500,000 sites hosted in the public clouds. Amazon and Rackspace together control ninety-four percent, and all the rest of the providers retain but a sliver of control.[2] Based on these statistics, and to illustrate the ease of moving to the cloud, I've chosen to demonstrate using Amazon web services and some related offerings from other vendors that make Amazon's offerings easier to use.

6.1.1   Amazon is Just an Illustrative Example

Jeff Bezos (Figure 6.2) and his company Amazon were the first to realize the potential for offering rent-a-cloud service on the massive cloud that Amazon maintains. Its Amazon Simple Storage Service[3] (Amazon S3) is for simply renting storage space in the cloud. Its Amazon Elastic Compute Cloud[4] (Amazon EC2) provides a complete environment, a processor, memory, numerous flavors, or preconfigured software. It offers scalability within minutes on a pay-as-you-go basis. Recently, in a series of announcements, not all of which are part of AWS, but may be used in conjunction with AWS, Amazon[5] released a set of hosted e-commerce payment services as well as an update to its Mechanical Turk service. The payment service, Checkout by Amazon, will allow online retailers to use Amazon's patented 1-Click[6] checkout system, calculate shipping costs and tax, as well as enable their customers to track shipments.

Amazon S3 is simply storage for the Internet (hence its name, Simple Storage Service). It is designed to make Web-scale computing easier for developers. It provides a simple Web services interface that can be used to store and retrieve any amount of data, at any time, from anywhere on the Internet. It gives any developer access to the same highly scalable, reliable, fast, inexpensive data storage infrastructure that Amazon uses to run its own

---

2. *State of the Cloud*, May 2010. See http://www.jackofallclouds.com/2010/05/state-of-the-cloud-may-2010/.

3. http://aws.amazon.com/s3/.

4. http://aws.amazon.com/ec2/.

5. http://www.amazon.com/.

6. http://en.wikipedia.org/wiki/1-Click.

Figure 6.2   Jeff Bezos (courtesy, Amazon Inc.).

global network of Web sites. The service aims to maximize benefits of scale and to pass those benefits on to developers.

6.1.2   Let's Do It Now

To sign up for Amazon S3, go to http://aws.amazon.com/s3/ and click "Sign Up for Amazon S3" (Sign Up For Amazon S3) [7] You can use your existing Amazon account, or create a new one (as shown in Figure 6.3).

That's it. You're in.

6.1.3   Amazon S3 Functionality

Amazon S3 is intentionally built with a minimal feature set.

Figure 6.3   Amazon S3 sign in.

- You can write, read, and delete objects containing from 1 byte to 5 gigabytes of data each. The number of objects you can store is unlimited.
- Each object is stored in a "bucket," which is the basic S3 container; it is retrieved via a unique, developer-assigned key.
- A bucket can be stored in one of several geographical Regions. You can choose a Region to optimize for latency, minimize costs, or address regulatory requirements. Amazon S3 is currently available in the US Standard, EU (Ireland), Asia (Singapore), and US-West (Northern California) Regions. The US Standard Region automatically routes requests to facilities in Northern Virginia or the Pacific Northwest using network maps.
- Objects stored in a Region never leave the Region unless you transfer them out. For example, objects stored in the EU (Ireland) Region never leave the EU.
- Authentication mechanisms are provided to ensure that data is kept secure from unauthorized access. Objects can be made private or public, and rights can be granted to specific users.
- Amazon S3 uses standards-based REST (*Representational State Transfer*) and SOAP (*Simple Object Access Protocol*) interfaces designed to work with any Internet-development toolkit. (see http://ajaxonomy.com/2008/xml/web-services-part-1-soap-vs-rest for a discussion of REST and SOAP).

- Built to be flexible so that protocol or functional layers can easily be added. Default download protocol is HTTP. A BitTorrent™ protocol interface (a peer-to-peer file sharing protocol used for distributing large amounts of data) is provided to lower costs for high-scale distribution. Amazon states that additional interfaces will be added in the future.
- Reliability is backed with the Amazon S3 Service Level Agreement.[8]

As with most cloud services, you pay for what you use (see Figure 6.4).

US – Standard		US – N. California		EU – Ireland	
Storage		**Data Transfer**		**Requests**	
Tier	Pricing	Tier	Pricing	Tier	Pricing
First 50 TB / Month of Storage Used	$0.150 per GB	All Data Transfer In	Free until June 30th, 2010*	PUT, COPY, POST, or LIST	$0.01 per 1,000 Requests
Next 50 TB / Month of Storage Used	$0.140 per GB	First 10 TB / Month Data Transfer Out	$0.150 per GB	GET and All Other Requests*	$0.01 per 10,000 Requests
Next 400 TB / Month of Storage Used	$0.130 per GB	Next 40 TB / Month Data Transfer Out	$0.110 per GB	* No charge for delete requests	
Next 500 TB / Month of Storage Used	$0.105 per GB	Next 100 TB / Month Data Transfer Out	$0.090 per GB		
Next 4000 TB / Month of Storage Used	$.080 per GB	Data Transfer Out / Month Over 150 TB	$0.080 per GB		
Storage Used / Month Over 5000 TB	$.055 per GB	* Data Transfer In will be $0.100 per GB after June 30th, 2010			

Data transfer "in" and "out" refers to transfer into and out of an Amazon S3 Region. There is no Data Transfer charge for data transferred within an Amazon S3 Region via a COPY request. Data transferred via a COPY request between Regions is charged at regular rates. There is no Data Transfer charge for data transferred between Amazon EC2 and Amazon S3 within the same Region or for data transferred between the Amazon EC2 Northern Virginia Region and the Amazon S3 US Standard Region. Data transferred between Amazon EC2 and Amazon S3 across all other Regions (i.e. between the Amazon EC2 Northern California and Amazon S3 US Standard Region) will be charged at Internet Data Transfer rates on both sides of the transfer.

Storage and bandwidth size includes all file overhead.

(Amazon S3 is sold by Amazon Web Services LLC.)

Figure 6.4   Amazon Cloud pricing.

A bill calculator for charges is provided by Amazon at http://calculator.s3.amazonaws.com/calc5.html and shown in Figure 6.5.

---

8.   http://aws.amazon.com/s3-sla/ (accessed June 25, 2010).

Figure 6.5   Amazon Cloud cost calculator. (Courtesy Amazon Corp.)

6.2   Using Amazon S3

S3 can be used in three ways:

- Programmatically, using HTTP protocol and standard Internet development tools (e.g., PHP, C#, Java, Perl, Ruby, Python)
- Through several tools for file transfer:
    - S3curl (For more information, go to http://developer.amazon-webservices.com/connect/entry.jspa?externalID=128).
    - S3 Fox Organizer (A free Firefox add-on, discussed below https://addons.mozilla.org/en-US/firefox/addon/3247).
    - S3 tool (Provides simple, command-line access to both Amazon S3 and Amazon EC2. See http://developer.amazonwebser-vices.com/connect/entry.jspa?externalID=739).
- Using AWS Import/Export.
  AWS Import/Export accelerates moving large amounts of data into and out of AWS using portable storage devices for transport. AWS transfers your data directly onto and off of storage devices using Amazon's high-speed internal network and bypassing the Internet. Amazon says that for significant data sets, AWS Import/Export is often faster than Internet transfer and more cost effective than upgrading your connectivity.[9]

6.3   Gladinet Puts a Desktop Face on S3

Gladinet is a solution based on Amazon's S3 and/or other cloud vendors. It offers the simplest method for users as well as businesses to store their information in the cloud and to access it seamlessly through existing applications.

---

9.   http://aws.amazon.com/importexport/.

We are going to work our way up to building cloud applications one step at a time.

First, let's consider Gladinet's solution. While it is limited in what it can do, it has been made to look very much like what you are already used to, as it looks and behaves like an external USB drive or a network drive, only it's physically in the cloud.

You can download Gladinet at its Web site (http://www.gladinet.com/ p/download_starter_direct.htm). The starter edition is free; the Professional Edition runs $39.99 for home use and $59.99 for business use. Volume and academic licenses are available.

Once installed, you will see Gladinet as a "Z" drive on your computer (as shown in Figure 6.6).

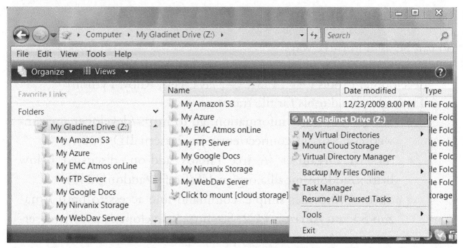

Figure 6.6   Gladinet "Z" drive. (Courtesy Gladinet, Inc.)

The Professional Edition of Gladinet Cloud Desktop is an open platform, with advanced features that provide seamless integration of cloud services with your desktop. These include advanced backup capabilities, enhanced security, compression, chunking, and ever-expanding support for integrated cloud storage. Gladinet Professional also leverages an ever-growing set of storage plugins that have been developed by either Gladinet or third parties. Plugins that are registered in the online Gladinet plugin directory may be downloaded on demand.

Gladinet is accessed through its Quick Launch Pad (see Figure 6.7).

The most interesting features of Gladinet go beyond its use as a backup tool. It is provider-agnostic, supporting, at this writing, Amazon S3, Google

Figure 6.7   Gladinet Launch Pad. (Courtesy Gladinet, Inc.)

Apps, Microsoft Azure, AT&T Synaptic Storage, Box.Net, and EMC Atmos, among others, so that customers can access storage from their desktop from many different clouds, each appearing as if it were on a local disk, simply by "mounting" the disk (Figure 6.8).

On my desktop, I mounted an Amazon S3 drive and a Google Apps drive, as shown in Figure 6.9.

6.3.1   Use Cases for Using Virtual Drives

How can a virtual drive be used in practice? Here are some use cases:

Direct Random Access

Broadband speeds vary from around 100KB/s to 800KB/s. A response time of <5s is required for good usability for direct access. This means direct random access to the cloud files with 500K to 4M in size will be very usable.

Online Backup

Online backup is write once and seldom read. At this stage, the cloud storage can't replace either the network attached storage or the local hard drive because of the speed, but it is perfect for backing up stuff.

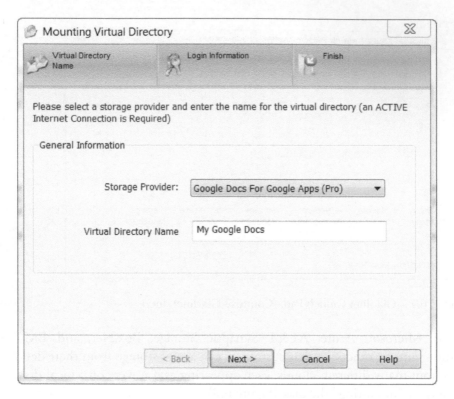

Figure 6.8   Mounting a Gladinet drive. (Courtesy Gladinet, Inc.)

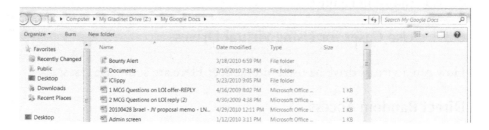

Figure 6.9   Multiple clouds appearing as local drives. (Courtesy Gladinet, Inc.)

File Server with Cloud Backup

An interesting twist is to combine the first two cases by moving the access point from user's desktop to a file server. Users can do direct random access on a network server while the network server is backed up by online storage. Gladinet's forthcoming Cloud Gateway fits this use case.

6.3.2   Beyond One-on-One: Use a Cloud Gateway

Cloud Gateway (Figure 6.10) is an extension of the virtual drive concept from one user to many users, providing a central access point for external cloud storage services. After an administrator has configured Cloud Gateway, it will mount all configured storage and deliver it to Cloud Desktop users as if it were a file server.

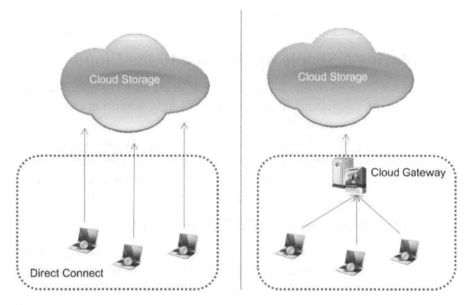

Figure 6.10   Gladinet Cloud Gateway. (Courtesy Gladinet, Inc.)

6.3.3   Benefits of Using Cloud Gateway

The benefits of using Cloud Gateway include:

- *Smart caching for faster access.* Cloud Gateway maintains local copies of the files stored by external cloud services. (This means that users usually have faster access to files at LAN speeds)
- *Centralized administration.* Users simply enter an IP address or DNS name and they are automatically connected to published storage. For example, Amazon S3 accounts can be configured at the Gateway and users will never need to know any account information, just the IP address of the Gateway server
- *Multiple offsite locations.* These can be accessed as if they were locally stored on users' desktops

- *Improved security.* The attack surface is reduced by reducing the number of external connections required

While this is certainly a method (a simple one) of using cloud storage, and is one of the simplest ways to start making use of the cloud for storage, the applications themselves are not running on the cloud but on individual desktops.

SMEStorage (http://smestorage.com) is a similar offering but at this writing, it does not support Microsoft Azure.

6.4   Moving A Simple Application to the Cloud

The Gladinet solution makes it easy to access cloud data from any application running on a desktop. The real power of cloud computing comes from running applications themselves up in the clouds.

Let's consider what it takes to move a simple application to the cloud and what the benefits might be. For this example, we'll look at Amazon's AWS. The process for other cloud vendors in very comparable, even if the mechanics and nomenclature are slightly different

6.5   Step One: Move Static Content to S3

The first and easiest step is to move all your static content—images, CSS, JavaScript files, etc.—to Amazon S3. The simplest way to do it is just a drop more complicated than if you were to create a Z drive with Gladinet.

Tip: Once your content has been stored on S3 you can also use Cloud-Front,[10] Amazon's CDN (Content Delivery Network), which provides edge servers in various locations around the globe to serve the stored data and to improve your application's performance. See http://aws.amazon.com/cloudfront/).

6.5.1   Using CloudFront

Amazon CloudFront has a simple Web services interface that lets you get started in minutes. In Amazon CloudFront, your objects are organized into distributions. A distribution specifies the location of the original version of your objects. A distribution has a unique CloudFront.net domain name (e.g., abc123.cloudfront.net) that you can use to reference your objects

---

10.   http://aws.amazon.com/cloudfront/.

through the network of edge locations. If you wish, you can also map your own domain name (e.g., images.example.com) to your distribution. You can create distributions to either download your content using the HTTP or HTTPS protocols, or stream your content using the RTMP protocol.

Amazon CloudFront employs a network of edge locations that cache copies of popular files close to users on the Internet. CloudFront ensures that end-user requests are served by the closest edge location. As a result, requests travel shorter distances to request objects, improving performance.

To use Amazon CloudFront, you:

- Store the original versions of your files in an Amazon S3 bucket
- Create a distribution to register that bucket with Amazon Cloud-Front through a simple API call
- Use your distribution's domain name in your Web pages, media player, or application. When end users request an object using this domain name, they are automatically routed to the nearest edge location for high performance delivery of your content
- Pay only for the data transfer and requests that you actually use

6.5.2   Other Tools for Moving Content to S3

There are many tools for loading your static content into S3. For computers running the free Firefox browser (Windows, Mac)S X, and Linux), perhaps the easiest is a free Firefox add-in called S3Fox. The AWS Management Console also includes support for Amazon S3. It runs in any browser.

Tip: For large amounts of data, AWS Import/Export (http://aws.amazon.com/importexport/) accelerates moving into and out of AWS using portable storage devices for transport. AWS transfers your data directly onto and off of storage devices using Amazon's high-speed internal network bypassing the Internet. For significant data sets, AWS Import/Export is often faster than Internet transfer and more cost effective than upgrading your connectivity. You can use AWS Import/Export for migrating data into the cloud, sending backups to AWS, exchanging data with others, and disaster recovery).

Here, we will assume that S3Fox is what you'll use to move content between your computer and the cloud.

6.5.3   Using Amazon S3 with Firefox S3Fox

1. S3Fox is a plugin for the Firefox browser, so if you don't have a Firefox browser installed in your machine, you'll first need to get one by downloading it free from http://www.mozilla.com/.

2. Next, download and install the S3Fox plugin (http://www.s3fox.net/),

3. Have your Access Key ID and Secret Access Key ready. If you have misplaced them, go to http://aws.amazon.com/security-credentials to view your S3 credentials (see Figure 6.11). To view your Secret Access Key, click on "Show."

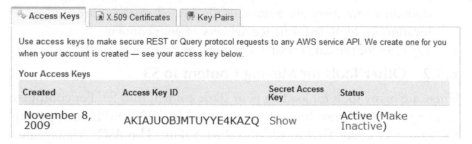

Access Credentials

There are three types of access credentials used to authenticate your requests to AWS services: (a) access keys, (b) X.509 certificates, and (c) key pairs. Each access credential type is explained below.

⚲ Access Keys	X.509 Certificates	Key Pairs

Use access keys to make secure REST or Query protocol requests to any AWS service API. We create one for you when your account is created — see your access key below.

Your Access Keys

Created	Access Key ID	Secret Access Key	Status
November 8, 2009	AKIAJUOBJMTUYYE4KAZQ	Show	Active (Make Inactive)

Figure 6.11   S3 Access Credentials.

Launch S3Fox Organizer

1. In Firefox, go to *Tools* and select *S3 Organizer* (as shown in Figure 6.12).

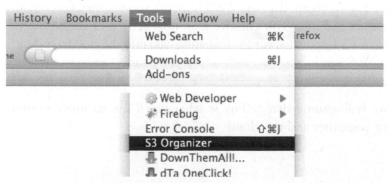

History	Bookmarks	Tools	Window	Help

Web Search	⌘K	irefox
Downloads	⌘J	
Add–ons		
🌐 Web Developer	▶	
🐛 Firebug	▶	
Error Console	⇧⌘J	
S3 Organizer		
⬇ DownThemAll!...		
🛢 dTa OneClick!		

Figure 6.12   Launching the S3 Organizer.

2.   Enter your S3 credentials.

3.   Enter a self-explanatory *Account Name*, your *Access Key* and *Secret Key* (click *Show* to see the secret key). Click *Add*. (See Figure 6.13.)

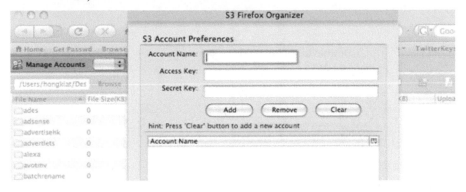

Figure 6.13   Entering S3 Credentials into the S3Fox Organizer.

Get Connected, Create First Bucket

Once you've entered the correct information, you'll be brought to your account which is blank, by default (In the screenshot in Figure 6.14, some files were previously created in S3 and are shown on the right panel).

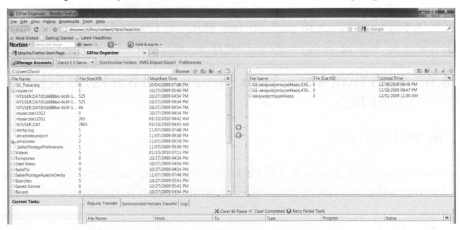

Figure 6.14   S3Fox Organizer Main Screen.

On the left side of S3Fox Organizer will be your local machine folders, and the Amazon S3 "buckets" will be on the right.

Right-click *Create Directory* (as shown in Figure 6.15). Anything created on the root level will be buckets. All files and folders will be stored/organized under buckets.

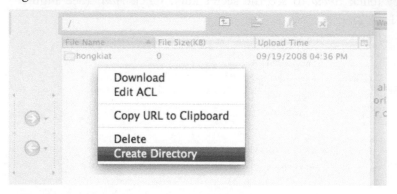

Figure 6.15   Create Directory in an S3 Bucket.

Create Folders, Upload Static Content

Double-click in your bucket and create a folder. Inside the folder, upload your content by dragging from the right-hand pane. By default, anything uploaded to your Amazon S3 account will not be accessible by public.

A similar solution (also available at no charge) is Cloudberry S3 Explorer (http://www.cloudberrylab.com), shown in Figure 6.16.

A Pro Version is also available (see Figure 6.17), and it adds additional features, including compression, security, search, and FTP support.

6.6   Step Two: Move Web Servers and Backend Servers to EC2

The Web Servers

Moving your Web servers to EC2 is fairly simple. You can set up EC2 images that are configured exactly the same way your current Web servers are.

Tip: If you require a queuing service as part of your architecture, consider switching to Amazon's SQS to make administration easier.

EC2 instances are virtual private servers that have some risk associated with them; if they crash, you can lose your data if you haven't made appro-

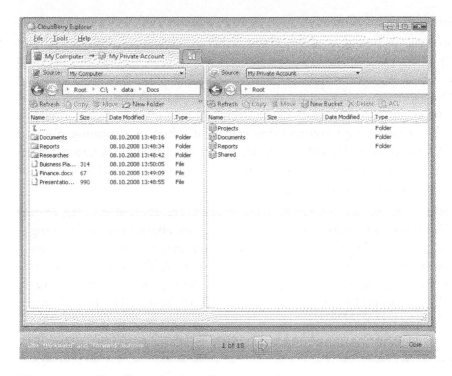

Figure 6.16   Cloudberry Explorer for Amazon S3.

Features	FREEWARE	PRO
Amazon S3	●	●
Amazon CloudFront	●	●
PowerShell	●	●
Number of accounts	1	Unlimited
Compression	-	●
Encryption	-	●
Search	-	●
Chunking	-	●
Multithreading	-	●
FTP Support(*)	-	●
Sync	-	●
Support	forum only	via email, 48 hours response
Expiration	every 3 months	doesn't expire
Price	FREE	$ 39,99

Figure 6.17   Cloudberry feature comparison.

priate provisions. Since you are building an architecture on a transient system, you are forced to think about flexibility, backups, and adaptability early in the development cycle. Amazon Elastic Block Store (EBS) provides block level storage volumes for use with Amazon EC2 instances. Amazon EBS volumes are off-instance storage that persists independently from the life of an instance. Amazon Elastic Block Store provides highly available, highly reliable storage volumes that can be attached to a running Amazon EC2 instance and exposed as a device within the instance. Amazon EBS is particularly suited for applications that require a database, file system, or access to raw block level storage.

Tip: If you wait until you must grow to think about how you're going to grow or migrate your system from one machine to another, you haven't done yourself any favors. Building on AWS puts building for resilience in the face of system failure at the top of your priority list, where it should be anyway. Using Elastic Block Storage (see below) goes a long way toward mitigating the risks associated with potential failure of an instance.

Let's do it.

Go to the Amazon EC2 Console Dashboard (https://console.aws.amazon.com/ec2/home) The screen should look something like the screenshot in Figure 6.18.

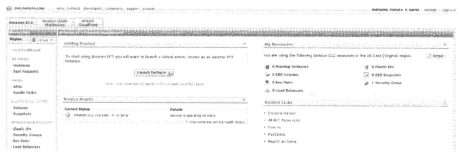

Figure 6.18   Amazon EC2 Console Dashboard.

Click the *Launch Instance* Button. Launch Instance

Choose an Amazon Machine Image (AMI) as shown in Figure 6.19.

We will select the LAMP Web Starter, a common image, of free, open source software, originally coined from the first letters of Linux (operating

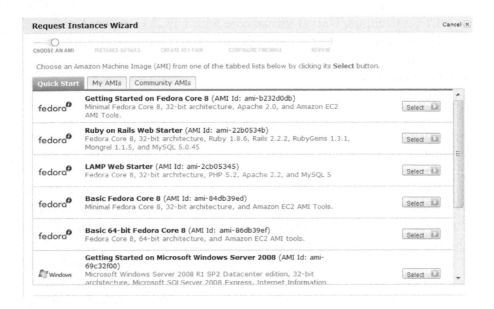

Figure 6.19   AWS Request Instances Wizard—1.

system), **Apache HTTP Server**, **MySQL** (database software), and **PHP**, **Python**, or **Perl** (scripting language)by clicking Select. Select

Next, we select the number of instances (easily changed), the availability zone (we will choose us-east-1a), and the type of instance we need (see Figure 6.20).

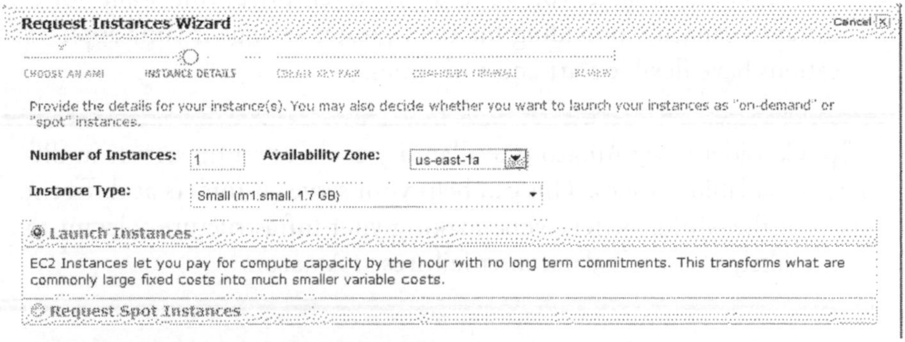

Figure 6.20   Request Instances Wizard.

A default "small instance" of EC2 provides:

- 1.7 GB memory

- 1 EC2 Compute Unit (1 virtual core with 1 EC2 Compute Unit)
  160 GB instance storage (150 GB plus 10 GB root partition)
- 32-bit platform
- I/O Performance: Moderate
- API name: m1.small

A large range of other instances can be selected to scale from this basic configuration. These provide more memory, more compute power, a 64-bit platform, enhanced I/O performance, and the like.

You can use a preconfigured software configuration running Linux, Windows, Sun or almost anything else. On-demand servers are available in three sizes, seven configurations, and with the operating system of your choice.

In addition to providing the flexibility to easily choose the number, the size and the configuration of the compute instances you need for your application, Amazon EC2 providesthree different purchasing models that give you the flexibility to optimize your costs.

- *On-Demand Instances* allow you to pay a fixed rate by the hour with no commitment
- *Reserved Instances* allow you to pay a one-time fee and in turn receive a significant discount on the hourly usage charge for that instance
- *Spot Instances* enable you to bid whatever price you want for instance capacity, providing for even greater savings if your applications have flexible start and end times.

Tip: Consider using Amazon's availability zones to set up servers in different availability zones. This can help your serve customers at different parts of the worlds better, while making your infrastructure tolerant to the unlikely event of a datacenter failures at Amazon.

We will choose a Small instance and click Continue. Continue
Next, select Advanced Instance Options (see Figure 6.21).

In this example, we can live with the defaults, so we just click Continue.

Next, we enter a name for the key pair identifying this instance, and click to create the key pair (as shown in Figure 6.22).

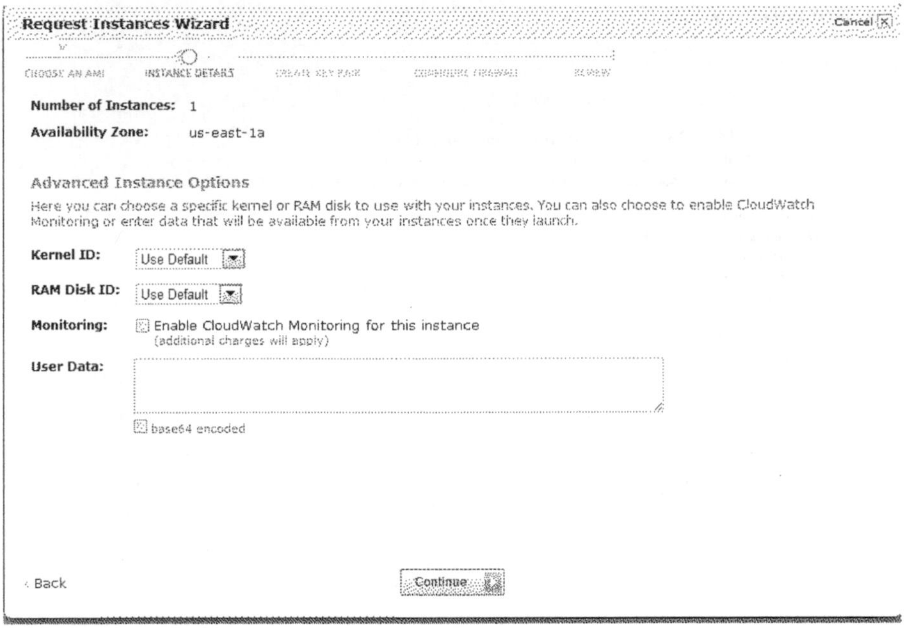

Request Instances Wizard   Cancel ☒

CHOOSE AN AMI   INSTANCE DETAILS   CREATE KEY PAIR   CONFIGURE FIREWALL   REVIEW

Number of Instances: 1
Availability Zone: us-east-1a

Advanced Instance Options

Here you can choose a specific kernel or RAM disk to use with your instances. You can also choose to enable CloudWatch Monitoring or enter data that will be available from your instances once they launch.

Kernel ID: Use Default ▼

RAM Disk ID: Use Default ▼

Monitoring: ☒ Enable CloudWatch Monitoring for this instance
                    (additional charges will apply)

User Data:

                    ☒ base64 encoded

‹ Back   Continue ▶

Figure 6.21   Advanced Instance Options.

Request Instances Wizard   Cancel ☒

CHOOSE AN AMI   INSTANCE DETAILS   CREATE KEY PAIR   CONFIGURE FIREWALL   REVIEW

Public/private key pairs allow you to securely connect to your instance after it launches. To create a key pair, enter a name and click **Create & Download your Key Pair**. You will then be prompted to save the private key to your computer. Note, you only need to generate a key pair once - not each time you want to deploy an Amazon EC2 instance.

○ Choose from your existing Key Pairs

◉ Create a new Key Pair

1. Enter a name for your key pair: *   BountyAlert   (e.g., jdoekey)

2. Click to create your key pair: *   🐾 **Create & Download your Key Pair**

                                         🐾 Save this file in a place you will
                                            remember. You can use this key pair to
                                            launch other instances in the future or visit
                                            the Key Pairs page to create or manage
                                            existing ones.

○ Proceed without a Key Pair

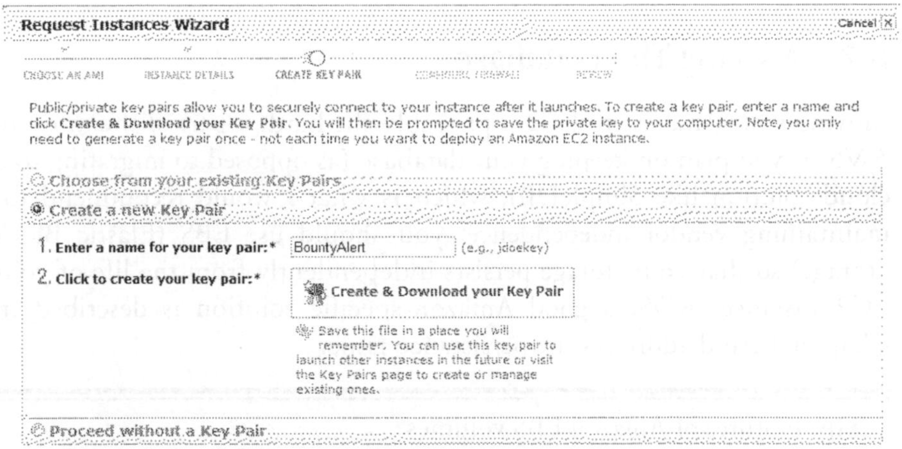

Figure 6.22   Create a key pair.

The key pair is created and downloaded to an encrypted file called a PEM file. It should be stored in a safe place. We can configure the firewall (port access) or use the default. We will accept the default. A review screen (Figure 6.23) shows us the results of our handiwork.

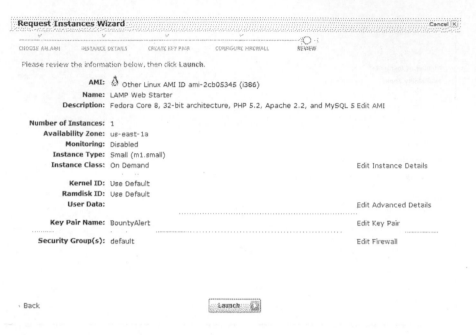

Figure 6.23   Review of Instance Characteristics.

Press Launch, and it's done.

6.7   Moving The Database

Moving your database to EC2 is probably the hardest part of the move to AWS. If you plan on keeping your database (as opposed to migrating to a cloud solution like SimpleDB), which is what I would recommend for maintaining vendor independence, you should use EBS (Elastic Block Storage) so that your storage persists independently from the life of your EC2 instance. RDS, a good Amazon-specific solution is described in Chapter 12 and addresses the persistance issue.

Tip: Features of Amazon EBS volumes

- Amazon EBS allows you to create storage volumes from 1 GB to 1 TB that can be mounted as devices by Amazon EC2 instances. Multiple volumes can be mounted to the same instance
- Storage volumes behave like raw, unformatted block devices, with user-supplied device names and a block device interface. You can

create a file system on top of Amazon EBS volumes or use them in any other way you would use a block device (like a hard drive)

- Amazon EBS volumes are placed in a specific Availability Zone and can then be attached to instances also in that same Availability Zone
- Each storage volume is automatically replicated within the same Availability Zone. This prevents data loss due to failure of any single hardware component
- Amazon EBS also provides the ability to create point-in-time snapshots of volumes, which are persisted to Amazon S3. These snapshots can be used as the starting point for new Amazon EBS volumes and protect data for long-term durability. The same snapshot can be used to instantiate as many volumes as you wish
- CloudFront lets you keep multiple copies in different zones

6.8   Using EBS for MySQL

The popular MySQL database included in the LAMP Web Starter runs well on EBS as does RDS (see Chapter 12). Some popular features include:

- *Persistent storage in the event of instance failure*—If an EBS volume is used as the storage for a MySQL database, then the data is protected from instance termination or failure. You can simply attach/mount the volume on another instance and MySQL will run its normal recovery procedures to bring the database up to date with the binary logs
- *Safety and replication*—According to Amazon, "EBS volume data is replicated across multiple servers." This makes your data safer than the default instance storage
- *Improved performance*—Studies on EBS disk IO performance indicate that EBS IO rates can be several times faster than ephemeral storage and even local disk IO. This has obvious benefits for databases, which are often IO bound
- *Large data storage capacity*—EBS volumes can be up to 1TB in size. In theory, you can support an even larger database with LVM or RAID across EBS volumes, or by placing different databases or table files on different EBS volumes. As always, paying attention to building your keys properly is essential for good performance
- *Instance type portability*—If you find that your current small EC2 instance is not able to handle your growing demand, you could

switch the EBS volume holding your MySQL database to one running an extra large instance in a matter of seconds without having to copy the database across the network. You can also downgrade instance types later to save money

■ *Fast and easy backups*—EBS snapshots alone could be a sufficiently attractive reason to move a database server to Amazon EC2. Being able to take live, consistent, binary snapshots of the database in just a few seconds is a thing of beauty. Add in the ability to create a new EBS volume from a snapshot so another EC2 instance can run against an exact copy of that database . . . and you've opened up new worlds of possibilities

AWS also enables you to create new volumes from AWS-hosted public data sets.[11]

Tip: Examples of popular public data sets include:

■ Annotated Human Genome Data, provided by ENSEMBL.
   The Ensembl project produces genome databases for human as well as almost 50 other species, and makes this information freely available.
■ Various U.S. Census Databases from The U.S. Census Bureau
   United States demographic data from the 1980, 1990, and 2000 U.S. Censuses, summary information about Business and Industry, and 2003–2006 Economic Household Profile Data.
■ UniGene provided by the National Center for Biotechnology Information
   A set of transcript sequences of well-characterized genes and hundreds of thousands of expressed sequence tags (EST) that provide an organized view of the transcriptome.
■ Freebase Data Dump from Freebase.com
   A data dump of all the current facts and assertions in the Freebase system. Freebase (www.freebase.com/) is an open database of the world's information, covering millions of topics in hundreds of categories. Drawing from large open data sets like Wikipedia, MusicBrainz, and the SEC archives, it contains structured

---

11.   http://aws.amazon.com/publicdatasets/.

information on many popular topics, including movies, music, people and locations—all reconciled and freely available.

■ *Backup.*—You can take scheduled snapshots of your EBS and store them on S3.

Tip: Consider replication and sharding. If you're using availability zone, you should consider sharding your data. For example, store data for European accounts data in Europe only. You should also consider replication between the different availability zones to ensure keep your site available even when one of the datacenter is unavailable.

6.9 Accessing Public Data

Amazon EC2 customers can access this public data by creating their own personal Amazon EBS volumes, using the public data set snapshots as a starting point. They can then access, modify and perform computation on these volumes directly using their Amazon EC2 instances and just pay for the compute and storage resources that they use. If available, researchers can also use preconfigured Amazon Machine Images (AMIs) with tools like Inquiry by BioTeam to perform their analysis.

6.10 Crawl, Walk, Run

Amazon's strategy for migrating enterprises to the cloud seems to be: crawl, walk, run. Start with simple things like S3 storage, move on to use AWS for development and test, and then watch how production is moved.

This has been well-articulated by James Governor, who wrote,[12]

> *It makes a great deal of sense to encourage its customers to adopt the pattern. That is—start with test, and go from there. Don't tell the customer to immediately migrate everything to, and run everything on, the cloud. Which would of course be insane. On the contrary recommend a low barrier to entry approach. Production is an end state where the customer finally just says: "remind me again why we aren't using this flexible infrastructure as a production environment?"*

---

12. http://developer.amazonwebservices.com/connect/kbcategory.jspa?categoryID=248.

He goes on to say, "Amazon is the new VMware. The adoption patterns are going to similar. Enterprise will see AWS as a test and development environment first, but over time production workloads will migrate there."

He may well be right.

6.11   Scaling and Monitoring: Taking Advantage of Cloud Services

Once an application is entirely running on Amazon's AWS cloud platform, it's time to take the full advantage of the platform and make it scale.

You can set up *Monitoring* to keep up with what's going on on your system. Amazon provides a service called *CloudWatch*[13] that allows you to monitor your machines and applications.

Based on the monitoring metrics, you may decide to use Amazon's auto-scaling and Elastic Load Balancing[14] capabilities to be able to consume and release computing resources according to demand.

Monitoring

Although Amazon is responsible for the physical well-being of its servers, and also for the system software, monitoring is still your responsibility. Nimsoft Monitoring Solution (NMS) for AWS[15] (see Figure 6.24) is one tool that allows customers to gain the insights they need to proactively monitor AWS performance so they can optimize service levels. NMS monitors the availability and performance of AWS' EC2 and S3 systems. NMS offers the scalability organizations require, whether they're looking to manage ten AWS instances or hundreds. NMS provides customers with visibility into resource utilization, operational issues, and overall demand patterns. CloudWatch also provides some of the features of NMS.

NMS can aggregate and report on metrics for CPU utilization, data transfer, and the disk usage and activity for each EC2 instance. It also monitors elastic load balancers for metrics such as request count and request latency.

Metrics available include:

- Overall AWS health

---

13.   http://developer.amazonwebservices.com/connect/entry.jspa?externalID=2283.
14.   http://developer.amazonwebservices.com/connect/entry.jspa?externalID=2320.
15.   "IBM, Red Hat adopt VMware Pattern for Cloud. Disruption Strategy Emerges," by James Governor, March 17, 2010, http://www.enterpriseirregulars.com/14945/ibm-red-hat-adopt-"vmware-pattern"-for-cloud-disruption-strategy-emerges/ (accessed June 10, 2010).

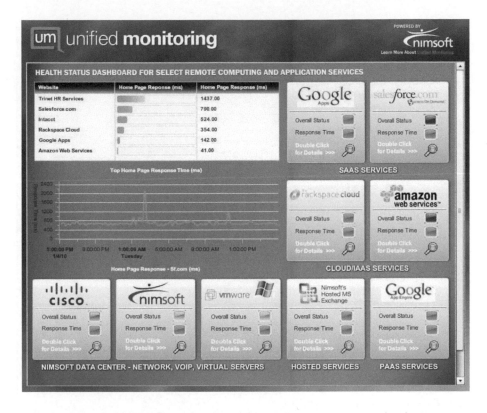

Figure 6.24 Nimsoft Monitoring Solution for AWS. (Courtesy, CA Technologies)

- CloudWatch values:
- CPUUtilization
- NetworkIn
- NetworkOut
- DiskWriteOps
- DiskReadOps
- DiskReadOps
- DiskReadBytes
- S3 file transfer times
- EC2 instance deployment time

See the screenshot in Figure 6.25.

6.12 Eucalyptus Enterprise Edition

In Chapter 2, we briefly discussed hybrid solutions, using the open source version of Eucalyptus as an example. Eucalyptus Enterprise Edition is built

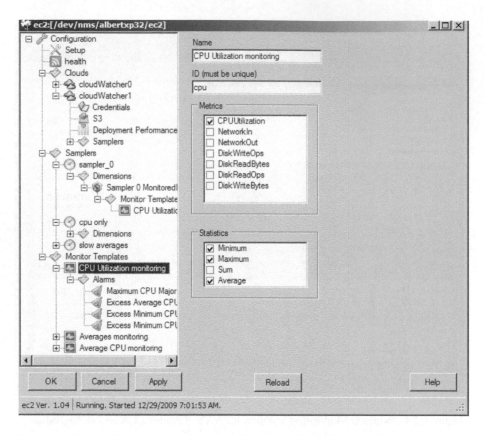

Figure 6.25   NMS Monitoring Settings. (Courtesy, CA Technologies)

on Eucalyptus—an open source software infrastructure for implementing a private cloud computing using an organization's own information technology (IT) infrastructure, without modification, special-purpose hardware, or reconfiguration. Eucalyptus turns data center resources such as machines, networks, and storage systems into a private cloud that is controlled and customized by local IT. Eucalyptus is, as far as I am aware, the only cloud architecture to support the same application programming interfaces (APIs) as public clouds. Eucalyptus is fully compatible with the Amazon Web Services™ cloud infrastructure.

Key Features and Functionality

- Many virtualization technologies are leveraged to provide a private cloud within your data center

- An image converter is included that helps users develop VMware-enabled Eucalyptus applications that are compatible with Amazon EC2 (see Chapter 7 on Virtualization for more details on VMware)
- Advanced storage integration (iSCSI, SAN, NAS) enables you to easily connect and manage your existing storage systems from within the Eucalyptus cloud
- Your data replication locations and even the degree of replication can be managed from an easy-to-use management console (no single point of failure for both data and services)

6.13   Nimbula—Roll Your Own Private EC2

Silicon Valley-based Nimbula (www.nimbula.com) was in stealth mode for over a year but emerged in June 2010. It's headed by Chris Pinkham and Willem van Bijon, a couple of Amazon developers credited with leading the development of EC2. The purpose of Nimbula is to "blend EC2-like scale, agility and efficiency with private infrastructure customization and control."

Nimbula brought in $5.75 million in Series A funding from venture capitalist Sequoia Capital and strategic partner VMware.

The Nimbula Cloud Operating System is an automated cloud management system delivering Amazon EC2-like services behind the firewall. Nimbula's technology allows customers to easily repurpose their existing infrastructure and build a computing cloud in the trusted environment of their own data center. Using simple and rapid deployment technologies, The Nimbula Cloud OS transforms underutilized private data centers into muscular, easily configurable computing capacity, quickly and cost effectively. With access to both on- and off-premise cloud services available via a common API, the Nimbula Cloud OS combines the benefits of capitalizing on internal resource capacity and controlled access to additional external compute capacity.

The Nimbula Cloud OS technology has been designed to respond to the following key requirements of an enterprise cloud solution:

- *Scalability*—The Nimbula Cloud OS is designed for linear scaling from a small cluster up to hundreds of thousands of computers. This allows an organization to grow and grow quickly.
- *Ease of use*—A highly automated, hands-off install requiring minimal configuration or interaction dramatically reduces the complexity of deploying an on-premise cloud. Racks come online

automatically in under 15 minutes. Management of cloud services is largely automated, significantly improving operational efficiency.

- *Ease of migration*—The Nimbula Cloud OS facilitates easy migration of existing applications into the cloud through its support for multiplatform environments and flexible networking and storage. It aims to avoid the dreaded lock-in problem discussed at length in Chapter 4.

- *Flexibility*—The Nimbula technology supports controlled federation to external private and public clouds like Amazon Elastic Compute Cloud (EC2) as needed by the customer: during peak times or for specific applications.

- *Reliability*—With no single points of failure, the Nimbula Cloud OS employs sophisticated fail-over mechanisms to ensure system integrity and resilience.

- *Security*—A robust and flexible policy based Authorization System supporting multitenancy provides mature and reliable security and sophisticated cloud management control.

Nimbula says it is in beta with a half-dozen international customers in financial services, tech and healthcare. More technical details are available at http://nimbula.com/technology. Interesting "use cases" from their beta customers are at http://nimbula.com/products/usecases.

CEO Chris Pinkham, who used to be VP of engineering at Amazon, said Nimbula wants "to help customers see beyond the false dichotomy of public versus private clouds" and let them feel all warm and secure about cloud computing.

Nimbula's other co-founder—and now its VP of products—Willem van Biljon wrote EC2s business plan and led its product development.

VMware co-founder and former CEO Diane Greene has just joined Nimbula's board.

The start-up's also got AWS's ex-biz dev and sales chief Martin Buhr as its VP of sales and ex-VMware exec Reza Malekzadeh as VP of marketing.

Summary

In this chapter, we looked briefly at Amazon's Web Services. We started with basic storage and used Gladinet to create a Z disk that appears local but connects to the cloud. We then used S3Fox Organizer to move our static content from our own computer to the Amazon cloud. We created a custom instance of a virtual server on EC2, configured just the way we wanted it. We can use CloudWatch to monitor EC2 instances and then Elastic Load Balancers in real time or Auto Scaling to dynamically add or remove Amazon EC2 instances based on Amazon CloudWatch metrics. Nimsoft's Nimsoft Monitoring Solution (NMS) for AWS is one tool for monitoring and controlling Amazon-hosted cloud solutions. Nimbula, a well-pedigreed start-up, aims to let enterprises create their own EC2 behind their own firewall.

Chapter 7

Virtualization: Open Source and VMware

Overview

In this chapter we discuss virtualization, the main ingredient of cloud computing, as well as the leading offerings. We shall see that while it's an old idea, it is modern, fast, low-cost, mass-produced hardware that has made virtualization cost-effective. Many powerful hypervisors, including Xen, KVM, and QEMU are open source. VMware is the commercial leader, but its products are based on open source. Citrix is a form of virtual desktop, but today it often rides on VMware. Amazon uses a modified version of Xen.

Monitoring is essential to managing the performance of virtual systems. Microsoft has its own patented approach to virtualization, which it deploys in Microsoft Azure. EMC's VPLEX is an important new technology for moving blocks of storage across the cloud. Interesting partnerships have been announced among VMware, Google, Salesforce.com, Eucalyptus, and Amazon that will help grow the entire industry and prevent lock-in to a single vendor.

> *OpenStack.org is open source that is compatible with Rackspace [see Chapter 13] and Amazon EC2 [see Chapter 6]. The goal of OpenStack is to allow any organization to create and offer cloud computing capabilities using open source software running on standard hardware. OpenStack Compute is software for automatically creating and managing large groups of virtual private servers. OpenStack Storage is software for creating redundant, scalable object storage using clusters of commodity servers to store terabytes or even petabytes of data.[1]*

---

1.   http://openstack.org/.

Virtualization Is an Old Story

At the heart of cloud computing is virtualization. As we noted in Chapter 2, virtualization's roots go back a long time, to the IBM 360 Model 67 and the CP operating system, which provided each user with a virtual "image" of an IBM 360 computer.

It's the virtual machine that makes cloud computing work.

In the years from 1995 to 2005, as PCs and client/server solutions took center stage, virtualization was relegated to the backwaters of computing.

Now, its time has come .. . . again.

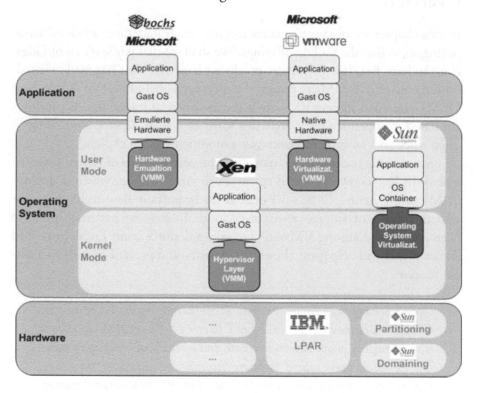

Figure 7.1   Overview of virtualization techniques.

7.1   The Hypervisor is the Secret Sauce

The software that allows multiple virtual images to share a single physical machine is today known as a *hypervisor*—a layer of software running directly on computer hardware and replacing the operating system, thereby allowing the computer hardware to run multiple guest operating systems concurrently, similar to what CP offered on the old IBM 360 Model 67. Microsoft Azure uses its own.

Certain hardware, such as Intel® architecture-based servers built with hardware-assisted Intel VT and AMD Opteron 64 servers with AMD-V, minimize the overhead associated with virtualization.

There are three leading open source hypervisors: Kernel-based Virtual Machine (KVM), Xen, and QEMU.

7.2 KVM

KVM is developed and maintained at www.linux-kvm.org. It has been embraced by Red Hat, a popular distributor of Linux software. A current FAQ (frequently asked questions) is maintained at http://www.linux-kvm.org/page/FAQ and includes information on supported processors. KVM offers a live migration feature to move virtual machines from one host to another without downtime.

7.3 Xen

The Xen hypervisor (Figure 7.2) is developed and maintained by the Xen.org community as a free solution licensed under the GNU General Public License.

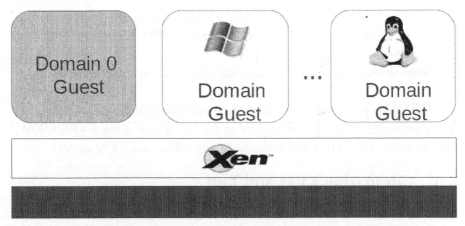

Figure 7.2   Xen hypervisor components.(Licensed under the GNU Free Documentation License).

A customized version of Xen is deployed by Amazon in EC2. Xen provides support for x86, x86-64, Itanium, Power PC, and ARM processors, which allows the Xen hypervisor to run on a wide variety of computing devices. Currently Xen supports Linux, NetBSD, FreeBSD, Solaris, Windows, and other common operating systems as guests running on the hypervisor. Xen can be downloaded without charge at http://www.xen.org/products/downloads.html.

Citrix also provides a free version of Xen, which it calls XenServer; it supports 64-bit versions of Intel and AMD processors.

Citrix Essentials for XenServer is a commercial product extension of XenServer (which is in the public domain, as it's based on open source technology). Citrix Essentialsoffers advanced virtualization management capabilities to server environments to help customers create highly scalable, manageable, and agile virtual infrastructures. Pricing is on a per-server basis and includes one year of support. Symantec Corporation also offers a Xen-based product.

7.4 QEMU

QEMU is a generic and open source machine emulator and virtualizer:

> *When used as a machine emulator, QEMU can run operating systems and programs made for one machine (e.g., an ARM board) on a different machine (e.g., your own PC). By using dynamic translation, it achieves very good performances.*
> *When used as a virtualizer, QEMU achieves near native performance by executing the guest code directly on the host CPU.*

> **Source:** *http://forums.techarena.in/operating-systems/1138990.htm*

QEMU supports virtualization when executing under the Xen hypervisor or using the KVM kernel module in Linux. When using KVM, QEMU can virtualize x86, server and embedded PowerPC, and S390 guests.

7.5 Comparing KVM and Xen

Xen is an external hypervisor; it assumes control of the machine and divides resources among guests. On the other hand, KVM is part of Linux and uses the regular Linux scheduler and memory management. This means that KVM is much smaller and simpler to use; it is also provides some features not available in Xen. For example KVM can swap guests to disk in order to free RAM.

However, KVM only runs on processors that support x86 hardware virtual machines (hvm), Intel Virtualization Technology (VT), and AMD SVM (Secure Virtual Machine) instruction sets, known as vt/svm, whereas Xen also allows running modified operating systems on non-hvm x86 processors using a technique called paravirtualization. KVM does not support paravirtualization for CPUs but may support paravirtualization for device drivers to improve I/O performance.

7.6   Comparing KVM and QEMU

QEMU uses emulation; KVM uses processor extensions (HVM) for virtualization.

7.7   Parallels

Parallels, Inc. (formerly SWsoft) has a product for the Apple Mac environment, Parallels Desktop for Mac, that is also based on hypervisor technology. Parallels Server for Mac is also hypervisor-based server virtualization software. It enables IT managers to run multiple Windows, Linux, and Mac OS X Server operating systems on a single Mac Xserve, Apple's line of 1U rack-mounted servers. At present, it is the only server virtualization solution for the Mac OS X server platform that allows users to virtualize the Mac OS X Leopard Server.

7.8   A Unique Hypervisor: Microsoft Azure and Hyper-V

Microsoft has included the Hyper-V hypervisor in Microsoft Server 2008 (code-named Viridian); Hyper-V is also available in a free, reduced-function stand-alone version. However, Hyper-V, which provides partition-level isolation, is *not* the basis for the Hypervisor in Microsoft Azure (discussed in Chapter 8). That was written, like the rest of Azure, from the ground up and is particularly optimized for multitenancy. The Windows Azure Hypervisor is tightly optimized with the Windows Azure kernel. However, Microsoft has stated that some of the features of the Azure Hypervisor will ultimately make their way into the next version of Hyper-V. For example, Second-level Address Translation will be available in Hyper-V v2.0. This concept is explained in U.S. Patent 7,428,626[2], invented by Rene Antonio Vega and assigned to Microsoft:

---

2.   http://www.google.com/patents/about?id=sbStAAAAEBAJ.

A method of performing a translation from a guest virtual address to a host physical address in a virtual machine environment includes receiving a guest virtual address from a host computer executing a guest virtual machine program and using the hardware oriented method of the host CPU to determine the guest physical address. A second level address translation to a host physical address is then performed. In one embodiment, a multiple tier tree is traversed which translates the guest physical address into a host physical address. In another embodiment, the second level of address translation is performed by employing a hash function of the guest physical address and a reference to a hash table. One aspect of the invention is the incorporation of access overrides associated with the host physical address which can control the access permissions of the host memory.

Microsoft released 20,000 lines of device-driver source code for virtualizing Linux over Windows. Some say that Microsoft made the move to rectify a violation of the open source General Public License v2. "The driver had both open-source components which were under GPL, and statically linked to several binary parts. The GPL does not permit mixing of closed and open source parts, so this was an obvious violation of the license," said Stephen Hemminger, a principal programmer with open-source networking firm Vyatta.[3]

7.8.1 Managing a Virtualized Infrastructure

Cloud management challenges are illustrated in Figure 7.3.

Managing a farm of physical servers, each running multiple virtual servers, is a management challenge that cries out for software solutions. We illustrate this in Figure 7.4 with ConVirt 2.0, which is an open source solution. But it's a rapidly growing area, and new products are announced frequently.

ConVirt 2.0 allows you to centrally monitor and configure your Xen and KVM virtual machines and proactively manage your virtualized infrastructure. The company's Web site claims that, "Armed with a consolidated view across all your Xen and KVM virtual machines, you can keep apprised of server utilization and easily respond to changes in application demand by reallocatingreallocating resources."[4] ConVirt may be downloaded at www.convirture.com/downloads.html.

---

3.   http://linux-network-plumber.blogspot.com/2009/07/congratulations-microsoft.html.
4.   http://www.convirture.com/solutions_datacenters.html.

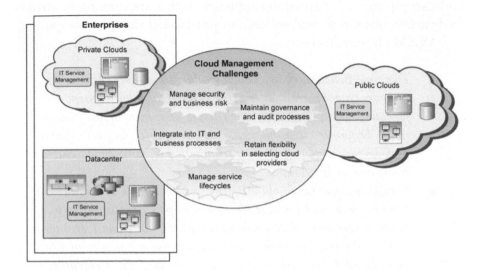

Figure 7.3   Challenges of cloud management (courtesy DMTF.org).

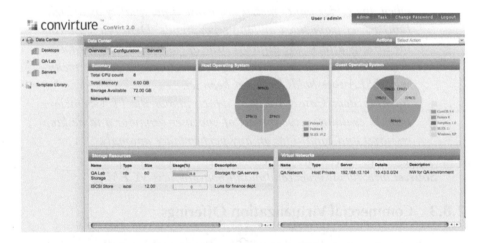

Figure 7.4   ConVirt 2.0 Centralized Monitor for Xen and KVM. The data center–
level configuration view provides detailed information about operating systems, storage, and networks resources in your environment.
(Licensed under the GNU Free Documentation License.)

7.8.2   Monitoring and Management

**Knoa, a commercial vendor, offers Virtual/Cloud Experience Manager
(VCEM),** an off-the-shelf product designed to monitor and manage real

end-user experience for enterprise applications that are running in virtualized environments, delivered via SaaS, or provisioned via cloud computing.

VCEM's features include:

- *Dynamic Benchmarking, which enables the IT organization to compare system performance prior to the change with system performance before and after each wave of infrastructure transition. Dynamic Benchmarking is available for all system performance metrics including transaction response times, system errors and utilization.*
- *Comprehensive Threshold Alerting, which allows IT organizations to create and manage alerts based upon established Service Level Agreements. Alerts can be delivered via e-mail or integrated into existing performance management consoles to provide the IT team with a "single pane of glass" for performance management.*
- *Dynamic Base-lining, which allows IT organization to monitor when any performance metric (response time, quality or utilization) varies from short or long-term trends. Dynamic base-lining directly attacks the difficult issue of ensuring no performance degradation for the thousands of transactions for which meaningful SLA thresholds have not been set.*
- *Advance Root Cause Analysis, which allows the IT Operations team to evaluation the impact of end-user behavior and desktop resources and conditions on any performance anomaly.*

Source: http://www.knoa.com/main/knoa-products-VCEM.jsp

7.8.3 Commercial Virtualization Offerings

We can't do justice to a discussion of virtualization without discussing Citrix and VMware.

7.8.4 Citrix

Citrix has been catching a wave.

Founded in 1989 by Ed Iacobucci, a former developer for IBM, Citrix's name is a portmanteau (blended word) of Citrus, the company's original name, a tribute to its headquarters in Coral Springs, Florida, and UNIX.

So right away, you know that they are into open source.

Citrix was an early pioneer in virtualization for PC architecture, Win-View, which provided remote access to DOS and Windows 3.1 applications on a multi-user platform. Microsoft agreed to license Citrix technology for Windows NT Server 4.0, resulting in Windows Terminal Server Edition, and Citrix agreed not to compete with a product of its own. However, it could (and did) offer extensions, which it initially called Metaframe XP and Presentation Server. The product, now called **XenApp,** provides application virtualization and application delivery. Citrix XenDesktop is **a** desktop virtualization and virtual desktop infrastructure (VDI) solution (see Figure 7.5) that delivers a complete Windows desktop experience as an on-demand service to any user, anywhere. In the virtual desktop market, Citrix and VMware are the main competitors.

Citrix's XenServer, discussed below, provides server platform virtualization.

First-generation VDI solutions were useful only to a narrow set of users, primarily those working all day using a small number of corporate applications.

Today, whether users are task workers, knowledge workers or mobile workers, XenDesktop can quickly and securely deliver individual applications or complete desktops while providing a high-definition user experience. Citrix calls its delivery technology FlexCast, and it enables IT to deliver any type of virtual desktop, on any device.

The most important benefits of the Citrix Xen Desktop are reduced administration and management costs.

7.8.5   VMware

Founded in 1998, VMware is the 800-pound gorilla in the virtualization room, with more than $2 billion in revenue. It offered its first virtualization platform (for x86 systems) in 1999. VMware was acquired by EMC in 2004, and partially spun-off from EMC in 2007, but EMC still overwhelmingly controls it.

Since parent EMC is a hardware vendor, primarily serving larger enterprises, VMware not surprisingly has private, secure data centers in its DNA, and has been going, as they say about themselves, "all in" on *private* clouds. It is a founding sponsor of PrivateCloud.com, an industry destination for news, resources, and conversation on enterprise cloud computing that's worth a visit. However, they are very active (through partners) in the public cloud space as well.

VMware has three offerings. vSphere™ 4 is VMware's offering for a private cloud solution and the current incarnation of its crown jewels.

XenDesktop Technology
How Desktop Delivery Works

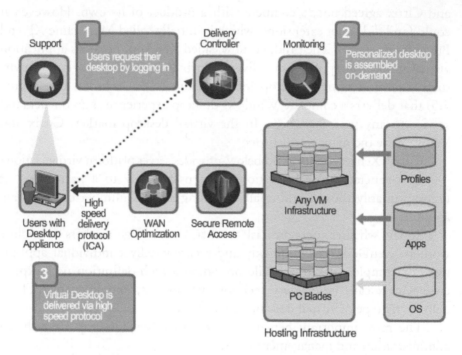

Figure 7.5   Xen desktop technology.technology. Licensed under the GNU Free Documentation License.

VMware ESXi is a free hypervisor solution somewhat comparable to Citrix XenServer, while VMware Server is a hosted solution. Table 7.1 compares VMware offerings:

VMware's special spices are a large variety of Virtual Appliances. VMware uses the term *Virtual Appliance* to describe the premade image that is similar to the Amazon Machine Image (AMI) described in Chapter 6, but goes a step further by allowing for preinstalled, pretested, packaged software from the VMware Virtual Appliance Marketplace. These may be highly specific. For example, the AllardSoft Secure Filetransfer Virtual Appliance is installed on a server in your own facilities to send big files securely to customers, clients, or other staff members. It integrates with your existing Active Directory or LDAP infrastructure to further assist with the deployment.

It's but one of hundreds of Marketplace offerings.

Table 7.1   Comparison of VMware offerings. © VMware, Reproduced by Permission

	Essentials for Retail	Essentials Plus for Retail	Standard	Advanced	Enterprise	Enterprise Plus
ESX/ESXi	✔	✔	✔	✔	✔	✔
vCenter Server Compatibility	vCenter Server for Essentials, vCenter Server Foundation & vCenter Server Standard	vCenter Server for Essentials, vCenter Server Foundation & vCenter Server Standard	vCenter Server Foundation & Standard	vCenter Server Foundation & Standard	vCenter Server Foundation & Standard	vCenter Server Foundation & Standard
Cores per Processor	6	6	6	12	6	12
vSMP Support	4-way	4-way	4-way	4-way	4-way	8-way
Memory Physical Server	256GB	256GB	256GB	256GB	256GB	*No license limit
Thin Provisioning	✔	✔	✔	✔	✔	✔
VC Agent	✔	✔	✔	✔	✔	✔
Update Manager	✔	✔	✔	✔	✔	✔
VMSafe	✔	✔	✔	✔	✔	✔

Table 7.1   Comparison of VMware offerings. © VMware, Reproduced by Permission

	Essentials for Retail	Essentials Plus for Retail	Standard	Advanced	Enterprise	Enterprise Plus
vStorage APIs for Data Protection	✔	✔	✔	✔	✔	✔
High Availability (HA)	✔	✔	✔	✔	✔	✔
Data Recovery			sold separately	✔	✔	✔
Hot Add				✔	✔	✔
Fault Tolerance				✔	✔	✔
vShield Zones				✔	✔	✔
VMotion			✔	✔	✔	✔
Storage VMotion					✔	✔
DRS DPM					✔	✔
**vNetwork Distributed Switch						✔

Table 7.1   Comparison of VMware offerings. © VMware, Reproduced by Permission

	Essentials for Retail	Essentials Plus for Retail	Standard	Advanced	Enterprise	Enterprise Plus
Host Profiles						✔
Third Party Multipath-ing						✔

*VMware ESX4.0 and ESXi 4.0 currently provide technical support for up to 1TB of memory.

Review the vSphere 4 Configuration Maximums document ((http://www.vmware.com/pdf/vsphere4/r40/vsp_40_config_max.pdf)) for more information.

**Enabler for third-party switch support.

At this writing, VMware itself is not in the public cloud business. It partners, as we shall discuss, with many leading cloud service providers.

Paul Maritz, who retired from Microsoft after 14 years, culminating as group vice president of platform strategy, is president and CEO of VMware, and Tod Nielsen, another senior Microsoft development executive, is its chief operating officer. Since these well-regarded folks spent significant parts of their careers at Microsoft, software is obviously in their DNA, but they are more used to selling software-in-a-box and per-seat licenses than they are to selling metered pay-as-you-go cloud computing.

Perhaps for this reason, VMware has partnered with third parties who provide external cloud infrastructure as a service that can integrate seamlessly with the internal cloud that VMware will be only too happy to sell you. vCloud Express is VMware's Infrastructure as a Service (IaaS) offering delivered by VMware's third-party service provider partners. It provides reliable, on-demand, pay-as-you-go infrastructure that ensures compatibility with internal VMware environments and with VMware Virtualized™ services. VMware's partners include

- Bluelock (http://vcloudexpress.bluelock.com/)
- Hosting.com (www.hosting.com/vcloudexpress)
- Terremark (http://vcloudexpress.terremark.com/)

Of these, Terremark Worldwide, Inc. is the most established VMware partner. Founded in 1982, Terremark offers Infrastructure as a Service and owns and operates purpose-built datacenters in the United States, Europe, and Latin America, and access to massive and diverse network connectivity from more than 160 global carriers. VMware holds a six percent equity interest in Terremark, which provides carrier neutral colocation, managed services, and exchange point services to approximately 1,300 customers worldwide including many government entities from three highly special-ized data centers, or Network Access Points (NAPs), that were purpose-built and have been strategically located to provide security, reliability, power availability and connectivity.

So far, the market is with VMware, in the sense that there are more private than public clouds. However, public clouds are growing quickly and maturing rapidly. As astute observers of the IT scene and as former Microsoft executives, VMware's management are well aware of three things: (1) Microsoft has, since its founding, derived substantially all of its revenue from software licensing, (2) Microsoft has made a huge bet on public cloud computing, which is our subject for the next chapter, and (3) Microsoft is under substantial pressure from free open source software. It will be interesting to look back in a few years to see if the largely propri-etary "software only" strategy of the dean of virtualization will prove to be the winning strategy.

7.9   EMC's VPLEX and VMware

Recently, EMC, VMware's controlling parent, introduced VPLEX as a vir-tual RAID (redundant array of independent disks or redundant array of inexpensive disks) for a storage area network (SAN) in order to access data anywhere within the private cloud. Wikipedia defines RAID[5] as

> . . . a technology that provides increased storage reliability through redundancy, combining multiple low-cost, less-reliable disk drive com-ponents into a logical unit where all drives in the array are interdepen-dent. The concept was first defined by David A. Patterson, Garth A. Gibson, and Randy Katz at the University of California, Berkeley in 1987 as redundant array of inexpensive disks.

VPLEX extends RAID beyond the datacenter and is storage agnostic. Two unique features of VPLEX are cache coherency and dirty region logs.

---

5.   http://en.wikipedia.org/wiki/RAID.

These facilitate high speed, long distance, and reliable operation. Prior to EMC VPLEX, information mobility was only available through the use of special purpose technologies and specifically designed applications. With VPLEX, you simply carve up storage and present it to the VPLEX; the VPLEX then claims the storage from the back-end and it presents it (makes it available) to your servers. You can claim storage from one SAN, claim storage from a different SAN that could be in the same data center or at another data center within synchronous distance (meaning that communication speed is very high) and then you can connect the two storages together in a RAID architecture. The servers behind the VPLEX just see this single virtualized storage unit even though it is being presented from multiple sources.[6]

The VPLEX is a hardware and software solution that comes in two configurations, Local and Metro. The Metro configuration extends a storage infrastructure by up to 100 Km. The goal, according to EMC, is to continue to extend this distance in future releases.

VPLEX Local provides local federation across heterogeneous arrays, whereas VPLEX Metro permits two clusters within limited distances to access the same physical Logical Unit Number (LUN). The VPLEX system architecture uses distributed cache coherence, active--active data sharing and scale--out performance, all new technology innovations developed by EMC.[7]

EMS controls VMware, so it is not surprising that VPLEX and VMware interact well together::

> *The combination of EMC VPLEX and VMware vMotion enables you to effectively distribute applications and their data across multiple hosts over synchronous distances. With Virtual Storage and virtual servers working together over distance, your infrastructure can provide load balancing, real-time remote data access, and improved application protection.*
>
> **Source:** *www.emc.com/campaign/global/vplex/index.htm ("vMotion over distance" tab)*
>
> *Within VMware, you can use Storage vMotion to enable a server live migration of virtual machine disk files across storage arrays. VMware*

---

6.   Adapted from Carlos Costanzo, "What is EMC's New VPLEX?" Available at http://www.vmwareinfo.com/2010/05/what-is-emcs-new-vplex.html.

7.   http://www.emc.com/collateral/analyst-reports/silverton-vplex-solutions-local-distributed-federation.pdf.

Storage vMotion lets you relocate virtual machine disk files between and across shared storage locations while maintaining continuous service availability and complete transaction integrity.

- *Reduce IT costs and improve flexibility with server consolidation*
- *Decrease downtime and improve reliability with business continuity and disaster recovery*
- *Increase energy efficiency by running fewer servers and dynamically powering down unused servers with our green IT solutions,*

Source: *www.vmware.com/products/storage-vmotion/*

When you use VPLEX and perform a vMotion movement between storage and even sites, the data is already there, so it seems as if it moves from site to site within seconds.

Key VPLEX features include:

- Active and very resilient
- Supports up to 8,000 virtual volumes per VPLEX cluster
- Maximum Logical Unit Number (LUN) size (as tested by EMC) of 32 TB (a LUN is the identifier of a SCSI logical unit, and by extension of a Fibre Channel or iSCSI logical unit)[8]
- 8 GBS fiber connection recommended between VPLEX devices
- Support maximum latency of 5 ms across locations
- Easiest migration path is through Storage vMotion

7.10   VMware Partners with Salesforce.com and Google

We first discussed Salesforce.com in Chapter 3. In late 2009, VMware acquired SpringSource, ". . . bringing VMware one of the most popular Java development frameworks, stewardship of the Apache Tomcat, Apache HTTP Server, Hyperic, Groovy, and Grails open source communities, as well as a group of engineers focused on the efficient development of applications for the cloud-computing era."[9] More recently, VMware acquired Rabbit Technologies, the company behind the popular open source cloud messaging technology RabbitMQ. These products, with others promised

---

8.   http://en.wikipedia.org/wiki/Logical_Unit_Number
9.   http://blogs.vmware.com/console/2010/04/vmforce-and-vmwares-open-paas-strategy.html

for the near future, are VMware's "vCloud Developer Services" and "vCloud Platform Services".

Salesforce.com and VMware have partnered to introduce VMforce—the first enterprise cloud for Java developers. With VMforce, Java developers can build apps that are instantly social and available on mobile devices in real time. And it's all in the cloud, so there's no hardware to manage and no software stack to install, patch, tune, or upgrade. Building Java apps on VMforce is easy!

- *Use the standard Spring Eclipse-based IDE*
- *Code your app with standard Java, including POJOs, JSPs, and Servlets*
- *Deploy your app to VMforce with 1 click*

Source: *www.salesforce.com/vmforce/category.jsp*

7.11   VMforce

The launch of VMforce is significant because it brings a mission critical deployment environment for enterprise Java apps in the cloud. Previously, Java developers had limited environments to deploy applications in the cloud. VMforce aims to provide a cloud-based application platform to the 6 million enterprise Java developers, including the 2 million members of Spring community. The offering allows Java developers to tap into Salesforce's Force.com application, which provides a cloud-based platform to run and operate business applications. Developers can access the Force.com database, workflow, analytics, search, and Chatter profiles and feeds.

VMforce will use the Spring Framework. The SpringSource Tool Suite, will allow applications will run on the tc Server, the Enterprise version of Apache Tomcat, and is optimized for virtual and cloud environments.

VMforce's platform will allows developers to incorporate collaboration services from recently launched Chatter in their applications. These pre-built services include profiles, status updates, groups, feeds, document sharing, the Chatter API.

Since VMforce will run on the Force.com platform, developers have access to a host of other pre-built business services that can be configured into their apps without requiring any custom coding. These services include search, identity and security, workflow, reporting and analytics, a robust web services integration API, mobile deployment, and more. Developers using VMforce will also be able to tap into Force.com's relational database, including automatic scalability, high availability, auto-tuning, back up and disaster recovery.

VMware's vCloud technology will manage the Java stack that powers VMforce applications and the underlying vSphere virtualization platform.

Salesforce previously didn't allow for Java-based applications to be deployed on the Force.com platform, says Ariel Kelman, VP of Product Marketing for Force.com. Kelman says the aim of VMforce is to bring a trusted cloud platform for the millions of Java developers and accelerate adoption of the new offering. While Amazon Web Services offers a Java platform for developers, says Kelman, VMforce manages many of the complexities for enterprise developers, such as analytics, search and more.

Source: http://www.techcrunchit.com/2010/04/27/salesforce-and-vmware-partner-to-launch-enterprise-java-cloud-platform-vmforce/

With VMforce, there's no hardware to manage—and no software stack to install, patch, tune, or upgrade. Just drag and drop your Java app to VMforce to deploy. Java developers can add built-in collaboration, mobile, and analytics components to their apps. Similar to other cloud infrastructures, all apps on VMforce are elastic, so you never have to worry about scaling up app servers, databases, or infrastructure.

Any enterprise with Java development resources and skillsets can now easily develop enterprise Java apps locally and then deploy them to the cloud. VMforce supports standard Java code, including POJOs, JSPs, and Servlets, along with the popular Spring Framework. With VMforce, you can also easily migrate existing enterprise Java apps to the cloud and avoid cloud lock-in.

Source: www.salesforce.com/vmforce/category.jsp

7.12   VMware and Google

VMware and Google are both known for *spring*ing (pun intended, as you'll see) out of Gates Computer Science Building at Stanford University at around the same time. Both have grown enormously, and executives of both companies stayed friendly. At some point, both companies realized that they shared similar visions of the cloud and similar passions for building great software to achieve this vision, including a shared vision to make it easy to build, run, and manage applications for the cloud, and to do so in a way that makes the applications portable across clouds. The rich applications should be able to run in an enterprise's private cloud, on Google's AppEngine, or on other public clouds committed to similar openness.

7.12.1   Spring for AppEngine

In May 2010, VMware committed to making Spring available as a language for Google App Engine and other cloud applications, even if that cloud, like Google's App Engine cloud is not currently based on VMware vSphere, and VMware is accepting that. Developers must be able to write applications without needing to know what underlying technology powers the cloud that they'll be deployed on. Furthermore, there are many use cases where portability between clouds makes great business sense. For example, they might want to develop and test their application on App Engine and then seamlessly move it to their own VMware-based private cloud for production execution. Or they might do it the other way around as well![10]

Paul Maritz, VMware CEO, stated at the 2010 Google I/O Conference, "VMware and Google are aligning to reassure our mutual customers and the Java community that choice and portability are of utmost importance to both companies. We will work to ensure that modern applications can run smoothly within the firewalls of a company's datacenter or out in the public cloud environment." For its part, Google announced support for Spring Java apps on the (recently enhanced) Google App Engine. VMware and Google are working together to combine the speed of development of Spring Roo, a rapid application development tool, with the power of the Google Web Toolkit (GWT) to build rich browser apps. These GWT-powered applications can leverage modern browser technologies such as AJAX and HTML5 to create a compelling end user experience on both smart phones and computers. In just one click, users of the new versions of SpringSource Tool Suite and Google Web Toolkit can deploy their application to Google App Engine for Business, a VMware environment or other infrastructure, such as Amazon EC2.

---

10.   Adapted from http://blogs.vmware.com/console/2010/05/google-and-vmwares-open-paas-strategy.html.

7.12.2   Spring Insight and Google Speed Tracer

The two companies are also collaborating to more tightly integrate VMware's Spring Insight performance tracing technology within the SpringSource tc Server application server with Google's Speed Tracer technology to enable end to end performance visibility of cloud applications built using Spring and Google Web Toolkit. Cloud-based SQL and SSL are also promised for delivery in 2010.[11]

eWeek reported, "Google App Engine for Business allows developers to use standards-based technology, such as Java, Python, the Eclipse IDE and Google Web Toolkit (GWT), to create applications that run on the platform. It also offers users dynamic scaling, consistent availability and flat-rate pricing."[12] The App Engine For Business Roadmap is maintained at http://code.google.com/appengine/business/roadmap.html and is updated regularly.

7.13   Eucalyptus and VMware

We briefly discussed Eucalyptus in Chapter 2 and Eucalyptus Enterprise Edition in Chapter 4. Users of VMware may appreciate the additional features that Eucalyptus Enterprise Edition provides, including:

- Run your Amazon Machine Image (AMI) instances on your VMware-based hypervisors on your own private cloud
- Seamlessly manage environments with multiple hypervisors (Xen, KVM,vSphere, ESX™ and ESXi™) under one management console
- Test, develop, and deploy on your private Eucalyptus EE cloud and smoothly transition to a public cloud or vice-versa, without any modifications
- Quickly and easily build hybrid clouds with your existing environment and other public clouds
- Leverage the ecosystem built around AWS (RightScale™, CohesiveFT™, Zmanda™ and rPath™ are among the vendors that deliver solutions for Amazon AWS that in-turn work seamlessly with Eucalyptus using VMware.)

---

11.   Adapted from www.cloudtweaks.com/2010/05/vmware-to-collaborate-with-google-on-cloud-computing/.
12.   http://www.eweek.com/c/a/Cloud-Computing/Google-Shows-Enterprise-Focus-with-App-Engine-VMware-Plans-810075/.

Recent VM Acquisitions

Beside acquiring SpringSource, which we discussed above, VMware has made several other acquisitions in 2010:

- Zimbra, a hosted e-mail service, acquired from Yahoo. *The New York Times* called it "the icing on the PaaS."[13]
- Parts of EMC's Ionix IT management business, including solutions aimed at delivering improved management and deployment of servers and applications in a virtualized data center. This deal gives VMware some tools to measure and automate the provisioning and management of virtualized machines. Since a platform can have hundreds of thousands of VMs, automation is essential. VMware is acquiring from EMC, its parent, all technology and intellectual property of FastScale, Application Discovery Manager, Server Configuration Manager, and Service Manager and will maintain engineering, marketing, sales, and support operations in the United States, Europe, Israel, India, and Australia. (As part of the agreement, EMC will retain the Ionix brand and have full reseller rights to continue to offer customers the products acquired by VMware.) VMware says that this "new capability will provide a holistic view of configuration compliance of complete IT services from underlying physical assets to applications. VMware plans to further optimize the acquired products for dynamic, VMware vSphere-based cloud infrastructure, to deliver unparalleled visibility, control and simplicity of enterprise IT management."[14]
- Rabbit MQ, an open-source messaging protocol acquired by VMware's SpringSource subsidiary. This acquisition "enables VMware to provide a messaging platform that is flexible enough to live on company servers, a platform or a private or public cloud computing environments"[15] according to *The New York Times*. RabbitMQ is a successful and well-regarded technology that forms the backbone for many cloud messaging systems environments, providing a multi-protocol, completely open, portable messaging system. The code was created by Open Source vendors Cohesive

---

13.   http://www.nytimes.com/external/gigaom/2010/06/11/11gigaom-what-should-one-make-of-vmwares-shopping-spree-45138.html.
14.   http://www.vmware.com/company/news/releases/emc-ionix.html.
15.   http://www.nytimes.com/external/gigaom/2010/06/11/11gigaom-what-should-one-make-of-vmwares-shopping-spree-45138.html.

FT[16] and LShift[17] based on the relatively young AMQP open standard[18] for messaging middleware, an industry effort backed by
major banks, Cisco, and a handful of smaller companies. As hardware is virtualized, translating some of the network equipment like
load balancers into software allows services running on the virtualized hardware to better scale.

- Gemstone, which "provides a distributed data caching technology
  to help analyze and crunch data across a number of servers or in
  the cloud——something VMware can use to make sure its PaaS
  can handle data without bogging down"[19] according to *The New
  York Times*.

- EngineYard? Maybe. As we go to press, EngineYard (the Ruby on
  Rails provider, discussed in Chapter 11)[20]) was also in talks to be
  acquired by VMware. EngineYard already works closely with
  VMware, because VMware provides its underlying software and is
  a strategic investor in Terremark, which hosts EngineYard's enterprise-class PaaS.

7.14   OpenStack

Rackspace and NASA, along with leaders Citrix, Dell, NTT Data, Right-
Scale, and others, have joined together to create OpenStack.org.

> *The goal of OpenStack is to allow any organization to create and offer
> cloud computing capabilities using open source software running on
> standard hardware. OpenStack Compute is software for automati-
> cally creating and managing large groups of virtual private servers.
> OpenStack Storage is software for creating redundant, scalable object
> storage using clusters of commodity servers to store terabytes or even
> petabytes of data"[21]*

The OpenStack project builds on efforts already underway by both
Rackspace and the space agency. Rackspace had been developing its own

---

16.   http://www.cohesiveft.com/.
17.   http://www.lshift.net/.
18.   http://www.amqp.org/confluence/display/AMQP/About+AMQP.
19.   http://www.nytimes.com/external/gigaom/2010/06/11/11gigaom-what-should-one-make-of-
      vmwares-shopping-spree-45138.html.
20.   http://dealbook.blogs.nytimes.com/2010/06/14/vmware-said-to-be-in-talks-to-acquire-engine-
      yard/.
21.   www.openstack.org.

cloud storage technology, while NASA, by way of its Nebula project, was building out a distributed compute fabric. Nebula is an open source cloud computing project and service developed to provide an alternative to the costly construction of additional data centers whenever NASA scientist or engineers require additional data processing. Nebula also provides a simplified avenue for NASA scientists and researchers to share large, complex datasets with external partners and the public.

All of the code for OpenStack is freely available under the Apache 2.0 license. Anyone can run it, build on it, or submit changes back to the project.

The combined OpenStack effort will challenge Amazon's cloud and S3 services; it will also provide a useful option for open source users.

OpenStack is another step towards high-speed interclouding. Though it hasn't happened yet, I believe that Amazon, Google, and VMware will all eventually support it.

Summary

Virtualization is a concept dating back to the 1960s for dynamically mapping virtual addresses to real addresses, allowing multiple virtual machines to share the resources of a single physical machine. This software is called a hypervisor. Xen, KVM, and QEMU are the leading open source hypervisors. Citrix is the leading commercial version of Xen, and mostly sells virtualized desktops. A custom variant of Xen is also used by Amazon's AWS. Microsoft has its own patented approach in Microsoft Azure.

VMware is the best-selling commercial virtualization software. It has been used together with Citrix CPS to improve performance. VMware has made a host of acquisitions, and aims to become what the NY Times calls "the concierge of the cloud."[22]

Interesting partnerships among VMware, Google, Salesforce.com, Eucalyptus, and Amazon will help grow the entire industry and prevent lock-in to a single vendor. Developments in standardization and interclouding (discussed in Chapter 4) will also allow for a great increase in the use of virtualization techniques.

---

22.   http://www.nytimes.com/external/gigaom/2010/06/11/11gigaom-what-should-one-make-of-vmwares-shopping-spree-45138.html.

Chapter 8

Securing the Cloud: Reliability, Availability, and Security

Cloud computing is about gracefully losing control while maintaining accountability even if the operational responsibility falls upon one or more third parties.
Cloud Security Alliance

Overview

In this chapter, we consider the issues that have caused the most ink to be spilled: reliability, availability, and security (RAS). Anyone relying on computing resources in general and cloud computing in particular has these three concerns:

- *Reliability*—How often is service available, and how often it fails. Reliability is often covered by a service level agreement.
- *Availability*—Are the resources I need available when I want them? How long does provisioning take new resources take? Can the service scale up and down quickly as my needs change?
- *Security*—Can those with approved access to data see only the data they are entitled to see, and no other data?

In this chapter, we review the standards that have been developed to independently audit whether a vendor's security standards are up to par.

8.1   The FUDD Factor

Probably nothing is more important to enterprises than the reliability, availability, and security of their systems. With that in mind, some make a career of peddling FUDD (fear, uncertainty, doubt, and disinformation), especially as these relate to reliability and security, usually in defense of the status quo.

8.2   Leakage

The major concern that we hear when transitioning to a public cloud is being considered is what I call *leakage*: Can one client's data be accessed (purposefully, inadvertently, or maliciously) by another client? Clearly, data in an access-restricted walled garden divorced from communications lines is the least vulnerable, but it's also the least accessible—it requires physical presence in the walled garden to access the data. At the other end of the spectrum is a multitenant environment in which multiple users share the same physical facilities and even the same programs, with access delivered over the Internet. In this case, the risks of inadvertent data-sharing or program corruption are greatest, but with suitable safeguards, may be perfectly acceptable. There is a belief (often a misbelief) that doing it all in-house automatically increases reliability, availability, and security. Conversely, the more things are outsourced, the greater the perceived risks that are assumed. It's not necessarily so.

8.3   Not All Threats Are External

Firstly, such a belief assumes that most threats are external. Experience teaches the opposite. Authentication-related challenges such as credential management, strong authentication (typically defined as multifactor authentication), delegated authentication, and managing trust across all types of cloud services are issues wherever the data resides, and it is likely (or at least possible) that cloud vendors have superior systems in place, and more experience in access restriction, than in the typical enterprise environment.

Secondly, larger service providers often provide superior protection against such forms of attack as distributed denial of service (DDoS), man in the middle (MitM), IP spoofing, port scanning, and packet sniffing by other tenants.

8.4   Virtualization Is Inherently More Secure

Additionally, with hypervisors such as Xen, guest operating systems run in a lessprivileged Ring 1 and applications in the least-privileged Ring 3. This explicit virtualization of the physical resources leads to a clear separation between guest and hypervisor, resulting in additional security separation between the two. Different instances running on the same physical machine are isolated from each other via the hypervisor. [1]

---

1.   http://www.slideshare.net/siostechnology/overview-of-cloud-computing-3823447.

8.5   Virtualization is Not Enough

Many IT organizations pursue virtualization in the belief that this will create their own private cloud, creating internal speed and efficiency benefits akin to Amazon and Google. But after enjoying server consolidation and other low-hanging fruit, virtualization initiatives typically hit a wall. Virtual sprawl replaces server sprawl. The abstracted and increasingly dynamic nature of virtualization makes it easy for rogue deployments to go undetected as they circumvent security and compliance processes, overwhelm networks, and obscure the root causes of business service problems. Organizations struggle to use virtual resources in more complex, mission-critical applications, as they must be assured, secured, and managed accordingly to their role in business services, something well beyond the capabilities and expertise of virtualization platform specialists.

Source: *www.ca.com/Files/SolutionBriefs/
enterprise_cloud_solutions_sb_236721.pdf, page 6*

8.6   The Best Security May Be Unavailable for (In-House) Private Clouds

Probably the most secure cloud computing available today is the Unisys patent-pending Stealth technology, which instantiates private communities of interest (COIs) based on FIPS 140-2, 256-bit AES encryption and cloaks the data with proprietary "bit splitting" so that data, even if intercepted, is both split-up and unreadable. Initially designed for government applications the technology, is now available to commercial clients. The Unisys Stealth technology enables encrypted "data in motion" to remain invisible as it traverses the infrastructure until it is reassembled upon delivery to authorized users. This type of security is not typically available in enterprise-managed data centers.

8.7   Providers Make Security Their Business

Finally, physical security is often better controlled by service providers. For example, Amazon says:

. . . datacenters are housed in nondescript facilities. Physical access is strictly controlled both at the perimeter and at building ingress points by

professional security staff utilizing video surveillance, state of the art intrusion detection systems, and other electronic means. Authorized staff must pass two-factor authentication a minimum of two times to access datacenter floors. All visitors and contractors are required to present identification and are signed in and continually escorted by authorized staff. AWS only provides datacenter access and information to employees and contractors who have a legitimate business need for such privileges. When an employee no longer has a business need for these privileges, his or her access is immediately revoked, even if they continue to be an employee of Amazon or Amazon Web Services. All physical access to datacenters by AWS employees is logged and audited routinely. AWS requires that staff with potential access to customer data undergo an extensive background check (as permitted by law) commensurate with their position and level of access to data. AWS understands that security and privacy of your confidential data is of paramount concern to you.

Source: *http://www.slideshare.net/AmazonWebServices/aws-jeff-barr-security, notes to Slide 6*

In most enterprise data centers, access restrictions fall short of those implemented by Amazon and other cloud vendors.

8.8   Cloud Security Providers Employ a Hierarchy of Containment Strategies

The inherent efficiencies of public clouds are hard to dispute; therefore the only reasons to employ a private cloud are the related concerns of privacy and security. Over the years, a hierarchy of containment strategies have been developed. Let's look at an extreme case.

The data in this case is so sensitive that it must be contained within a single secure room. Physical access is restricted by complex layers of physical access control and sally ports. The computer itself is unconnected to the Internet, may be protected from eavesdropping by expensive shielding, and log-in restrictions may include fingerprints, retina scans, and/or password control.

In this example, the data is pretty well protected, but the operation is costly, and access is both limited and extremely inconvenient. At the other extreme consider a site hosting public data that is accessible by all (such as a public Web site) but where the concerns relate to unauthorized changes to the data (hacking) or DoS attacks (massive high-speed pinging of the

Figure 8.1   A sally port to restrict access.

Figure 8.2   CIA Headquarters, Langley, Virginia.

server in an attempt to make a computer resource unavailable to its intended users).

These are real concerns, and they are not always limited to high-profile (well-known) sites; some hackers systematically troll the Internet seeking out vulnerable sites that are ripe for attack.

8.9   How a Denial of Service Attack Is Carried Out

Although the means to carry out, motives for, and targets of a DoS attack may vary, an attack generally consists of the concerted efforts of a person or people to prevent an Internet site or service from functioning efficiently or at all, temporarily or indefinitely. Perpetrators of DoS attacks typically target sites or services hosted on high-profile Web servers such as banks, credit card payment gateways, and even root nameservers.

A DoS attack can be perpetrated in a number of ways. The five basic types of attack are:

- Consumption of computational resources, such as bandwidth, disk space, or processor time
- Disruption of configuration information, such as routing information
- Disruption of state information, such as unsolicited resetting of TCP sessions
- Disruption of physical network components
- Obstructing the communication media between the intended users and the victim so that they can no longer communicate adequately

A DoS attack may include execution of malware intended to:

- Max out the processor's usage, preventing any work from occurring
- Trigger errors in the microcode of the machine
- Trigger errors in the sequencing of instructions, so as to force the computer into an unstable state or lock-up
- Exploit errors in the operating system, causing resource starvation and/or thrashing, i.e., to use up all available facilities so no real work can be accomplished
- Crash the operating system itself

Source: http://en.wikipedia.org/wiki/Denial-of-service_attack

Generally, DoS attacks capitalize on the fact that the call is cheap (a laptop in Starbucks can easily issue 4,000 HTTP requests per second). If servicing the calls is resource intensive, 4,000 such calls per second can easily overwhelm the server.

8.10   Cloud Computing Offers Enhanced Defenses for Thwarting DoS Attacks

DoS attacks are equal opportunity challenges that are thwarted by firewalls, security software, redundancy, and vigilance. It's an ongoing battle. The technique for effectively dealing with DoS is called maneuver warfare. This concept holds that strategic movement can bring about the defeat of an opposing force more efficiently than by simply contacting and destroying enemy forces until they can no longer fight. The following definition of maneuver was prepared by Kevin L. Jackson, and is reprinted with permission:

The U.S. Marine Corps concept of maneuver is a "warfighting philosophy that seeks to shatter the enemy's cohesion through a variety of rapid, focused, and unexpected actions which create a turbulent and rapidly deteriorating situation with which the enemy cannot cope." It is important to note, however, that neither is used in isolation. Balanced strategies combine attrition and maneuver techniques in order to be successful on the battlefield.

With cloud computing, IT security can now use maneuver concepts for enhance[d] defense. By leveraging virtualization, high speed wide area networks and broad industry standardization, new and enhanced security strategies can now be implemented. Defensive options can now include the virtual repositioning of entire datacenters. Through "cloud-bursting", additional compute and storage resources can also be brought to bear in a defensive, forensic or counter-offensive manner. The IT team can now actively "fight through an attack" and not just observe an intrusion, merely hoping that the in-place defenses are deep enough. The military analogy continues in that maneuver concepts must be combined with "defense in depth" techniques into holistic IT security strategies.

A theoretical example of how maneuver IT security strategies could be use[d] would be in responding to a denial of service attack launched on [an application]. After picking up a grossly abnormal spike in inbound traffic, targeted applications could be immediately transferred to virtual machines hosted in another datacenter. Router automation would immediately re-route operational network links to the new location (IT defense by maneuver). Forensic and counter-cyber attack applications, normally dormant and hosted by a commercial infrastructure-as-a-service (IaaS) provider (a cloudburst), are immediately launched, collecting information on the attack and sequentially blocking zombie machines. The rapid counter would allow for the immediate, and automated, detection and elimination of the attack source.

Source: *http://cloudcomputing.sys-con.com/node/994396. Reprinted with permission.*

8.11   Who's Responsible? Amazon's AWS EC2 and Salesforce.com Compared

The security responsibilities of both the provider and the services consumer need to be clearly understood and greatly differ among cloud service models. The Cloud Security Alliances' Security Guidance states:

Amazon's AWS EC2 infrastructure as a service offering, as an example, includes vendor responsibility for security up to the hypervisor, meaning they can only address security controls such as physical security, environmental security, and virtualization security. The consumer, in turn, is responsible for security controls that relate to the IT system (instance), including the operating system, applications, and data.

Quite the inverse is true for Salesforce.com's customer resource management (CRM) SaaS offering. Because the entire 'stack' is provided by Salesforce.com, the provider is not only responsible for the physical and environmental security controls, but it must also address the security controls on the infrastructure, the applications, and the data. This alleviates much of the consumer's direct operational responsibility.

Source: *www.cloudsecurityalliance.org/csaguide.pdf, p. 25.*

8.12   VMForce.com

VMforce is a new offering, delivered by two of the most trusted industry leaders, salesforce.com and VMware. VMware provides the virtualization technology. Force.com claims to be the world's most secure cloud computing platform. Thus Java apps can now run on an infrastructure that's passed the most stringent security certifications, including ISO 27001, SysTrust, and SAS 70 Type II.

8.13   Azure and Security

Security is, of course, a key issue for prospective users of cloud computing. Microsoft argues that its Azure system is more secure than current corporate software, since it can spot attacks and patch flaws in the system from a central location (an argument made by its leading competitors, as well).

8.14   OASIS and SPML

Identity provisioning and control are key aspects of security. Where a vendor's offerings for identity provisioning are insufficient, and Cloud Security Alliance (CSA, discussed later in the chapter) says that capabilities currently offered by cloud providers are not currently adequate to meet enterprise requirements, Service Provisioning Markup Language (SPML) provides a way to leverage standard connectors provided by cloud providers without resorting to proprietary solutions such as creating custom connectors unique to cloud providers, as these exacerbate management complexity, restrict mobility and are maintenance-intensive. Oasis (Organization for the Advancement of Structured Information Standards) offers SPML an XML-based framework for exchanging user, resource and service provisioning information between cooperating organizations. It's a good technique for avoiding the single greatest risk in using public clouds. Enhanced credentialing is facilitated by creating a dedicated VPN tunnel to the corporate network.

8.15   Trust, but Verify

Enterprises today recognize the value of a concept called *trust, but verify*, which was a signature phrase of President Ronald Reagan. He usually used it while discussing relations with the Soviet Union, and he almost always presented it as a translation of the Russian proverb *doveryai, no proveryai*. For example, he used it at the signing of the Intermediate-Range Nuclear Forces Treaty (INF Treaty) in 1987, and his counterpart Mikhail Gorbachev responded: "You repeat the phrase every time we meet," to which Reagan answered "I like it." (The phrase has been attributed to Damon Runyan, 1884–1947.)

8.16   Independent Third-Party Validation is a Prerequisite

Increasingly, cloud service providers must get third-party validation (verification) of the efforts they make for security, policy enforcement and authentication in order to land business customers. SAS 70, which predates the popularity of cloud computing, has been pressed into action as a validation tool, in the absence of cloud-specific standards. The SAS 70.com Web site says:

> *A service auditor's examination performed in accordance with SAS No. 70 (a "SAS 70 Audit") is widely recognized, because it represents that a service organization has been through an in-depth audit of their control objectives and control activities, which often include controls over information technology and related processes.*

8.17   Standards and Vendor Selection

In selecting a vendor, and in evaluating what services and data you can entrust to the vendor, you need both criteria and a methodology.

In general, information technology is evaluated by reference to two applicable standards, SAS 70 and ISO 27001. SAS 70, especially has become the measure of cloud security.

We consider ISO 27001 first.

8.17.1   ISO 27001

> *ISO 27001 is an Information Security Management System (ISMS) standard published in October 2005 by the International Organization for Standardization (ISO) and the International Electrotechnical Commission (IEC). Its full name is ISO/IEC 27001:2005 -- Information technology -- Security techniques -- Information security management systems -- Requirements but it is commonly known as "ISO 27001".*
>
> *Compliance with ISO 27001 requires that management:*
> - *Systematically examine the organization's information security risks, taking account of the threats, vulnerabilities and impacts;*
> - *Design and implement a coherent and comprehensive suite of information security controls and/or other forms of risk treatment (such*

as risk avoidance or risk transfer) to address those risks that are deemed unacceptable; and

■ *Adopt an overarching management process to ensure that the information security controls continue to meet the organization's information security needs on an ongoing basis.*

Source: *http://en.wikipedia.org/wiki/ISO/IEC_27001*

ISO/IEC 27001 provides a model for establishing, implementing, operating, monitoring, reviewing, maintaining and improving an information security management system (ISMS). The design and implementation of an ISMS is influenced by the organization's needs and objectives, security requirements, processes, size, and structure.[2]

An ISMS may be certified compliant with ISO/IEC 27001 by a number of accredited registrars worldwide, also called an Accredited Certification Body (CB).[3] Certification against any of the recognized national variants of ISO/IEC 27001 (e.g., JIS Q 27001, the Japanese version) by an accredited certification body is functionally equivalent to certification against ISO/IEC 27001 itself.[4] In the United States, accreditation is managed bu ANSI-ASQ National Accreditation Board.

 ANSI ASQ National Accreditation Boarc

Figure 8.3   ANAB Accreditation for ISO/IEC 27001 Information Security Management Systems.

The ISO/IEC 27001 certification, like other ISO management system certifications, usually involves a three-stage audit process:

■ *Stage 1 is a preliminary, informal review of the ISMS, for example, checking the existence and completeness of key documentation such as the organization's information security policy, Statement of Applicability (SoA), and Risk Treatment Plan*

---

2.   http://www.daminda.com/downloads/ISO27001.pdf.
3.   The CB is accredited by a recognized accrediting body for its competence to audit and issue certification confirming that an organization meets the requirements of a standard (http://en.wikipedia.org/wiki/Accredited_registrar).
4.   http://en.wikipedia.org/wiki/ISO/IEC_27001.

(RTP). This stage serves to familiarize the auditors with the organization and vice versa.

■ *Stage 2 is a more detailed and formal compliance audit, independently testing the ISMS against the requirements specified in ISO/IEC 27001. The auditors will seek evidence to confirm that the management system has been properly designed and implemented, and is in fact in operation (for example by confirming that a security committee or similar management body meets regularly to oversee the ISMS). Certification audits are usually conducted by ISO/IEC 27001 Lead Auditors. Passing this stage results in the ISMS being certified compliant with ISO/IEC 27001.*

■ *Stage 3 involves follow-up reviews or audits to confirm that the organization remains in compliance with the standard. Certification maintenance requires periodic re-assessment audits to confirm that the ISMS continues to operate as specified and intended. These should happen at least annually but (by agreement with management) are often conducted more frequently, particularly while the ISMS is still maturing.*

Source: *http://en.wikipedia.org/wiki/ISO/IEC_27001*

8.17.2 SAS 70 (Statement on Auditing Standards No. 70): Service Organizations[5]

The Statement on Auditing Standards No. 70, commonly known as SAS 70, is an auditing statement put forth by the Auditing Standards Board as designated by the American Institute of Certified Public Accountants (AICPA). Over the years, more than 110 "SAS" have been issued, ranging on a number of critical subjects for auditing matters.

Source: *http://www.sas70.us.com/what-is/history-and-overview.php*

SAS 70 is part of the AU Section 324 Codification of Auditing Standards, which is used to report on controls placed in operation and the testing of the operating effectiveness of those controls. Put simply, it's a widely used compliance audit for assessing the internal control framework on service organizations that provide critical outsourcing activities for

---

5. Adapted from information available at http://www.sas70.us.com/.

other entities. Introduced in 1992, SAS 70 audits were used in the early and mid-1990s. They still are used for very traditional standards, such as evaluating a service organization's services if those services are part of the user organization's information system:

> *For example, if the ABC company used the XYZ company, which is a service organization, to perform and conduct transactions and procedures that are considered significant to the ABC company's "information system" or business environment, then the XYZ service organization would need to be SAS 70 compliant.*

> *Source: http://www.sas70.us.com/what-is/history-and-overview.php*

Think of it as an audit that examines and tests the characteristics of internal controls for service organizations. Service organizations are the entities that undergo the SAS 70 audit. Who requires the audit to be done and why? Generally speaking, compliance legislation in recent years has revolved around corporate governance and the ability to have a strong mechanism of internal controls within organizations. Laws such as The Sarbanes-Oxley Act of 2002 (SOX), the Health Insurance Accountability and Portability Act (HIPAA), and the Gramm-Leach-Bliley Act (GLBA), have emphasized themes such as governance, privacy, security, confidentiality, and segregation of duties.[6]

8.17.3   Type I and Type II Audits

> *Initially, service organizations undergo a SAS 70 Type I audit, gradually migrating towards Type II compliance in subsequent years. The main difference between the two "types" (I vs. II) is that a Type II requires a "testing period", that is, a generally accepted allotted time frame (usually no less than six months) for conducting testing on a service organization's control environment. A Type I, on the other hand, is just for a specified date, with no testing period whatsoever.*

> *Source: http://www.sas70.us.com/white-papers/introduction-to-the-auditing-standard.php*

---

6.   http://www.sas70.us.com/white-papers/introduction-to-the-auditing-standard.php

At the end of the audit, the service auditor issues an important report called the *Service Auditor's Report:*[7]

- *Type I* includes an opinion written by the service auditor. Type I reports describe the degree in which the service organization fairly represent its services in regards to controls that have been implemented in operations and its inherent design to achieve objectives set forth.
- *Type II* reports are similar to Type I, however an additional section is added; the additional section includes the service auditor's opinion on how effectively controls operated under the defined period during the review (usually the defined period is six months, but can be longer).

Type II reports are more th[o]rough, because the auditors gives an opinion on how effective the controls operated under the defined period of the review. Type I only lists the controls, but Type II tests the efficacy of these controls to reasonably assure that they are working correctly. Because Type II reports require a much more thorough audit they are usually much more expensive.

Source: http://www.tech-faq.com/sas-70.html

8.18   SAS 70 and Cloud Computing

Increasingly, vendors point to SAS 70 and ISO 27001 certifications as evidence of their security credentials.

Vendor Security Credentials	
Google	"Asked to flash its cloud security credentials at an industry forum, Google pointed to its SAS 70 certification, giving more support to that set of standards as a measure of how well cloud providers lock down customer data. 'We need to prove we are secure,' says Rajen Sheth, the product manager at Google who came up with Google Apps, speaking at a panel on cloud services at the Enterprise 2.0 conference in Boston.*"

---

7.   http://www.tech-faq.com/sas-70.html.

Microsoft	Microsoft announced that it recently gained SAS 70 Type I and Type II attestations and ISO/IEC 27001:2005 certification.
Amazon	Amazon Web Services (AWS) has successfully completed SAS 70 Type II Audit from independent auditors, and has stated that it will continue to obtain the appropriate security certifications and accreditations to demonstrate the security of our infrastructure and services. An overview of Security Processes applicable to Amazon Web Services is available at http://awsmedia.s3.amazonaws.com/pdf/AWS_Security_Whitepaper.pdf.
Rackspace	Rackspace has achieved ISO/IEC 27001, ISO 17799, SAS 70 Type II audit process, Microsoft Gold Partner, Gartner Leader, Dell Partner, and Cisco Powered Network Certification.
Salesforce.com and Force.com	Salesforce.com and Force.com are SAS 70 Type 2, SysTrust, and ISO 27001 compliant.
ServePath	In addition to SAS 70 and ISO 27001 certifications, Serve-Path has a particularly rigorous service level agreement (SLA), which they call 10,000% Guaranteed®. It states: For every minute ServePath fails to deliver, we will provide you with 100 minutes of service credit. ■ The SLA covers the following elements of service: ■ Network performance ■ Hardware replacement (within 60 minutes) ■ Support response time (30 minutes for server down, packet loss, or routing issues) ■ Domain name services ■ Power availability and performance ■ Cooling and environment ■ Server power cycling ■ Physical security ■ 24 x 365 onsite engineering However, no credit will exceed one hundred percent (100%) of Customer's fees for the service feature in question for the then-current billing month. Details of the SLA are available at http://servpath.com/pdfs/ServePathSLA.pdf

Unisys	The Unisys Secure Cloud Solution allows balancing work-loads across a global network of Unisys data centers, which are certified to key international standards such as ISO/IEC 27001:2005 for security, ISO/IEC 20000 for service management and the SAS 70 Type II auditing standard.
Verizon	Verizon announced that it had successfully completed the first annual SAS 70 Type II examination of controls for its cloud computing data centers.
IBM	IBM offers customers Security Assessment services. Of course, its own cloud offerings are fully compliant.

* http://www.networkworld.com/newsletters/vpn/2009/062309cloudsec1.html?hpg1=bn

8.19   Cloud Security Alliance

Doug Cornelius, chief compliance officer for Beacon Capital Partners, says he already believes that the providers serve up security that equals what his firm could put in place itself. "I'm past the security," Cornelius says. "I assume [your] security has got to be as good as my security."

Security news and analysis Web site DarkReading.com reports that a first-ever security certification dedicated to cloud services is in the works amid enterprise concerns of the safety of their data in the cloud. "There needs to be a certification that is specifically for cloud providers," says Jim Reavis, co-founder and executive director of the Cloud Security Alliance (CSA), a non-profit organization formed to promote the use of best practices for providing security assurance within cloud computing, and to provide education on the uses of cloud computing to help secure all other forms of computing.[8]

8.20   SysTrust Certification

SysTrust certification was developed jointly by the American Institute of Certified Public Accountants (AICPA) and the Canadian Institute of Chartered Accountants (CICA).

A SysTrust engagement is performed by a licensed CPA to evaluate a system's reliability as measured against the SysTrust principles and criteria. The CPA performs tests to determine whether the system was available for operation and use at times set forth in service level statements or

---

8.   http://www.darkreading.com/securityservices/security/government/showArticle.jhtml?articleID=221600333.

agreements. If the system meets the requirements of the Trust Services Principles and Criteria, an unqualified attestation report is issued.

Source: *https://www-935.ibm.com/services/us/index.wss/summary/iss/ a1029093*

Trust Services are defined as:

A set of professional assurance and advisory services based on a common framework (i.e., a core set of principles and criteria) to address the risks and opportunities of IT.[9]

The objective in developing Trust Services was to establish a core set of principles and related criteria for key areas related to IT, e-commerce, e-business, and systems, all of which form the measurement basis for the delivery of the related service(s).

The SysTrust seal indicates that this core set of principles have been examined by an independent auditing firm in conformity with the rigorous AICPA and CICA Trust Services Principles & Criteria. The certification attests that:

- The system was available for operation and use at times set forth in service-level statements or agreements
- The system was protected against unauthorized physical and logical access
- Information designated as confidential was protected as committed or agreed

Source: https://www-935.ibm.com/services/us/index.wss/summary/iss/ a1029093

8.21 Cloud Security Alliance Working Toward Cloud-Specific Certifications[10]

The Cloud Security Alliance (CSA) is working with other key players in cloud security and auditing to determine which organizations should provide the

9.   www.webtrust.org/overview-of-trust-services/index.aspx.
10.   Adapted from Kelly Jackson Higgins. "New Security Certification on the Horizon for Cloud Services." *Dark Reading*, November 4, 2009. Available at www.darkreading.com/securityservices/security/government/showArticle.jhtml?articleID=221600333 (accessed July 27, 2010).

certification, as well as what such a certification should include.[11] Certification is likely to be managed by multiple bodies.

> *[The CSA's] research identifies the vulnerabilities that threaten to hinder cloud service offerings from reaching their full potential. For example, companies must be aware of "abuse and nefarious use of cloud computing," which includes exploits such as the Zeus botnet and InfoStealing trojan horses, malicious software that has proven especially effective in compromising sensitive private resources in cloud environments. However, not all of the threats in this category are rooted in malicious intent. As the social Web evolves, more sites are relying on application programming interfaces (APIs), a set of operations that enable interaction between software programs, to present data from disparate sources. Sites that rely on multiple APIs often suffer from the "weakest link security" in which one insecure API can adversely affect a larger set of participants. Together, these threats comprise a combination of existing vulnerabilities that are magnified in severity in cloud environments as well as new, cloud-specific techniques that put data and systems at risk. Additional threats outlined in the research include:*

- *Malicious Insiders*
- *Shared Technology Vulnerabilities*
- *Data Loss/Leakage*
- *Account/Service and Traffic Hijacking*

> **Source:** *http://www.hp.com/hpinfo/newsroom/press/2010/100301b.html*

The entire cloud model of computing as a utility and its dynamic characteristics makes this a whole new ballgame for certification. Jim Reavis, CSA's Co-founder and Executive Director, quoted in Dark Reading, says, "[Cloud computing] brings everything into question: where the machines are, what is the nature of data. If data is encrypted on the public cloud providers' [systems] and the key held by a separate cloud [provider]—is that even data? There's some rethinking we need to do."[12]

---

11.   Kelly Jackson Higgins. "New Security Certification on the Horizon for Cloud Services." *Dark Reading*, November 4, 2009. Available at www.darkreading.com/securityservices/security/government/showArticle.jhtml?articleID=221600333 (accessed July 27, 2010).

12.   Ibid.

In the same article, Bret Hartman, chief technology officer at the RSA, states that an enterprise's own security controls and their cloud security provider's controls must go hand in hand as well. "It's complicated with cloud computing because there are multiple parties involved," Hartman says. "I think it's time for us to think about what a cloud certification would be ... and there would be different levels of certification required,"[13] Hartman says. "It would be different than SAS 70."

CSA Goes Beyond SAS 70 and ISO 27001

SAS 70 is a set of self-defined certifications for the internal business controls of an organization: everything from how human resources handles backup checks to data backup, patch management, and client administration. However, it doesn't specifically address issues affecting cloud-based services.

The issue is that one company's SAS 70 certification isn't the same as another's: "You define the controls as the service provider and the auditor comes in and makes a judgment whether these controls are sufficient or not" with testing, says Chris Day, chief security architect at cloud computing provider Terremark, a major cloud services provider, which holds a SAS 70 certification. "SAS 70 is very enterprise-specific: my SAS 70 is different from yours or IBM's, for example. It's difficult to know whether my SAS 70 is more comprehensive as yours, which would be troubling for something as complex as cloud security."[14] Day says that the PCI Security Standards[15] Council (PCI) is actually a better standard for gauging data security, because it dictates a series of controls, how they should be implemented, and what level of logging should be deployed.

PCI is an open global forum for the ongoing development, enhancement, storage, dissemination and implementation of security standards for account data protection.

The PCI Security Standards Council's mission is to enhance payment account data security by driving education and awareness of the PCI Security Standards. The organization was founded by American Express, Discover Financial Services, JCB International, MasterCard Worldwide, and Visa, Inc.

Source: *https://www.pcisecuritystandards.org/index.shtml*

---

13.   Ibid.
14.   Ibid.
15.   https://www.pcisecuritystandards.org/index.shtml

Continues Day, "We have SAS 70, but that it doesn't necessarily tell the whole story. SAS 70 is a foundational certification.[16]"

Reavis of the CSA says ISO 27001 is actually better for cloud services than SAS 70. "It's more holistic and covers more ground," he says.[17] ISO 27001 specifies how an organization should handle its information security management, including security controls, risk assessment, and other issues.

However, like SAS 70, ISO 27001 is self-defined by each organization that uses the certification. "You can exclude from the certification some very important things," Reavis says. Even so, he says, ISO 27001 makes the most sense for now: "We feel that until we can get a cloud security certification, ISO is a better interim step" because it's more broad than SAS 70, he says.[18]

8.22 Customers Demand Better Proof

Prospective cloud customers are asking more questions about the security of their data in the cloud. "What I hear from customers is 'how do I know my data is being protected by this cloud service?'" RSA's Hartman says.[19] They want to be assured that their sensitive data is protected, and they want to be able to demonstrate that assurance to their auditors and upper management. "If there were a widely accepted and reliable certification for this, it would be a great way to address those requirements [for customers]," Hartman says.[20]

RSA has authored *The Role of Security in Trustworthy Cloud Computing*.[21] Included in its recommendations are:

- Policies for protecting data
- Transparency of the cloud provider, enabling customers to see their logs and events (among other things)
- Adoption of data encryption and masking, so that one customer's data cannot be accessed by another customer of the cloud provider
- Federated identity management[22]

16.   Kelly Jackson Higgins. "New Security Certification on the Horizon for Cloud Services." *Dark Reading*, November 4, 2009. Available at www.darkreading.com/securityservices/security/government/showArticle.jhtml?articleID=221600333 (accessed July 27, 2010).
17.   Ibid.
18.   Ibid.
19.   Ibid.
20.   Ibid.
21.   https://rsa-email.rsa.com/servlet/campaignrespondent?_ID_=rsa.4696&WPID=9921
22.   Kelly Jackson Higgins. "New Security Certification on the Horizon for Cloud Services." *Dark Reading*, November 4, 2009. Available at www.darkreading.com/securityservices/security/government/showArticle.jhtml?articleID=221600333 (accessed July 27, 2010).

CSA has released a worthwhile document entitled *Security Guidance for Critical Areas of Focus in Cloud Computing*. As we go to press, the latest version, V2.1, can be downloaded at www.cloudsecurityalliance.org/csaguide.pdf.

There are many efforts centered around the development of both open and proprietary APIs which seek to enable things such as management, security, and interoperability for cloud. Some of these efforts include:

- The Open Cloud Computing Interface Working Group
- Amazon EC2 API
- VMware's vCloud API
- Sun's Open Cloud API
- Rackspace API
- GoGrid's API

Open standard APIs will play a key role in cloud portability and interoperability as well as common container formats, such as the DMTF's Open Virtualization Format (OVF).

8.23   CloudAudit

CloudAudit[23] (codename: A6) has the following goal:

> . . . *to provide a common interface and namespace that allows cloud computing providers to automate the Audit, Assertion, Assessment, and Assurance (A6) of their IaaS, PaaS, and application (SaaS) environments and allow authorized consumers of their services to do likewise via an open, extensible and secure interface and methodology.*

> **Source:** *http://www.cloudaudit.org/page3/page3.html*

A draft specification, still undergoing revision, is available.[24] It has been submitted to the Internet Engineering Task Force (IETF):

> *The first CloudAudit release is designed to be as simple as possible so as it can be implemented by creating a directory structure and uploading files to a standard web server that implements HTTP.[25] Subsequent*

---

23.   http://www.cloudaudit.org/.
24.   http://cloudaudit.googlecode.com/svn/trunk/docs/draft-hoff-cloudaudit.html.
25.   http://cloudaudit.googlecode.com/svn/trunk/docs/draft-hoff-cloudaudit.html#RFC2616.

releases may add the ability to write definitions and assertions, and to request new assertions be generated (e.g. a network scan). That is, while 1.x versions are read-only, subsequent releases may be read-write.

A . . . client will typically interrogate the service and verify compliance with local policy before making use of it. It may do so by checking certain pre-defined parameters (for example, the geographical location of the servers, compliance with prevailing security standards, etc.) or it may enumerate some/all of the information available and present it to an operator for a manual decision. This process may be fully automated, for example when searching for least cost services or for an alternative service for failover.

As it is impossible to tell in advance what information will be of interest to clients and what service providers will be willing to expose, a safely extensible mechanism has been devised which allows any domain name owner to publish both definitions and assertions.

Source: *http://cloudaudit.googlecode.com/svn/trunk/docs/draft-hoff-cloudaudit.html*

Summary

Cloud users are rightly concerned about reliability, availability, and security (RAS) of their data. However, many commercial service providers have better tools and facilities for ensuring RAS than do their clients. ISO 27001 and SAS 70 are two recognized standards designed for independently ensuring that third parties handling data have sufficient controls in place. These standards have been adapted for cloud security. The Cloud Security Alliance (CSA) has been developing cloud-specific standards that will further improve on such standards. CloudAudit is developing an open, extensible and secure interface that allows cloud computing providers to expose Audit, Assertion, Assessment, and Assurance (A6) information for cloud infrastructure (IaaS), platform (PaaS), and application (SaaS) services to authorized clients.

Chapter 9

Scale and Reuse: Standing on the Shoulders of Giants

9.1   Objectives

This chapter reviews the two principle attributes of cloud computing—scalability and code reuse—and considers service-oriented architecture (SOA), Web 2.0, and SOA 2.0 for promoting code reuse in a cloud environment. We also look at some cloud-specific techniques for code reuse.

9.2   Cloud Computing on One Foot

Figure 9.1   Sir Isaac Newton.

Sir Isaac Newton (1643–1727), paraphrasing the Jewish tosaphist Isaiah di Trani[1] (c. 1180–c. 1250) famously said, "If I have seen a little further it is by standing on the shoulders of Giants."[2] There is also the famous story of the heathen who came before Hillel the Elder (c.110 BCE–10 CE, during the reign of King Herod) and said to him, "Make me a proselyte, on the condition that you teach me the whole Torah while I stand on one foot," Hillel replied, "What is hateful to you, do not do to your neighbor: that is the whole Torah; the rest is commentary; go and learn it."[3]

How are these stories connected?

The connection is this: If someone had come to me and asked that I teach him the essence of cloud computing while standing on one foot, I would say to him, "Stand on tall shoulders. The rest is commentary. Go and learn."

Let's face it. Writing debugged code is difficult, time-consuming, and expensive (in the range of $30–$40 per line of code, about half of which is spent on debugging[4]). I have been preaching the gospel of reuse for many years, dating back to the early 1990s, and even back in those days, I was a "johnny-come-lately" to the reuse party.

By reusing blocks of debugged software, you are standing on broad shoulders. Call them what you will—objects, API calls, libraries, Ajax calls, whatever—code reuse has been going on since the 1950s. As much as it's sometimes taken for granted, it's often underused, and millions of lines of code are developed for which duplicate code has already been written, tested, and debugged.

Fortunately, there are more robust ways than ever to reuse code in a cloud environment.

9.3 Just Make the Call; Let Google Do It

Cloud computing offers a huge advantage for code reuse, as it solves many problems, chief among them version control. Many different applications, for example, can make a call "to the cloud" for a service, and can be assured that the service being provided uses the latest release. For example, Google's AJAX APIs[5] let you implement rich, dynamic Web sites entirely in JavaScript and HTML. You can add a map, a dynamic search box, or download feeds to a Web site with just a few lines of JavaScript. The Google API libraries for Google Web Toolkit[6] (GWT) are a collection of libraries that provide Java language bindings for popular Google JavaScript APIs. These

1. *Teshuvot haRid* 301–303. Quoted in Shnayer Z. Leiman, "Dwarfs on the Shoulders of Giants," *Tradition* (Spring 1993). In *Isaac Newton, Historian,* Frank Edward Manuel (Harvard University Press, 1963) demonstrates that Isaac Newton was familiar with the Talmud, and had a copy in his personal library.
2. Letter to his rival Robert Hooke in 1676.
3. B. Talmud Shabbat 31a.
4. http://www.ghs.com/products/doublecheck.html.
5. http://code.google.com/apis/ajax/.
6. http://code.google.com/webtoolkit/.

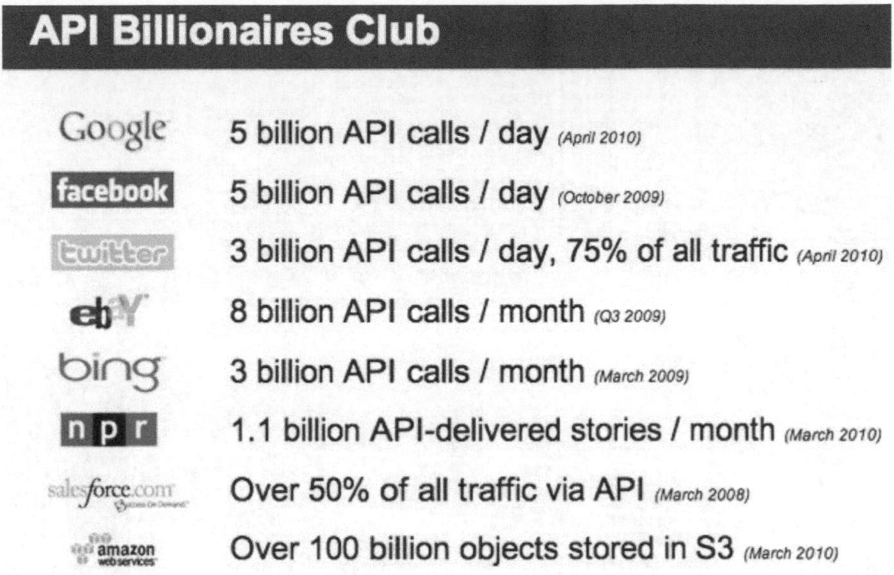

API Billionaires Club

Google   5 billion API calls / day *(April 2010)*

facebook   5 billion API calls / day *(October 2009)*

twitter   3 billion API calls / day, 75% of all traffic *(April 2010)*

ebY   8 billion API calls / month *(Q3 2009)*

bing   3 billion API calls / month *(March 2009)*

n p r   1.1 billion API-delivered stories / month *(March 2010)*

salesforce.com Over 50% of all traffic via API *(March 2008)*

amazon   Over 100 billion objects stored in S3 *(March 2010)*
web services

Figure 9.2   API Billionaires Club. (Courtesy ReadWriteWeb)

libraries make it quick and easy for developers to use Google JavaScript APIs for building and optimizing complex browser-based applications. Google eats its own dogfood, and GWT is used by many products at Google, including Google Wave (of blessed memory) and Google AdWords. It's open source, completely free, and used by thousands of developers around the world. The libraries are supported by the Google Web Toolkit team, and calls are executed in the cloud, on Google-maintained servers, with Google worrying about load balancing, performance, and maintenance. Just ask, and ye shall receive.

9.4   Hardware Reuse

For a long time, equipment reuse was limited. However, as we discussed in Chapter 5, virtualization allows for reuse (and parallel use) of hardware. Multiple virtual servers each go about doing their own thing, with the hypervisor allocating resources efficiently. EMC's VPLEX, discussed in Chapter 7, applies the same concepts to storage. Managing hundreds or thousands of virtual servers to efficiently use dozens or even hundred of physical servers can be a management challenge, but hardware efficiency (maximum utilization) requires scale, so that servers (of both the virtual and physical varieties) can be provisioned and de-provisioned from a large pool.

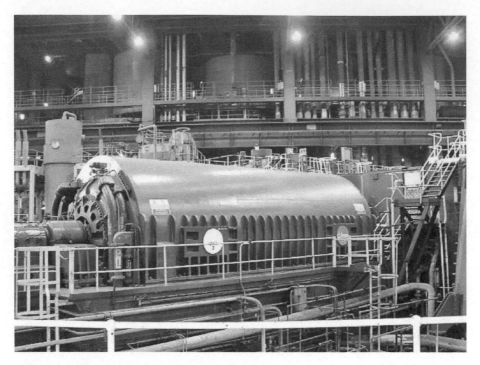

Figure 9.3   Drax Power Station generator.

9.5   Scale and Reuse (Use it or Lose it)

Think of your electric utility. A generator in a power plant converts mechanical energy to electrical energy and produces a fixed amount of electricity (the source of mechanical energy may be a reciprocating or turbine steam engine, water falling through a turbine or waterwheel, an internal combustion engine, a wind turbine, a hand crank, compressed air or any other source of mechanical energy). The electricity generated goes out to "the grid" for delivery to customers. If it's not used, it's usually wasted, as electricity is usually too expensive to store (in a battery) for later use. The idea behind the grid is that many plants contribute to the grid, and many, many users consume electricity from the grid at varying times and in varying amounts. Inevitably, there are peaks and valleys in demand. At consumption low points, only the most efficient (least costly) generators are used. At peak, the most expensive generators are fired up. Since at times of reduced demand, the same amount of electricity is generated by the generator, unconsumed (excess) power is sold off to a distant utility where possible. Selling power over longer distances takes advantage of the fact that the consumption peaks shift with the time zone changes. For example, at the

8:00 P.M. peak in the West Coast it's already 11:00 P.M. on the East Coast, when demand is slacker, so sending excess power from East to West helps smooth out local peaks and valleys.

It's the same concept with computing power, only on steroids.

Not only does user demand vary wildly (Oprah Winfrey praises a Web site on her show and demand instantly skyrockets), but transactions themselves have their own sharp peaks and valleys in resource consumption, at one moment demanding lots of processing cycles and at another almost no processing cycles while file (database) access is demanded. Cloud computing and virtualization allow for more effective use of computer resources, smoothing out the peaks and valleys and increasing average equipment utilization. The larger the overall cloud network, the more efficiently the smoothing can be done. Thus public clouds enjoy an inherent efficiency advantage over private clouds, which in turn have efficiency advantages over farms of older single-purpose (dedicated) servers. In Chapter 5, on capacity planning and economics, this topic is covered in greater detail.

9.6   Service-Oriented Architecture

A service-oriented architecture (SOA) is inextricably linked to cloud computing. This flexible set of design principles is used during the phases of systems development and integration.

> *An SOA-based architecture will provide a loosely-integrated suite of services that can be used within multiple business domains.*
>
> *SOA also generally provides a way for consumers of services, such as web-based applications, to be aware of available SOA-based services. For example, several disparate departments within a company may develop and deploy SOA services in different implementation languages; their respective clients will benefit from a well understood, well defined interface to access them. XML is commonly used for interfacing with SOA services, though this is not required.*
>
> *SOA defines how to integrate widely disparate applications for a web-based world that uses multiple implementation platforms. Rather than defining an API, SOA defines the interface in terms of protocols and functionality. An endpoint is the entry point for such an SOA implementation.*

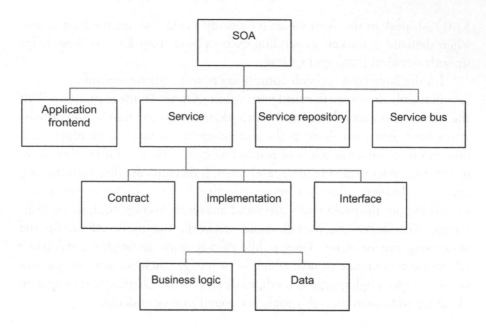

Figure 9.4   Service-Oriented Architecture.

Figure 9.4 Elements of SOA, by Dirk Krafzig, Karl Banke, and Dirk Slama[1], *Enterprise SOA*. Prentice Hall, 2005. (Reproduced under GNU Free Documentation License)

> *Service-orientation requires loose coupling of services with operating systems, and other technologies that underlie applications. SOA separates functions into distinct units, or services,[7] comprised of unassociated, loosely coupled units of functionality that have no calls to each other embedded in them. Developers make accessible over a network in order to allow users to combine and reuse them in the production of applications. These services and their corresponding consumers communicate with each other by passing data in a well-defined, shared format, or by coordinating an activity between two or more services[8].*

Source: *http://en.wikipedia.org/wiki/Service-oriented_architecture*

---

7.   Michael Bell. "Introduction to Service-Oriented Modeling." *Service-Oriented Modeling: Service Analysis, Design, and Architecture*, p.3. Wiley & Sons. (2008).

8.   Michael Bell. *SOA Modeling Patterns for Service-Oriented Discovery and Analysis*, p. 390. Wiley & Sons. 2010.

9.7   Web 2.0[9]

Tim O'Reilly coined the term "Web 2.0" to describe a quickly-growing set of Web-based applications.[10] The concepts of complexity-hiding and reuse, and loosely coupling services very obviously suggested the potential of combining technologies and principles of both Web 2.0 and SOA.[11]

As the world migrates to the Internet of Services, people, machines, and goods will have access via the network infrastructure. The multiplicity of available services will require a complex services infrastructure based on Cloud Computing, including service-delivery platforms bringing together demand and supply. Building blocks for the Internet of Services include SOA, Web 2.0, as well as novel business models, and approaches to systematic and community-based innovation.[12] Gartner analysts and others call this "advanced SOA," "SOA 2.0," or event-driven SOA. The idea is to combine the intelligence and proactiveness of event-driven computing architecture with the organizational capabilities found in SOA. Before event-driven SOA, the typical SOA platform orchestrated services centrally, through pre-defined business processes, assuming that what should have already been triggered is defined in a business process. This older approach does not account for events that occur across, or outside of, specific business processes.[13]

9.8   Summary

Scalability and code reuse are two of the greatest benefits of cloud computing, increasing the utilization of (physical) hardware and facilitating use of blocks of tested and debugged code, wherever they may reside, with better tools to ensure that that points of interface don't break. SOA and SOA 2.0 are techniques for promoting massive code reuse that are especially applicable to the cloud.

---

9.   Section adapted from http://en.wikipedia.org/wiki/Service-oriented_architecture and http://en.wikipedia.org/wiki/Event-driven_SOA.

10.   Tim O'Reilly. "What Is Web 2.0." September 30, 2005. Available at http://oreilly.com/web2/archive/what-is-web-20.html (retrieved June 10, 2008).

11.   Christoph Schroth and Till Janner. Web 2.0 and SOA: Converging Concepts Enabling the Internet of Services. *IT Professional 9* (2007), Nr. 3, pp. 36-41. IEEE Computer Society. Available at http://www.alexandria.unisg.ch/Publikationen/37270 (retrieved February 23, 2008).

12.   Rainer Ruggaber. Internet of Services—A SAP Research Vision. IEEE Computer Society, 2007. Available at http://csdl2.computer.org/comp/proceedings/wetice/2007/2879/00/28790003.pdf (retrieved February 23, 2008).

13.   Yefim Natis and Roy Schulte. Advanced SOA for Advanced Enterprise Projects. *Gartner.* July 13, 2006. Available via http://www.gartner.com/DisplayDocument?ref=g_search&id=493863.

Chapter 10

Windows Azure

Chapter Objectives

We discussed virtualization in Chapter 7. We noted that it's the hypervisor that provides the essential ingredient that makes cloud computing possible. While most vendors build on open source hypervisors, Microsoft chose to roll their own, starting from the bottom up.

More than being just another cloud offering, Windows Azure represents a major evolution, both of operating systems and in Microsoft's overall strategy. In this chapter, we'll look at the history that led up to this point, understand the Azure offering, and understand where it fits in with competitive offerings.

10.1 Back to the Future

It's "Back to the Future" time at Microsoft, folks. In 1992, I wrote a long piece on *The Road to Cairo* about Microsoft's plans for an Object File Store (OFS), an object-oriented database designed to make it easy to search documents and other structured data by content no matter where it was located. It was announced by Jim Allchin in 1991 and planned for release in 1993. In part, it was developed from the distributed object-oriented operating system that was based on Allchin's 1983 doctoral thesis at Georgia Institute of Technology[1]. Still, ten years later in 2002, Computerworld reported[2] that "Windows remains uncontaminated by many of the features originally slated for Windows NT and Cairo, including [its Object File System] OFS." It was, to use the poet Robert Frost's words, the road not taken[3]. While some of Cairo made it out the door as Windows NT 4.0, its charter

---

1. Allchin, James, *An Architecture for Reliable Decentralized Systems* http://portal.acm.org/citation.cfm?id=911173 (1983).
2. http://www.computerworld.com/softwaretopics/os/story/0,10801,69882,00.html.
3. http://www.poemhunter.com/poem/the-road-not-taken/.

to build technologies for a next-generation operating system that would ful-fill Bill Gates' vision of "information at your fingertips" promulgated[4] in 1994 and made into a book published in 1995 called *The Road Ahead*,[5] has sadly, never been fulfilled.

As the poet Robert Frost famously wrote,

Two roads diverged in a yellow wood,
And sorry I could not travel both . . .[6]

Why was the road to Cairo not taken?

Simply put, the infrastructure and technology just was not there yet. Moore's Law,[7] famously first stated in 1965, predicts that the number of transistors on a chip will double about every two years, a prediction that has held true for more than 40 years now. Indeed, computers today are 128 times more powerful than they were back then, at least. The average con-nection speed over the Internet has increased at least twenty-five-fold. Goo-gle gives each (free) user of Google Apps more than 7 GB of managed network storage (paid users get 25 GB), and services complex searches in fractions of a second. So we've made great strides in the past fourteen years in these areas.

10.2   But Windows had not kept pace.

Its kernel accumulated too much baggage. Windows became overly com-plex, and scalability became a serious issue. Windows XP was released on October 25, 2001, so it was about eight years old by the time it was finally replaced by Windows 7. Vista, Microsoft's ill-fated, supposed-to-be replace-ment for the venerable Window XP, was released to the world on January 31, 2007, but it failed. It was acknowledged by all to be a buggy, resource-hogging failure, and many enterprises never adopted it. In the meantime, Linux and open source blossomed. As Microsoft was forced to acknowledge in its SEC filings, Linux and open source posed a significant threat to Microsoft's long period of domination and control of the operating system and desktop.

---

4.   http://ourworld.compuserve.com/homepages/r_harvey/iayf2005.htm.
5.   http://www.amazon.com/Road-Ahead-Bill-Gates/dp/0453009212/ref=ed_oe_h.
     http://www.sec.gov/Archives/edgar/data/789019/000119312509158735/
     d10k.htm#tx73014_3.
6.   Robert Frost, "The Road Not Taken," Mountain Interval, New York: Henry Holt and Company,
     1920 , Bartleby.com, 1999. www.bartleby.com/119/. Accessed June 11, 2010.
7.   http://www.intel.com/technology/mooreslaw/index.htm.

10.3   Billionaire's Agita

Suffering from an acute case of Billionaire's Agita, Steve Ballmer saw that he needed to do something radical. He turned to a veteran Microsoftie, Eric Rudder, senior vice president for technical strategy, who worked closely with Bill Gates, and headed the Servers and Tools group until 2005. Rudder's initial mission was to "incubate" a project called Singularity[8] that came out of Microsoft Research and to turn it into a project code-named Midori (the Japanese word for green, and a common Japanese name for females). Midori was named after Midori Sugiura, a character in the anime and manga series *My-HiME* and *My-Otome*. It's also a character who appears in *Guitar Hero III: Legends of Rock*, a video game in which the player uses a guitar-shaped controller to simulate the playing of lead, bass, and rhythm guitar parts in rock songs by playing in time to scrolling notes on the screen The name is an encoded hat-tip to Jim Allchin, who is an accomplished musician.[9]

As it turns out, Midori has emerged from its shroud of mystery and has become a new, scalable, saleable product for cloud computing called Windows Azure, a platform that is unburdened with the accumulated baggage of Microsoft Windows.

In choosing Rudder, Ballmer chose well. Rudder is an out-of-the-box thinker. I first met Eric shortly after he joined Microsoft in 1988. He is not only a clear-thinking, very smart and hard-working fellow; he is one of a handful of really nice people within the senior ranks of Microsoft. He is rumored to be Ballmer's ultimate successor, when the time comes (really, he would be Bill's successor). In turn, Rudder convinced Ray Ozzie, famed developer of Lotus Notes and now Microsoft's Chief Software Architect (a Microsoft title previously held only by Bill Gates) to spearhead Windows Azure.

10.4   Prologue to Windows Azure

To properly appreciate Azure, we have to understand Midori.

David Worthington at *SD Times* wrote[10] that he had seen the Midori documents. He said (and this was prior to any official announcement),

---

8.   http://research.microsoft.com/os/Singularity/.
9.   See http://www.jimallchin.com/officialsite.cfm.
10.   See http://www.sdtimes.com/link/32627.

. . . building Midori from the ground up [in order to] to be connected underscores how much computing has changed since Microsoft's engineers first designed Windows; there was no Internet as we understand it today, the PC was the user's sole device and concurrency was a research topic.

Today, users move across multiple devices, consume and share resources remotely, and the applications that they use are a composite of local and remote components and services. To that end, Midori will focus on concurrency, both for distributed applications and local ones.

According to the documentation, Azure was built with an asynchronous-only architecture designed for task concurrency and parallel use of local and distributed resources, with a distributed, component-based and data-driven application model, and dynamic management of power and other resources.

Concurrency (vital to support cloud computing) is a basic design principle. The technically inclined reader can work through this paper from Microsoft Research for some insight: "SCOPE: Easy and Efficient Parallel Processing of Massive Data Sets," available at http://research.microsoft.com/en-us/um/people/jrzhou/pub/Scope.pdf.

While I was conceited enough to think I was alone in observing the similarities to Cairo (which at one time employed more than 1,000 developers), Mary Jo Foley of ZD Net seems to have found some other old geezers with long memories.[11] We all see Cairo written all over Midori.

10.5   Introducing Windows Azure

Windows® Azure is a cloud services operating system that serves as the development, service hosting, and service management environment for the Azure Services Platform, which provides developers with on-demand compute and storage to host, scale, and manage Web applications on the Internet through Microsoft® data centers.

Source: *http://www.microsoft.com/windowsazure/windowsazure*

Microsoft Azure competes with other hosted services, such as Amazon's offerings. In case you were wondering about its name, Windows Azure probably is named for The Temple of Azure Clouds,[12] a Buddhist temple

---

11.   See http://www.zdnet.com/blog/microsoft/might-microsofts-midori-be-cairo-revisited/1473).

located just outside the north gate of Fragrant Hills Park, a northwestern suburb of Beijing, China. It was built in the 14th century (possibly in 1331) during the Yuan Dynasty (1271–1368) and was expanded in 1748 (see Figure 10.1).

Figure 10.1   Temple of Azure Clouds.

Obviously, Windows Azure is Microsoft's first foray into cloud computing; now that a free Community Technology Preview has ended, it can be accessed "for the money" at www.microsoft.com/windowsazure.

Based on what has been released so far (as of June 2010), Azure certainly incorporates some of the major elements of Midori, and just as certainly, lacks some of the key features of Cairo, such as its Object File System.

10.6   What is Windows Azure?

Windows Azure[13] is a software *cum* services platform (see Figure 10.2), an operating system in the cloud providing services for hosting, management, and scalable storage with support for simple blobs, tables,

---

12.   See http://en.wikipedia.org/wiki/Temple_of_Azure_Clouds.
13.   http://msdn.microsoft.com/en-us/windowsazure/default.aspx.

and queues, as well as a management infrastructure for provisioning and geo-distribution of cloud-based services, and a development platform for the Azure Services layer.

Figure 10.2   Windows Azure Services Platform. (Used with permission from Microsoft.)

Ray Ozzie has a lot riding on Windows Azure. So does Microsoft. Azure's debut is a critical step both for Ozzie and for his employer. Ozzie sees Azure as a chance to remake Microsoft's businesses for years to come, changing the way it produces software and is paid for its products.

10.7   Microsoft's Secret Datacenter

Forbes reported[14] that in a suburb outside Chicago, Microsoft has been showing off its cloud data center:

> *The 707,000-square-foot building will hold, at top strength, 162 sealed cargo containers of up to 2,500 computer servers each, plus thousands more servers in conventional racks. The cost: $500 million. . . .*
> *All the computers will run on a single operating system . . . that, eventually, will let big companies run applications like e-mail and house data at this and other Microsoft data centers. . . . The idea is to cut the cost of the labor, the hardware and the energy that go into data processing, and to make files accessible to workers who move around a lot. Proponents promise cost reductions between 30% to 90%. At the Chicago center only three Microsoft employees and a few contractors can run over*

---

14.   http://www.forbes.com/forbes/2009/1116/outfront-ibm-cloud-microsoft-new-cloud-computing.htm.

400,000 servers catering to more than 670 million e-mail and instant
messaging accounts and drawing 60 megawatts of electricity.

Microsoft has a principle of "eating its own dog food," so it will initially use this center to run 250 of its businesses, including the Bing search service and the Xbox Live gaming platform, which currently run on servers all over the world. But Forbes says, "The real goal is to persuade big companies like Coca Cola, Fujitsu, and Pitney Bowes (which have all taken a peek) to trust their data to the megacomputers and then trust Azure to manage it."

Microsoft's "special seasoning," which it hopes will distinguish it from a growing array of competitors is to convince developers that with Microsoft development tools, there is "one way to write for everything, everywhere: the cloud, the server, the desktop, and mobile," according to Timothy O'Brien, Microsoft's senior director for platform strategy. "That is a really big deal," he claims.

The *Forbes* article goes on to say:

Microsoft does not expect wholesale corporate adoption at first. Busi-
nesses will start with just a few components, like sending a portion of e-
mail or little-used data off to Microsoft's care. As it builds trust, Azure
will grow in size and complexity, says Arne Josefsberg, Microsoft's gen-
eral manager of infrastructure services: "It's going to be a negotiation
every day." But Josefsberg insists that if Azure absorbs both Microsoft's
online empire and a fair amount of corporate assignments, it may be the
Internet's largest single piece of software, in terms of the amount of data
it runs, within a year.

10.8   Azure is an Open Platform

Interestingly, Windows Azure is an open platform that will support both Microsoft and non-Microsoft languages and environments. To build applications and services on Windows Azure, developers can use their existing Microsoft® Visual Studio® 2008 expertise. Windows Azure is not grid computing, packaged software, or a standard hosting service. It is an integrated development, service hosting and management environment maintained at Microsoft datacenters. The environment includes a robust and efficient core of compute and simple storage capabilities and support for a rich variety of development tools and protocols.

Jon Brodkin of *Network World* quotes Tim O'Brien, senior director of Microsoft's Platform Strategy Group, as saying that Microsoft's Windows

Azure and Amazon's Elastic Compute Cloud tackle two very different cloud computing technology problems today, but are destined to emulate each other over time.[15]

10.9   How does the Windows Azure SDK for PHP fit in?

Many existing applications were built on the LAMP platform (Linux, Apache, MySQL and PHP).

While Microsoft would certainly like to convince you to build applications on its .NET platform using Microsoft development tools, it has recognized that restricting Azure to .NET and proprietary tools will limit its use and slow its growth.

Accordingly, it has provided a Windows Azure SDK for PHP that provides access to Windows Azure's storage, computation and management interfaces by abstracting the REST/XML interface Windows Azure provides into a simple PHP API. This is shown in Figure 10.3.

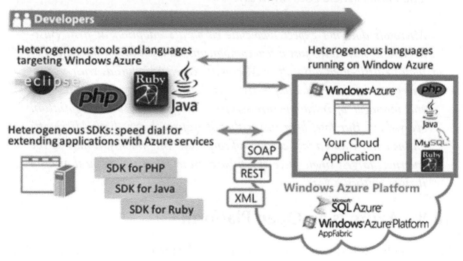

Figure 10.3   Heterogeneous tools in an Azure environment. (Used with permission from Microsoft.)

10.10   Deployment Scenarios

Any server accessible through the Internet can communicate with Windows Azure, even one hosting your PHP application, as shown below.

---

15.   http://www.networkworld.com/news/2010/062510-microsoft-azure-amazon-ec2.html (accessed June 25, 2010).

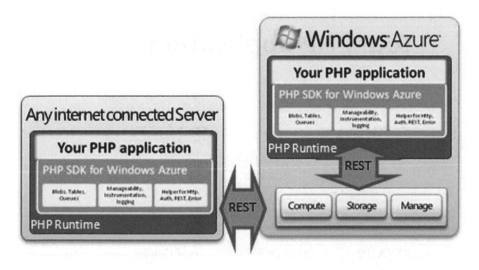

Figure 10.4   Connecting any Internet server to Azure. (Used with permission from Microsoft.)

However, in addition, an application built using Windows Azure SDK for PHP can access Windows Azure's features, no matter whether it is hosted on the Windows Azure platform or on an in-premise Web server.

10.11   Recent Enhancements[16]

Windows Azure has now been updated with .NET Framework 4.0, and there are new tools for Visual Studio and an updated SDK. The tools are much improved. You can now view the status of your Azure-hosted services and get read-only access to Azure data from within the Visual Studio IDE.

Debugging Azure applications is now easier, thanks to a feature called IntelliTrace that keeps a configurable log of application state so you can trace errors later. Deployment is now streamlined, and it can now be done directly from the IDE rather than through an Azure portal.

The Azure database service, SQL Azure, has been updated too. It now supports spatial data types and databases up to 50GB. There is also a new preview of an Azure Data Synch Service, which controls synchronizing data across multiple datacenters, and a web manager for SQL Server on Azure.

---

16.   Tim Anderson, "Conviction and confusion in Microsoft's cloud strategy: With progress comes ambiguity." *The Register.* June 8, 2010. Accessed July 26, 2010.

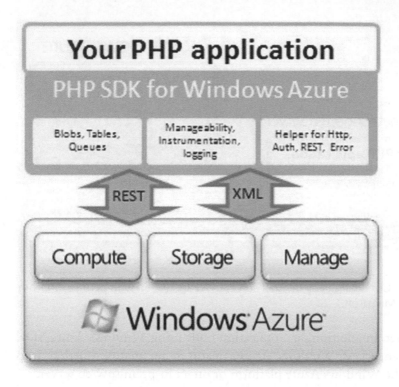

Figure 10.5   Accessing Azure from anywhere. (Used with permission from Microsoft.)

> *Microsoft AppFabric, a free add-on for Microsoft's web server, is now done. AppFabric has two features which are only loosely related. One is a distributed cache, which lets you scale web sites by caching data across multiple servers. The other is a promising runtime for workflow applications. Workflow applications with long-running state can be tricky to implement, and AppFabric in conjunction with new tools in Visual Studio 2010 is an interesting and rapid development approach.*

Source: *www.theregister.co.uk/2010/06/08/teched_microsoft_cloud*

10.12   Open Source Embraced

We see that, though it was very late to the game, Microsoft has of late embraced open source. Another recent Microsoft product reflecting this trend is the Open XML File Format Converter for Mac 1.1.4, which can be downloaded at www.microsoft.com/downloads/details.aspx?FamilyID=4c5487d5-c912-4087-8c83-769e3fb78ea9&displaylang=en. Additional resources are

Microsoft's open source Web site (http://www.microsoft.com/opensource/ default.aspx) and CodePlex, Microsoft's hosting site for open source (http:// codeplex.codeplex.com/).

10.13   Azure: IaaS or PaaS?[17]

"It's a double edged sword," O'Brien said in an interview with *Network World*:[18]

> *The reason people like infrastructure-as-a-service is because it's pro-gramming model agnostic. The bare metal VM doesn't care what language you wrote the application in, it doesn't matter what tools you use and what runtimes you've targeted. If it runs on Windows or Linux, give it a virtual machine and it will run just fine. The problem is it's a lot of extra work. You are responsible for that virtual machine the same way you're responsible for a server sitting under your desk. You're responsible for turning it on. You're responsible for turning it off. You're responsible for applying the a patch or update. If Red Hat applies a Linux patch, and you have a (customized) Linux VM running on Amazon [rather than an Amazon-maintained Amazon Machine Image], you have to apply that patch yourself. They won't do that for you.*

But, O'Brian says, there are shortcomings in the platform-as-a-service model as well. The biggest problem with PaaS may be difficulty migrating existing applications from the internal data center to the cloud:

> *Platform-as-a-service has a different set of tradeoffs. All of that stuff is completely abstracted away, it's a friction-free development, you basi-cally code up an application, you hit deploy and it'll go run on the plat-form that's supplied by those runtimes. So in our case its PHP, C Sharp, in the case of Google [App Engine] it [may be] Python and Java.*

While building new applications is easy, and removes the need for own-ing internal hardware and software, other than a Web browser, "part of the

---

17.   Adapted from Jon Brodkin, "Microsoft Windows Azure and Amazon EC2 on collision course." *Network World*, June 25, 2010. Available at http://www.networkworld.com/news/2010/ 062510-microsoft-azure-amazon-ec2.html (accessed July 27, 2010).

18.   Ibid.

challenge there is it's not necessarily optimal for migrating existing applications," O'Brian says.

Nonetheless, Microsoft has already announced that "at some point [in the next 12 months] we will be offering the ability to provision a bare-metal VM, and run your application on that," according to O'Brien.

O'Brien also believes that just as Microsoft moves into IaaS, Amazon will build a PaaS offering that more closely resembles Azure than anything that Amazon offers today.

Microsoft's goal in the cloud is to offer customers the same functionality they would expect if they installed the software themselves, he said. "If you can write an app for Windows Server you should be able to write an app for Windows Azure," O'Brien said.

10.14   Competition with Salesforce.com

In competition with Salesforce.com, Microsoft Dynamics CRM, Microsoft's solution for Customer Relationship Management will be available on Windows Azure. It provides a full suite of sales, service, and marketing functionality built on a set of data and application services that can be used to build other types of business systems. CRM Services in Azure will provide building blocks that developers can use to build new applications. In contrast, because Azure was built from the ground up and is a totally new platform, applications certified for Windows Server will *not* run on Windows Azure unless the code is ported.

10.15   Salesforce.com is Microsoft's Real Concern

While O'Brien spoke of competition between Microsoft and Amazon in his interview with *Network World*, it appears that Microsoft is more concerned about Salesforce.com as a competitor, and with the announcement of Force.com and the alliance with Google discussed in Chapter 11, probably rightly so. In fact, Microsoft sued Salesforce.com in Washington[19] for patent infringement in May 2010[20] over a variety of back-end and user interface features, ranging from one covering a "system and method for providing and displaying a Web page having an embedded menu" to another that covers a "method and system for stacking toolbars in a computer display"[21] About a month later, Salesforce.com sued Microsoft in Delaware[22]

---

19.   Microsoft Corp. v. Salesforce.com Inc., 10cv825, U.S. District Court, Western District of Washington (Seattle). The suit was settled by Salesforce.com a licensing fee.

20.   http://news.cnet.com/8301-13860_3-20005306-56.html (accessed June 25, 2010).

for infringement patent of its patents, hiring David Boies, who defeated Microsoft ten years earlier in the U. S. Justice Department's landmark antitrust case against them.

Salesforce.com's CEO Marc Benioff responded to the Microsoft lawsuit by saying, "I guess you know you've made it in software when Microsoft is protesting your event. Or maybe when they've sued you. This is the greatest thing that's ever happened in my career."[23]

10.16   Preparing for Midori[24]

Recent additions to the .NET Framework adhere to the concurrent programming principles outlined in the Midori documents that SD Times viewed in 2008.[25] Silverlight (a Web application framework that provides functionalities similar to those in Adobe Flash, integrating multimedia, graphics, animations, and interactivity into a single runtime environment)[26] and the Windows Azure platform could also be complementary to a potential future release of Midori, according to analysts familiar with the project.

Midori is to be Internet-centric, with an emphasis on distributed concurrent systems. It also introduces a new security model that sandboxes applications.

Larry O'Brien, a private consultant and author of the "Windows & .NET Watch" column for *SD Times*, said,

Midori is an attempt to create a new foundation for the operating system that runs "inside the box," on the desktop and in the rack. As such, it's willing to break with compatibility (or at least wall off compatibility to a virtual machine).

Source: http://www.sdtimes.com/link/34251

21.   http://i.i.com.com/cnwk.1d/i/ne/pdfs/MSFTvSalesforceComplaintWDWashington.pdf?tag=mncol;txt (accessed June 25, 2010).
22.   Case 1:10-cv-00555-UNA Salesforce.com, Inc. v. Microsoft Corporation, filed 6-24-2010. Complaint may be viewed at http://assets.bizjournals.com/cms_media/pdf/salesforcevmicrosoft.pdf?site=techflash.com (accessed June 25, 2010).
23.   http://mobile.venturebeat.com/2010/06/22/microsoft-salesforce-com-ipad/ (accessed June 25, 2010).
24.   Adapted from David Worthington. "Midori concepts materialize in .NET." SDTimes, April 5, 2010. Available at http://www.sdtimes.com/link/34251 (accessed July 27, 2010).
25.   http://www.sdtimes.com/content/article.aspx?ArticleID=32627&page=4.
26.   http://en.wikipedia.org/wiki/Microsoft_Silverlight.

Microsoft may be laying a foundation for Midori in Azure and in its existing development stack through its development language tools and the Silverlight runtime. Microsoft Research is also increasingly focused on concurrent programs, O'Brien added.

It won't be pain-free. Major architectural transitions such as these require developers to make a conceptual leap to a new model of programming and to relearn how to program in an efficient manner, noted Forrester Research principal analyst Jeffrey Hammond, adding:

> *We're seeing a gulf opening up right now between serial and parallel programming; only a small minority of rocket-scientist types can actually write code that works effectively in a parallel, multicore world. I think it's pretty clear that Midori is on the other side of that scale-out gulf. From a development point of view, those that can make the leap solidify their skills and employment opportunities for the next decade and beyond.*
>
> **Source:** *http://www.sdtimes.com/link/34251*

10.17   F# and Midori[27]

> *F# (pronounced F Sharp) is a multi-paradigm programming language, targeting the .NET Framework. It encompasses functional programming as well as imperative, object-oriented programming disciplines. It is a variant of the ML programming language developed by Robin Milner and others in the late 1970s at the University of Edinburgh. F# was initially developed by Don Syme at Microsoft Research but is now part of the Developer Division (where Microsoft's development tools are built) and is being distributed as a fully supported language in the .NET Framework and Visual Studio as part of Visual Studio 2010*
>
> **Source:** *http://en.wikipedia.org/wiki/F_Sharp_(programming_language)*

F# "hugely fits" the Midori programming model that was outlined in Microsoft's documents, Larry O'Brien said, explaining that F# is designed with restrictions that are intended to make it easier for developers to automatically parallelize applications.

---

27.   Adapted from David Worthington. "Midori concepts materialize in .NET." SDTimes, April 5, 2010. Available at http://www.sdtimes.com/link/34251 (accessed July 27, 2010).

For instance, F# is highly immutable—meaning that object states cannot be modified once created—and has an implicit type system. Midori requires developers to follow a similarly constrained model. O'Brien explains:

Immutable variables are [more like constants,] pretty much the opposite of how most programmers think about variables ("A variable that doesn't vary?"). So just a few years ago, the idea that functional programming was going to catch on seemed very dubious, and it was very surprising that F# became a first-class language so quickly. Similarly, immutability and strong typing make it easier to reason about security.

Source: *www.sdtimes.com/content/article.aspx?ArticleID=34251&page=2*

Microsoft also has rapidly developed its Silverlight runtime. The Midori programming model includes Bartok, "an optimizing compiler and managed runtime system for Common Intermediate Language (which .NET languages compile to)."[28] It is also a Microsoft Research project whose objective was to create a lightweight, compiled and managed runtime system that was more efficient than the .NET Framework.

"There's no question that Microsoft is seeing Silverlight as the lightweight platform for delivering applications (Web-based and mobile). As far as Midori and [Windows] Azure go, what I can see is that a Silverlight front end is a good front end for an Azure-powered back-end system," O'Brien said.[29]

10.18   An Azure Tie-In-to Midori?

It would make sense for Microsoft to use the Azure platform as a vehicle for introducing Midori, Forrester Research principal analyst Jeffrey Hammond said in an interview with SDTimes.com:[30]

It's essentially a .NET-centric (and Internet-centric) scale-out runtime. A distributed network-aware OS is the perfect thing to host in the cloud, and what better place to knock out the kinks than your own data center, where you have 100% control over the hardware and infrastruc-

---

28.   http://en.wikipedia.org/wiki/Bartok_(compiler).
29.   http://www.sdtimes.com/content/article.aspx?ArticleID=34251&page=2.
30.   David Worthington. "Midori concepts materialize in .NET." SDTimes, April 5, 2010. Available at http://www.sdtimes.com/link/34251 (accessed July 27, 2010).

ture you're testing on? This also allows them to test it underneath parts of the overall infrastructure: for example, hosting an individual service.

Microsoft is battling for new territory—distributed applications—with the Windows Azure platform. This is appropriate, as the platform has little legacy codebase. Rumor has it that Azure has ample funding in money and talent.

10.19 Azure Pricing

Pricing, of course is subject to change. Basic pricing parameters are:

- Compute = $0.12 / hour
- Storage = $0.15 / GB stored / month
- Storage transactions = $0.01 / 10K
- Data transfers = $0.10 in / $0.15 out / GB - ($0.30 in / $0.45 out / GB in Asia)[31]

10.20 Microsoft Intune: A New SaaS-based Service

Intune[32] is (at this writing) a forthcoming cloud-based platform (currently in a beta test) for remote Windows PC administration. It is of interest to enterprises for two reasons:

- It's a useful, cloud-based application that reduce management time and increase reliability.
- It's a likely harbinger of other SaaS based applications o be offered by Microsoft on the Azure platform.

Microsoft says MSPs and end-customers can use the Windows Intune to:

- Manage updates
- Protect PCs from malware
- Proactively monitor PCs
- Provide remote assistance
- Track hardware & software inventory
- Set security policies[33]

Other goals of Microsoft Intune are included in Table 10.1.

---

31.   No charge for inbound data transfers during off-peak times through October 31, 2010.
32.   https://www.microsoft.com/online/windows-intune.mspx.
33.   Microsoft, "Windows Intune: Things You Need to Know." Available at http://www.microsoft.com/windows/windowsintune/windowsintune-faq.aspx (accessed July 27, 2010).

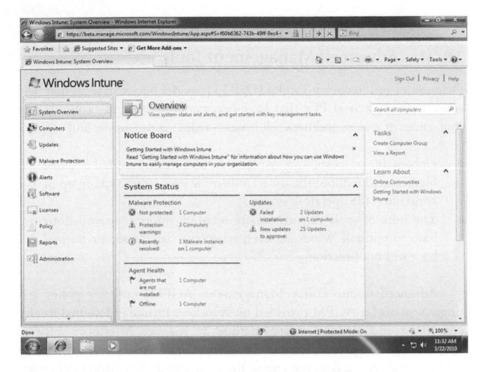

Figure 10.6   Microsoft Intune Overview Screen. (Used with permission from Microsoft.)

Table 10.1   Microsoft Intune goals.

Stay current with Windows 7 Enterprise.	Upgrade your PCs to Windows 7 Enterprise, providing users with an improved and intuitive user interface, advanced search capabilities, and BitLocker drive encryption to help protect confidential data.
Standardize on the Windows you want.	Get the flexibility to standardize your PC environment on a single Windows platform—Windows 7 Enterprise, Windows Vista, or even Windows XP—and automatically get the rights to future versions of Windows, so you never have to worry about purchasing upgrade licenses.
Advanced tools to manage Windows.	Ensure that you get the best PC experience with advanced on-site tools delivered through the Microsoft Desktop Optimization Pack (MDOP) that complement the online service to help you diagnose and repair even unbootable PCs, manage Group Policy, and deploy virtualized applications and operating systems.

(Table used with permission from Microsoft.)

10.21   Advanced Management Tools

Diagnostics and Recovery Toolkit (DaRT) provides powerful tools that help administrators recover PCs that have become unusable and easily identify root causes of system and network issues—reducing downtime and costs:

- Unbootable or locked-out systems can be quickly repaired and lost files restored without the time-consuming process of backing up or reinstalling the operating system.
- The suite of tools provides many recovery options, so you don't have to reinstall Windows, even when the Safe Mode or normal boot will not function.

Advanced Group Policy Management (AGPM) enforces policy settings. Support for AGPM provided by Windows Intune is designed to give you a fast and straightforward method to manage Microsoft software updates, malware protection, and firewall policies. However, the Windows Intune cloud service does not enable the configuration of Group Policy settings. Businesses with an ongoing need to manage Group Policy settings will be able to download and use AGPM. Group Policy provides a more comprehensive set of controls but also introduces more complexity. With AGPM, you can reduce the possibility of errors and better respond to requests to implement new or modified policies.

- AGPM provides a layer of protection and process on top of Group Policy to ensure that organizations can get the most out of this technology while making sure that errant changes are not introduced into their environment until they are tested and approved. The key benefits of AGPM are:
    - Offline editing of Group Policy
    - Simple workflow
    - Rollback to previous state
    - Role-based delegation
    - Change control
- You can also use AGPM to define workflows to ensure that approvers and reviewers are aware of the pending changes. And it lets you know when changes have been reviewed. It can even help bridge organizational gaps, such as departmental policies that

may prevent desktop administrators from managing PCs using Group Policy when server Group Policy objects are managed by server administrators.

10.22   Intune is Microsoft-Centric

Implicit in the foregoing discussion is that Intune is Windows-centric. Additionally, the Intune Web console requires a Web browser that supports Silverlight 3.0, such as Internet Explorer 7.0 or higher.

Mixed environment shops will find that Intune addresses only some of their needs. Note that some of the benefits that Intune provides are similar to the Microsoft Software Assurance program for Windows.[34] Pricing and licensing details have not yet been announced.

An online demo of Microsoft Intune is available at http://www.microsoft.com/showcase/en/us/details/ba0b0831-375f-4650-88de-cad15e46cb67.

In many respects, Intune is a basic, cloud-based remote monitoring and management platform for PCs running Windows 7 (Enterprise, Ultimate and Professional), Windows Vista (Enterprise, Ultimate and Business) and/ or Windows XP Professional (Service Pack 2 or 3). Plus, InTune is based on Windows Server Update Services (WSUS)[35] .

10.23   Microsoft Resources

- Webcasts, videos, virtual labs and podcasts:
  www.microsoft.com/events/series/azure.aspx
- Azure training kit (including PHP samples):
  www.microsoft.com/azure/trainingkit.mspx
- Other Azure SDKs:
  www.microsoft.com/azure/sdk.mspx
- "How do I . . . ?" videos:
  http://msdn.microsoft.com/en-us/azure/dd439432.aspx
- PHP on Windows Training Kit:
  www.microsoft.com/downloas/details.aspx?displaylang=en&Fami-lyID=c8498c9b-a85a-4afa-90c0-593d0e4850cb
- Azure   Pricing: www.microsoft.com/windowsazure/offers/popup.aspx?lang=en&locale=en-US&offer=COMPARE_PUBLIC

---

34.   http://www.microsoft.com/licensing/software-assurance/default.aspx.
35.   http://support.microsoft.com/kb/894199.

Summary

Microsoft Azure is an new and interesting competitor that comes with a long, mostly distinguished and expensive pedigree. It seems to be the first to-market component of Midori, the descendant of Cairo, Microsoft's two-decades-ago planned, never-released object-oriented distributed operating system. Midori's strong emphasis on concurrency issues, a willingness to break compatibility, and the idea of using a hypervisor "as a kind of Meta-OS" fits Microsoft's long-term strategy.

There is no generally available concrete knowledge about the state of Midori or even whether its design is necessarily attractive for a data center OS. However, the here and now is that Azure is a great place to develop and host .NET applications, an adequate place to build and host LAMP applications, and a very good place for hosting applications developed in a mixed environment.

We can expect Microsoft to add PaaS to its current IaaS offerings.

It will also be interesting to see how Salesforce.com slugs it out with Microsoft, as they head on a collision course.

Chapter 11

Google in the Cloud

> *You might just as well say, . . . that*
> *"I like what I get" is the same thing as "I get what I like"!*
> The March Hare, in *Alice's Adventures in Wonderland* by Lewis Carroll[1]

Overview

Yes, Virginia, there is a cloud vendor called Google.[2] They're a very large cloud vendor.

No one knows for sure, but it is believed that Google manages one of the two or three largest server farms in the world. For a long time, all its content was made available free; it was entirely advertising-supported. Its servers were proprietary and used only by Google. Recently, it has begun making its infrastructure available to others, for a fee. Its first widely-marketed offering was Google Apps for Business, priced simply at $50 per head per year, which includes a bundle of services, such as e-mail and cloud storage. It operates a plethora of popular services, among them Google Maps, Google Finance, and Google Voice. More recently, it has introduced Google App Engine, and in its own unique way, it is now a general cloud services provider.

---

1. The Millennium Fulcrum Edition 3.0, Chapter VII, www.cs.cmu.edu/~rgs/alice-table.html, accessed June 11, 2010.
2. In 1897, Dr. Philip O'Hanlon, a coroner's assistant on Manhattan's Upper West Side, was asked by his then eight-year-old daughter, Virginia (1889–1971), whether Santa Claus really existed. Virginia O'Hanlon had begun to doubt there was a Santa Claus, because her friends had told her that he did not exist. Dr. O'Hanlon suggested she write to the New York Sun, a prominent New York City newspaper at the time, assuring her that "If you see it in The Sun, it's so." She did. Is There a Santa Claus? was the title of an editorial appearing in the September 21, 1897 edition of the New York Sun. It included the famous reply "Yes, Virginia, there is a Santa Claus."

11.1   Free is Good

Google searches have always been free. To service the huge volume of search requests, Google created the world's largest cloud-based infrastructure. Then they kept those servers even busier, offering free public e-mail that provided the then-unheard of 1.0 GB of free storage per account. Over the next few years, Google repeatedly upped the ante.

Following on the heels of Amazon's rent-a-cloud service, Google's initial cloud offering was, with a bow to Google's "it's free to the consumer" mantra, offered without charge, subject to limitations. This free version of Google Apps now allows free hosting of your e-mail server (with your own domain name), up to 7.3 GB of storage per free user account, and free Google Talk, Google Calendar, Google Docs (for creating and sharing documents, spreadsheets and presentations, collaboration in real-time right inside a Web browser window), Google Sites (for easily creating and sharing a group Web site) and Start Page, and so forth. Recently, IMAP support was added to e-mail hosting, and offline support for Google Docs was added too. (For $50 per user per year, storage is upped to 25 GB per user, and many other features are added.) All these goodies were initially targeted primarily at end-users, though now there are over 1 million paying, and presumably mostly business, users. Recently, Google Docs was enhanced to support storage of all types of files, up to 250 MB per file. At present there is a 1.0 GB storage limit for files you upload that are not converted to Google Docs format (e.g., Google documents, spreadsheets, and presentations). Following Apple's lead this time, Google recently launched Apps Marketplace,[3] allowing Apps users to add other layers to their environments from companies like SocialWok and Zoho.

11.2   Reaching Out to the Development Community

Google, having seen the potential of cloud computing as a business, has extended its largess to the development community in a big way, much as Microsoft did in the 1990s, when it was trying to woo corporate developers to its platforms and away from UNIX, then king of the Corporate Mountain.

Free "cloud computing" and a free and robust toolkit to deploy applications are both now available. The free version of Google App Engine™ enables developers to build their Web apps on the same infrastructure that

---

3.   www.google.com/enterprise/marketplace/.

powers Google's own applications. More information about Google App Engine is available at http://code.google.com/appengine.

11.3   App Engine Cost Structure

In terms of commercial pricing for the new "for a charge" versions, each application costs $8 per user per month, up to a maximum of $1,000 per month. To woo the enterprise developer, Google is promising to add more enterprise-level functionality in the future, including hosted SQL databases, SSL on a company's domain for secure communications, and access to advanced Google services.

Creating an App Engine application is easy and it costs nothing. As Google says, "You can create an account and publish an application that people can use right away at no charge, and with no obligation. An application on a free account can use up to 500MB of storage and up to 5 million page views a month."[4] Beyond that, you need to pay. As of June, 2010, the cost for renting Google computing resources is shown in Table 11.1.

Table 11.1   Google App Engine pricing[*]

Resource	Unit	Unit cost
Outgoing Bandwidth	gigabytes	$0.12
Incoming Bandwidth	gigabytes	$0.10
CPU Time	CPU hours	$0.10
Stored Data	gigabytes per month	$0.15
Recipients emailed	recipients	$.0001

*   http://code.google.com/appengine/docs/billing.html

11.4   Google Web Toolkit™

Google Web Toolkit™ (at this writing it's up to Release 2.0) now includes Java 5 language support so that developers can use the full capabilities of the Java 5 syntax. With Google Web Toolkit (GWT), Web applications can be developed and debugged in the Java programming language familiar to the developer, and then deployed as highly optimized JavaScript. With this approach, developers sidestep common AJAX issues, such as

---

4.   http://code.google.com/appengine/docs/whatisgoogleappengine.html

browser compatibility, and achieve significant improvements in performance and productivity.

GWT is a development toolkit for building and optimizing complex browser-based applications. Its goal is to enable productive development of high-performance web applications without the developer having to be an expert in browser quirks, XMLHttpRequest ("an API available in Web browser scripting languages such as JavaScript . . . used to send HTTP or HTTPS requests directly to a web server and load the server response data directly back into the script"[5]), as well as JavaScript. GWT is used by many products within Google, and the new version of AdWords. It's open source, completely free, and used by thousands of developers around the world.

11.5   Google Cloud Applications Built on GWT

Google has also built a number of applications using GWT. For example, Google Health (https://health.google.com) is a recently launched cloud-based application developed on GWT.

Google also announced the free availability of the Google Earth API and browser plug-in, which allows Web developers to quickly and easily turn their Web pages into 3D map applications. Its key features are:

Key Features
- *Embed Google Earth inside any web page with only a few lines of code*
- *Use the JavaScript API to enable rich Earth-based web applications*
- *Manipulate KML and the 3D environment: create polygons, lines, placemarks, and more*
- *Convert your existing Google Maps API site to 3D with as little as one line of code*

Source: *http://www.google.com/intl/en/press/annc/ earthapi_20080528.html*

11.6   Google Gears R.I.P.

Google Gears is an open source project that powers the offline features of Google Reader and Google Docs by providing a local database. It has been

---

5.   http://en.wikipedia.org/wiki/XMLHttpRequest.

renamed simply Gears. It provides additional support for other browsers, and Google has made it available for all developers.[6] Its key capabilities are:

- Let Web applications interact naturally with the desktop
- Store data locally in a fully-searchable database
- Run JavaScript in the background to improve performance

Google Gears, however, appears not to be long for this world. Google has decided instead to support HTML5, which subsumes the functionality that Gears was intended to supply. The specification for HTML5 is still being finalized.[7] As one Google rep told *The Los Angeles Times*,[8] "We are excited that much of the technology in Gears, including offline support and geolocation APIs, are being incorporated into the HTML5 spec as an open standard supported across browsers, and see that as the logical next step for developers looking to include these features in their websites." You can keep up with progress of standardization process at W3.org.[9]

Clearly, Google has decided to spare no expense to win the hearts and minds of developers. And it is appears to be succeeding. Free is an attractive price, isn't it?

11.7   Google Apps Script

We aren't all coders. Google Apps Script[10] is a powerful way to automate business processes ranging from expense approvals to time-sheet tracking to ticket management and order fulfillment. Scripts are an efficient way for customers to add custom functionality beyond Google's expanding suite of Web-based applications. Google Apps Script now offers:

- *Data interoperability through JDBC (Java Database Connectivity): Now, Google Apps Script can connect to any MySQL database, including business databases running on servers behind firewalls.*
  [Google still prefers that developers use The App Engine datastore, but it has bowed to reality.]

---

6.   http://tinyurl.com/2a6ph6.
7.   see http://dev.w3.org/html5/spec/Overview.html.
8.   http://latimesblogs.latimes.com/technology/2009/11/google-gears.html.
9.   http://dev.w3.org/html5/spec/Overview.html and www.whatwg.org/specs/web-apps/current-work/multipage/.
10.   http://code.google.com/appengine/docs/billing.html.

- *Custom user interfaces for scripts: Google Apps Premier Edition users can now script graphical interface elements and menus. For example, a company could power an internal application for purchasing office supplies. Users could shop via a customized menu interface, and the script could email the employee's selections to their manager for purchasing approval before routing the order to fulfillment team.*
- *Standalone invocation of scripts: It's now possible to call a script from any website, so you're able to build web pages where users can submit entries that will be collected in a Google spreadsheet.*
- *More integrations with other Google properties: New integrations with Google Docs and Google Maps add the ability to create and modify files in the Google Documents List and retrieve directions from Google Maps.*

Source: *http://googleenterprise.blogspot.com/2010/05/automating-business-processes-with.html*

11.8   What Is Google App Engine?[11]

Google App Engine lets you run (host) your own Web applications on Google's infrastructure. However, by no means is this a "rent a piece of a server" hosting service. With App Engine, your application is not hosted on a single server. There are no servers to maintain: You just upload your application, and it's ready to serve your users. Just as servicing a Google search request may involve dozens, or even hundreds of Google servers, all totally hidden and satisfied in a fraction of a second, Google App Engine applications run the same way, on the same infrastructure. This is the unique aspect of Google's approach. Yes, you cede some control to Google, but you are rewarded by being totally free of the infrastructure, capacity management, and load balancing tasks that enterprise typically have to manage, irrespective of whether they are self-hosting or hosting on someone else's PaaS or IaaS.

You can serve your app from your own domain name (such as http://www.example.com/) using Google Apps or, you can serve your app using a

---

11.   Adapted from "What is Google App Engine?" available at http://code.google.com/appengine/docs/whatisgoogleappengine.html (accessed July 28, 2010) and Kenneth Corbin. "Google Takes to The Cloud With App Hosting Platform." InternetNews.com. April 8, 2008. Available at www.internetnews.com/dev-news/article.php/3739401/Google+Takes+to+The+Cloud+With+App+Hosting+Platfor.htm (accessed July 28, 2010).

free name on the appspot.com domain. You can choose to share your application with the world, or limit access to members of your organization.

Google App Engine supports apps written in several programming languages:

> *With App Engine's Java runtime environment, you can build your app using standard Java technologies, including the JVM, Java serv-lets, and the Java programming language—or any other language using a JVM-based interpreter or compiler, such as JavaScript or Ruby. App Engine also features a dedicated Python runtime environment, which includes a fast Python interpreter and the Python standard library. The Java and Python runtime environments are built to ensure that your application runs quickly, securely, and without interference from other apps on the system.*
>
> ***Source:*** *http://code.google.com/appengine/docs/whatisgoogleap-pengine.html*

As with most cloud-hosting services, with App Engine, you only pay for what you use. Google levies no set-up costs and no recurring fees. Similar to Amazon's AWS, resources such as storage and bandwidth are measured by the gigabyte.

App Engine costs nothing to get started. All applications can use up to 500 MB of storage and enough CPU and bandwidth to support an efficient app serving around 5 million page views a month, absolutely free. When you enable billing for your application, your free limits are raised, and you only pay for resources you use above the free levels.

Application developers have access to persistent storage technologies such as the Google File System (GFS) and Bigtable, a distributed storage system for unstructured data. The Java version supports asynchronous non-blocking queries using the Twig Object Datastore interface.[12] This offers an alternative to using threads for parallel data processing.

"With Google App Engine, developers can write Web applications based on the same building blocks that Google uses," Kevin Gibbs, Google's technical lead for the project, wrote in *The Official Google Blog*. "Google

---

12.   Twig is an object persistence interface built on Google App Engine's low-level datastore which overcomes many of JDO-GAEs limitations, including full support for inheritance, polymorphism, and generic types. You can easily configure, modify or extend Twig's behavior by implementing your own strategies or overriding extension points in pure Java code. See http://code.google.com/p/twig-persist/.

App Engine packages those building blocks and provides access to scalable infrastructure that we hope will make it easier for developers to scale their applications automatically as they grow."[13]

Google App Engine has appeared at a time when an increasing number of tech companies are moving their operations to the cloud; it places Google squarely in competition with Amazon's Elastic Cloud Computing (EC2) and Simple Storage Service (S3) offerings.

Google says its vision with Google App Engine is to offer developers a more holistic, end-to-end solution for building and scaling applications online. Its servers are configured to balance the load of traffic to developers' applications, scaling to meet the demand of an influx of traffic. App Engine also includes APIs for user authentication to allow developers to sign on for services, and for e-mail, to manage communications.

InternetNews.com reported,

Through its initial preview, Google's App Engine will be available free to the first 10,000 developers who sign up, with plans to expand that number in the future.

During that period, users will be limited to 500MB of storage, 10GB of daily bandwidth and 5 million daily page views, the company said. Developers will be able to register up to three applications.[14]

11.9   Google App Engine for Business[15]

In May 2010, Google announced enhancements to Google Apps for business and Google App Engine as Google's public cloud offering—making Google a more mainstream cloud services provider. With Google App Engine for Business, Google is introducing new enterprise-level capabilities, including centralized administration, premium developer support and an uptime Service Level Agreement (SLA), flat monthly pricing, and soon, access to premium features like cloud-based SQL and SSL.

The new version included centralized administration, which is an administration console that lets you manage all the applications in your

13.   Kevin Gibbs. "Developers, start your engines." *The Official Google Blog.* Available at http://googleblog.blogspot.com/2008/04/developers-start-your-engines.html (accessed July 27, 2010).
14.   Kenneth Corbin. "Google Takes to The Cloud With App Hosting Platform." *InternetNews.com.* April 8, 2008. Available at www.internetnews.com/dev-news/article.php/3739401/Google+Takes+to+The+Cloud+With+App+Hosting+Platfor.htm (accessed July 28, 2010).
15.   Adapted from Leena Rao, "Google Launches Business Version of App Engine; Collaborates with VMware." *TechCrunchIT.com,* May 19, 2010. Available at http://www.techcrunchit.com/2010/05/19/google-launches-business-version-of-app-engine-collaborates-with-vmware/ (accessed July 28, 2010).

domain. Google promises reliability, with a 99.9% uptime service level agreement and premium developer support available. Additionally, Google addresses security concerns by only allowing users from a Google Apps domain to access applications, with an administrator's security preferences implemented on each individual app.

11.10   Collaboration with VMware[16]

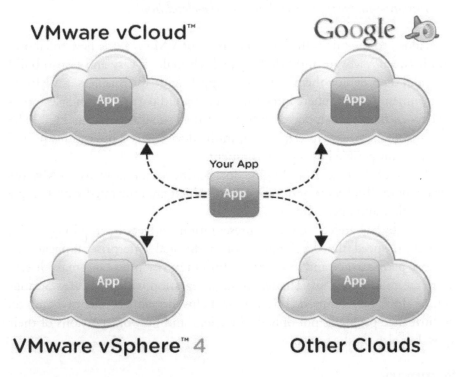

Figure 11.1   VMware and Google collaborate. (Courtesy, VMware)

In May 2010, Google announced a collaboration with VMware for deployment and development of apps on the new cloud infrastructure.

VMware and Google have a shared vision to make it easy to build, run, and manage applications for the cloud, and to do so in a way that makes applications portable across clouds. With this joint initiative,

---

16.   Adapted from Leena Rao, "Google Launches Business Version of App Engine; Collaborates with VMware." *TechCrunchIT.com*, May 19, 2010. Available at www.techcrunchit.com/2010/05/19/google-launches-business-version-of-app-engine-collaborates-with-vmware/ (accessed July 28, 2010).

Spring becomes the preferred Java programming model for Google App Engine. Additionally, the two companies have been working to integrate Google's GWT (Google Web Toolkit) technology with the Spring framework and development tools, to enable Spring developers to easily and rapidly build rich internet applications.

Source: *http://blogs.vmware.com/vcloud/2010/05/vmware-and-google-initiative-supports-javabased-apps-in-the-cloud.html*

Added to the mix is the announcement of VMforce, the new collaboration between VMware and Salesforce, which make it easy and fast to build apps and then deploy them to Google App Engine for Business, a VMware environment (on a vSphere infrastructure, vCloud partner, or on Salesforce's VMforce), or other supported infrastructures, such as Amazon EC2. The aim is to make it easy to create rich, multi-device Web applications hosted in a Java-compatible hosting environment.

Users of Google App Engine for business can now use VMware's SpringSource Tool Suite and Spring Roo, which are integrated with Google Web Toolkit and Speed Tracer.

Google has added new data presentation widgets in its Google Web Toolkit to speed the development of traditional enterprise applications, increase performance and interactivity for enterprise users, and make it easier to create mobile apps. Thanks to the integration with VMware's SpringSource Tool Suite, Speed Tracer now helps developers identify and fix performance problems not only in the client and network portions of their apps, but also on the server.

Summary

In addition to its traditional strengths in search and public e-mail, Google is aiming to be an enterprise cloud vendor. Its approach to development in the cloud may be summarized as:

- Stand on our tall shoulders (use Google's extensive code base)
- Develop your applications in Java, PHP, or Python
- Use the GQL datastore as an alternative to SQL
- Let Google worry about resource allocation, load balancing, and scalability

Google Web Toolkit, Google App Engine, and Google Apps Script offer clear evidence of Google's big push to bring enterprise development to the cloud. By offering a powerful and interoperable environment and toolset to developers, Google App Engine should prove to be a worthy competitor with Amazon Web Services, which is one of App Engine's major competitors for hosting environments.

Chapter 12

Enterprise Cloud Vendors

Overview

It feels just like the weeks before prom night. The guys and gals are looking each other over and pairing up. They all want the most attractive partner, but they also know they need a date for the dance, because they can't go alone.

In Chapter 11, we looked at Google's cloud offerings and how the company collaborates with VMware (discussed in Chapter 7) to provide for application portability across clouds. In this chapter, we consider how the traditional vendors to the enterprise have evolved their respective strategies to adapt to the cloud, and also at how they have partnered with other companies.

We look at IBM, who has partnered with Red Hat, SOASTA, RightScale and others; HP, who has partnered with Microsoft; and Oracle, who bought Sun outright and partners with Amazon AWS.

We provide some additional details about Amazon AWS, beyond what we discussed in Chapter 6.

CA Technologies, Inc. (formerly Computer Associates) is a tool vendor that can partner with almost everyone. It has extended its partnership with NetApp, integrating CA's virtualization, automation, and service assurance offerings with NetApp's storage management solutions. It also partners with Carnegie Mellon University and a host of resellers.

Unisys has partnered with VMware on the software side and with its parent, EMC, on the hardware side, among others.

While there are obvious differences, they have more in common than not, and we highlight the divergences.

12.1 IBM

"Cloud is an important new consumption and delivery model for IT and business services. Large enterprises want our help to capitalize on what this

233

model offers in a way that is safe, reliable and efficient for business," said Erich Clementi, General Manager, Enterprise Initiatives at IBM.[1]

The company believes the digital and physical infrastructure are converging as a result of the instrumentation of all kind of business and IT assets, but that while the impact will be vary from industry to industry, cloud will be the delivery engine for emerging industry systems. Analytics are also going to play a huge role in collaborative industry clouds. To extract valuable insights, clients need tools to mine the massive amounts of data and pull out actionable information. Software is a focus as well—IBM is integrating software into services that can be sold through the cloud to deliver the high-value solutions enterprise clients are requesting, including integrated hardware, software, and services packages.

IBM was a very early proponent of both virtualization and cloud computing. IBM Smart Business cloud solutions support clouds built behind the enterprise firewall, or the IBM cloud. IBM's public cloud offering is still new, while its private cloud offerings are, for the cloud, very mature.

Unlike Google, who has collaborated with VMware (as discussed in Chapter 11), IBM's strategy is to handhold enterprises into the cloud both by providing services and also by working with Red Hat to offer Red Hat's EL, bypassing VMware with the announcement of Smart Business Development & Test on the IBM Cloud.[2] IBM has also partnered with SOASTA, who makes "CloudTest,"[3] and is a leading provider of cloud testing. SOASTA also partners with CA (discussed later in this chapter), Amazon (discussed in Chapter 6), and Microsoft (discussed in Chapter 10). It is competing head-on with VMforce and Salesforce.com (discussed in Chapter 7). IBM also partners non-exclusively with RightScale, which offers Hyperic HQ (see Chapter 13).

12.1.1 Consistent Development Experience[4]

IBM was relatively early in recognizing the advantages of cloud computing for development. IBM has offered a *private* cloud solution for development and test since June 2009, and now offers development and test services in three delivery models:

---

1. IBM, "IBM Readies Cloud for Business" (press release), available at http://www-03.ibm.com/press/us/en/pressrelease/27720.wss (accessed July 28, 2010).
2. http://www-03.ibm.com/press/us/en/pressrelease/29685.wss#release.
3. http://soasta.com/.
4. Adapted from IBM. "IBM Extends Development and Test to the IBM Cloud" (press release). Available at http://www-03.ibm.com/press/us/en/pressrelease/29685.wss#release (accessed July 28, 2010).

- *IBM Smart Business Development and Test Cloud.* A private cloud service behind the client's firewall, built and managed by IBM. The service now includes enhanced capabilities for collaborative cloud development using Rational Software Delivery Services for Cloud Computing.
- *IBM Smart Business Development and Test on the IBM Cloud.* Application development and test featuring Rational Software Delivery Services for Cloud Computing over IBM's secure, scalable cloud.
- *IBM CloudBurst for Development and Test.* IBM CloudBurst is a pre-integrated set of hardware, storage, virtualization, and networking, with a sophisticated built-in service management system to allow clients to rapidly deploy an internal/private cloud environment.

"Workload characteristics continue to drive the rate and degree of standardization of IT and business services," said Rich Esposito, vice president, IT Strategy & Architecture and Middleware Services, IBM. "Standardization is key to bringing discipline, efficiency and simplicity to the most complex corners of big businesses."

12.1.2   Eleven Cloud Computing Competency Centers Worldwide

IBM's cloud computing competency centers are designed to showcase IBM cloud computing infrastructures, applications, and services capabilities through specific competency and training solutions, as well as offer additional services to clients. By June 2010, IBM had opened eleven centers:

- Singapore
- Dublin, Ireland
- Beijing, China
- Tokyo, Japan
- Johannesburg, South Africa
- Sao Paulo, Brazil
- Bangalore, India
- Seoul, South Korea
- Hanoi, Vietnam
- The Netherlands
- Wuxi, China

Craig Sowell, Director, Cloud Marketing and Communications at IBM, was kind enough to discuss IBM's cloud strategy with me. The points that IBM stresses are that IBM cloud solutions:

- Assist in reducing capital and licensing expenses as much as fifty to seventy-five percent using virtualized resources
- Help reduce operating and labor costs as much as thirty to fifty percent by automating development and testing resource provisioning and configuration
- Facilitate innovation and time to market by helping reduce development and testing setup time from weeks to minutes
- Improve quality through more accurate configurations and enhanced modeling to help reduce defects by as much as fifteen to thirty percent
- Achieve better utilization, as the average enterprise devotes up to fifty percent of its entire technology infrastructure to development and test, but typically up to ninety percent of it remains idle

IBM purchased Rational a number of years ago, and is particularly strong in supporting application development and testing. Smart Business Development and Test on the IBM Cloud offers flexible provisioning on demand, at a predetermined cost.

The IBM Smart Business Development and Test on the IBM Cloud is a dynamically provisioned and scaled runtime environment that provides a complete environment to develop and test application code; of course, it highlights IBM's software offerings. These include tools to configure and manage the dynamic execution environment, an IDE that facilitates the direct use of the execution environment, and build and test tools that can exploit the execution environment. Other areas supported include SaaS solutions for collaboration and governance infrastructure and resource repositories for source and reusable assets. It is available now in North America.

The IBM Smart Business Development and Test Cloud provides an on-premises cloud, built by IBM Services. IBM CloudBurst offers pre-integrated hardware, storage, virtualization, and networking to create an on-premises cloud environment. Service management capability is delivered via IBM Tivoli Service Automation Manager V7.2.

IBM's Smart Business Desktop Cloud Solution is an on-premise approach providing virtualized desktops to provide replication of a standardized desktop to enterprises.

In May 2010, IBM acquired Cast Iron Systems, a cloud integrator, to deliver industry-leading cloud integration software, appliances, and services. It does this on a cross-vendor basis; for example, it integrates cloud applications from providers (such as Salesforce.com, Amazon, NetSuite, and ADP) with on-premise applications (such as SAP and JD Edwards). Cast Iron has hundreds of prebuilt templates and services expertise, reducing custom coding and allowing cloud integrations to be completed in the space of days, rather than weeks or longer. These results can be achieved using a physical appliance, a virtual appliance, or a cloud service. IBM also strengthened its offerings by acquiring Sterling Commerce from AT&T.

PayPal, the online payment system discussed in Chapter 1, is extending its global payments platform, PayPal X, into the cloud. PayPal is working with the IBM Cloud Labs to quickly monetize new applications developed and made available via smart phones. "We want to provide a very simple way to make payments available on all platforms, including mobile applications," said Osama Bedier, PayPal's vice president of platform and emerging technologies. "The IBM cloud provides a platform for developers to come together as a community, to create, develop and test new applications. We look forward to seeing the payments innovations our developers create through the IBM cloud and bringing the wallet into the cloud."[5]

One of I.B.M.'s test beds for cloud computing has been the Interior Department's National Business Center, a service center that handles payroll, human relations, financial reporting, contracting services and other computing tasks for dozens of federal agencies. The center runs two large data centers, one in Northern Virginia and another outside Denver. Douglas J. Bourgeois, the center's director, said he is introducing several cloud-style applications over the next nine months including Web-based training, and staffing and recruitment software. In tests with financial and procurement software, the cloud-computing environment has delivered efficiencies of 40 to 60 percent in productivity and power consumption, he stated. "For us, like other data centers, the volume of data continues to explode," Mr. Bourgeois said. "We want to solve some of those problems with cloud computing, so we don't have to build another $20 million data center."

---

5.   IBM, "IBM Extends Development and Test to the IBM Cloud" (press release). Available at http://www-03.ibm.com/press/uk/en/pressrelease/29696.wss (accessed July 28, 2010).

Source: http://www.nytimes.com/2009/06/15/technology/business-computing/15blue.html

Internationally, IBM has several interesting collaborations:

- Nissay Information Technology is collaborating with IBM to build a cloud-based development and test environment for Japan's Nippon Life Insurance that will support the development of mission critical Web systems and allow more flexibility for the allocation of IT resources. Prior to the cloud environment, developers needed a month to allocate resources; now the process takes only hours.[6]
- IBM has created Malaysia's first animation cloud for Multimedia Development Corporation (MDeC). The new center is allowing animators, start-ups, and creative content companies to take advantage of cloud computing to significantly reduce in-house production time—animators can perform rendering jobs up to 8 times faster than with local workstations—and produce high quality images for computer-generated content.[7]
- IBM partnered with Spanish hotel company Sol Meliá to manage the company's technology infrastructure, including its central IT platform and applications (including e-mail and reservation system) and host the Web site (used by guests to book hotel rooms) and the equipment used daily by 4,500 users in an effort to reduce operational cost and foster innovation. As part of the deal, IBM is providing desktop cloud services to Sol Meliá's users in Spain, Europe and 19 hotels in Latin America.[8]
- Options IT, a leading provider of high-performance financial technology infrastructure-as-a-service (IaaS) to buyside and sellside firms, is working with IBM to deliver an optimized private cloud environment for financial services firms. With the new infrastructure, Options IT is able to help clients take advantage of global trading opportunities with new resources.[9]

---

6. http://www-03.ibm.com/press/us/en/pressrelease/32053.wss.
7. http://cloudcomputing.sys-con.com/node/1453372.
8. http://prensa.solmelia.com/en/view_object.html?obj=84,c,4416.
9. ftp://public.dhe.ibm.com/common/ssi/pm/ab/n/blc03055gben/BLC03055GBEN.PDF.

12.1.3   IBM Cloud Resources

- IBM's Cloud Computing Portfolio and Overview: http://www.ibm.com/ibm/cloud/
- IBM developerWorks: http://www.ibm.com/developerworks/
- IBM Cloudburst: http://www-01.ibm.com/software/tivoli/products/cloudburst/
- Small Business Development and Test Cloud: http://www-935.ibm.com/services/us/index.wss/offering/midware/a1030965

12.1.4   Recent IBM Cloud Press Releases

- IBM Advances Cloud Initiatives with Acquisition of Cast Iron Systems: http://www-03.ibm.com/press/us/en/pressrelease/30580.wss
- IBM LotusLive Expands with Business Tools and Services from UPS, Skype, Salesforce.com and Silanis to Serve Growing Demand for Cloud Computing: http://www-03.ibm.com/press/us/en/pressrelease/29887.wss
- IBM Extends Development and Test to the IBM Cloud: http://www-03.ibm.com/press/us/en/pressrelease/29685.wss
- IBM Launches Initiative to Foster Cybersecurity Collaboration with Public and Private Sector Clients (mentions U.S. Air Force cloud work): http://www-03.ibm.com/press/us/en/pressrelease/29580.wss
- IBM Launches Academic Cloud to Speed Delivery of Technology Skills to College Students: http://www-03.ibm.com/press/us/en/pressrelease/29367.wss
- Panasonic Ushers in the Cloud Computing Era with IBM LotusLive: http://www-03.ibm.com/press/us/en/pressrelease/29189.wss

12.2   Amazon AWS

We discussed Amazon's AWS in Chapter 6, so in this chapter we only focus on the more advanced features not discussed in Chapter 6.

12.2.1   Amazon RDS[10]

Amazon Relational Database Service (Amazon RDS) is a web service that makes it easy to set up, operate, and scale a relational database in

---

10.   Adapted from http://aws.amazon.com/rds.

the cloud. It provides cost-efficient and resizable capacity and manages time-consuming database administration tasks.

Source: *http://aws.amazon.com/rds*

Amazon RDS looks and feels like the familar MySQL database, and is code-compatible. This means the code, applications, and tools you already use with your existing MySQL databases work seamlessly with Amazon RDS. Amazon RDS automatically patches the database software and backs up your database, storing the backups for a user-defined retention period.

The compute resources or storage capacity associated with your relational database instance can be scaled via a single API call. In addition, Amazon RDS allows you to easily deploy your database instance across multiple Availability Zones (different locations where Amazon has data centers), providing enhanced availability and reliability for critical production deployments.

12.2.2   Amazon CloudWatch[11]

Amazon CloudWatch is a Web service that provides monitoring for AWS cloud resources, beginning with Amazon EC2. It provides visibility into resource utilization, operational performance, and overall demand patterns—including metrics such as CPU utilization, disk reads and writes, and network traffic.

To use Amazon CloudWatch, simply select the Amazon EC2 instances that you'd like to monitor; almost immediately Amazon CloudWatch will begin aggregating and storing monitoring data that can be accessed using the AWS Management Console, Web service APIs or Command Line Tools.

Amazon CloudWatch enables you to monitor the following in real time:

- Amazon EC2 instances
- Amazon EBS Volumes
- Elastic Load Balancers
- RDS database instances

Amazon CloudWatch enables Auto Scaling, which allows you to dynamically add or remove Amazon EC2 instances based on Amazon

---

11.   Adapted from http://aws.amazon.com/cloudwatch.

CloudWatch metrics. Amazon CloudWatch customers are not charged for CloudScaling.

Amazon CloudWatch fees are only incurred for Amazon EC2 instances you choose to monitor. There are no additional charges for monitoring Amazon EBS volumes, Elastic Load Balancers, orRDS Database Instances.

12.3   Hewlett Packard

Hewlett Packard is primarily selling cloud solutions to the enterprise and the enterprise is typically hosting the solutions in private clouds. Its SaaS offerings are still specialized and limited, as discussed later in this section.

Russ Daniels, CTO of HP's Cloud Service Strategy, has a vision of the cloud as a unified, persistent repository for data that applications or people can access anywhere. HP sees clouds primarily as a means to deliver IT as a service *inside* the enterprise.

HP advocates using data already in the cloud as a way to offer IT as a service. So instead of getting the IT department to write an application for human resources, the IT department shows someone in HR the types of data that can be accessed and builds a service around that.

HP is also "eating its own dog food." In 2006, it cut the number of data centers to six from eighty-five. And in May 2010, it announced that it would cut 9,000 jobs and take a $1 billion restructuring charge, spread out through the end of its 2013 fiscal year, as the company seeks to automate its data centers so it can deliver enterprise business services. As HP noted in its filings with the SEC, "As part of this multi-year transformation plan, HP intends to (i) invest in fully automated, standardized, state-of-the-art commercial data centers, (ii) invest to facilitate the migration of client applications to modernized infrastructure platforms, and (iii) consolidate the enterprise services business's commercial data centers, management platforms, networks, tools and applications."[12] Reading a little between the lines, HP is set to offer PaaS and IaaS both for its own use and for sale to its clients. HP expects annualized net savings, after reinvestment in salespeople and other efforts, to be between $500 million and $700 million by its 2013 fiscal year. (We also noted in Chapter 10, on Microsoft Azure, that Microsoft and HP are together investing $250 million in "infrastructure to application solutions.")

---

12.   www.sec.gov/Archives/edgar/data/47217/000110465910031672/a10-11066_18k.htm.

12.3.1   HP's SaaS Offerings

HP has taken a number of its complex products (which require substantial installation and ongoing maintenance efforts) and have made them accessible as SaaS offerings in a public cloud environment. These include:

- HP Business Availability Center
- HP Performance Center
- HP Service Manager
- HP Project and Portfolio Management Center
- HP Quality Center
- HP Site Seer

They all can be used to manage an enterprise's efforts worldwide.

Another interesting offering is *HP's Cloud Assure* service, designed to help ensure security, performance, and availability in the Cloud. It too is delivered as a SaaS offering for performing security risk assessments to detect and correct security vulnerabilities. It provides common security policy definitions, automated security tests, centralized permissions control, and Web access to security information. HP Cloud Assure can scan networks, operating systems, middleware layers, and Web applications and perform automated penetration testing to identify potential vulnerabilities—giving you an accurate security-risk picture of your cloud services.

12.3.2   HP Business Service Management

The HP Business Service Management (BSM) software suite, version 9.0, works on automating comprehensive management across applications lifecycles, with new means to bring a common approach to hybrid-sourced app delivery models. Whether apps are supported from virtualized infrastructures, on-premise stacks, private clouds, public clouds, software as a service (SaaS) sources, or outsourced IT, they need to managed with commonality.

The objective of BSM is to help companies automate applications and services management amid complexity "We did a study last October that showed our clients believe innovation is going to help them even through uncertain economic times—and they see technology as central to their ability to succeed in a changing environment," said Paul Muller, vice president of Strategic Marketing, Software Products, HP Software & Solutions.[13]

---

13.   http://h30501.www3.hp.com/t5/BriefingsDirect-by-Dana-Gardner/New-HP-products-take-aim-at-managing-complexity-in-hybrid-data/ba-p/2497.

12.3.3   HP's View of the Hybrid World[14]

HP wants to help IT combat skepticism by equipping them with HP BSM 9.0. The solutions not only address hybrid delivery models, but also what Muller calls the "consumerization of IT," referring to people who use non-company-owned devices on a company network. As Muller sees it, employees expect to have the same dependable experience while working from home as they do at work.

"We believe organizations will struggle to deliver the quality outcomes expected of them unless they are able to deal with the increase rate of change that occurs when you deploy virtualization or cloud technologies," Muller said. "It's a change that allows for innovation, but it's also a change that creates opportunity for something to go wrong."

Bill Veghte, HP Executive Vice President for HP Software and Solutions, said that three major trends are converging around IT: virtualization, cloud, and mobile. "We need to continuously simplify" management to head off rapid complexity acceleration around this confluence of trends. "Users want a unified view in a visually compelling way, and they want to be able to take action on it," said Veghte.

HP's solution to this challenge is HP BSM 9.0.

12.3.4   HP BSM 9.0[15]

BSM 9.0 offers several unusual features, one of which is automated operations that work to reduce troubleshooting costs and hasten repair time. BSM 9.0 also offers cloud-ready and virtualized operations that aim to reduce security risks with strategic management services.

"The active interest of our clients in cloud computing has just exploded," said Robin Purohit, Vice President and General Manager of HP Software Products:

I think last year was a curiosity for many senior IT executives something on the horizon, but this year it's really an active evaluation. I think

---

14.   Adapted from Dana Gardner. "New HP products take aim at managing complexity in 'hybrid data center' era." *HP BriefingsDirect*, June 15, 2010. Available at http://h30501.www3.hp.com/t5/BriefingsDirect-by-Dana-Gardner/New-HP-products-take-aim-at-managing-complexity-in-hybrid-data/ba-p/2497 (accessed July 28, 2010).

15.   Adapted from Dana Gardner. "New HP products take aim at managing complexity in 'hybrid data center' era." *HP BriefingsDirect*, June 15, 2010. Available at http://h30501.www3.hp.com/t5/BriefingsDirect-by-Dana-Gardner/New-HP-products-take-aim-at-managing-complexity-in-hybrid-data/ba-p/2497 (accessed July 28, 2010).

most customers are looking initially at something a little safer, meaning a private cloud approach, where there is either new stack of infrastructure and applications are run for them by somebody else on their site, or at some off-site operation. So that seems to be the predominant new paradigm.

Source: *http://h30501.www3.hp.com/t5/BriefingsDirect-by-Dana-Gardner/New-HP-products-take-aim-at-managing-complexity-in-hybrid-data/ba-p/2497*

BSM 9.0 is designed to come to grips with the "hybrid data center." The solution offers a single, integrated view for IT to manage enterprise services in hybrid environments, while new collaborative operations promise to boost efficiency with an integrated view for service operations management. Every IT operations user receives contextual and role-based information through mobile devices and other access points for faster resolution.

"BSM 9 is our solution for end-to-end monitoring of services in the data center. It's been a great business for us, and we now have a breakthrough release that we reveled to our customers today, that's anchored around what we call the Runtime Service Model," said Purohit. The Runtime Service Model works to save time by improving organizational service impact analysis and troubleshooting processing times.

12.3.5 HP Business Availability Center[16]

The HP Business Availability Center (BAC)[17] 9.0 offers an integrated user experience as well as applications monitoring and diagnostics with HP's twist on the run-time service model. Paul Muller explains:

The rate of change in the way infrastructure elements relate to each other—or even where they are from one minute to the next—means we've moved from an environment where you could scan your infrastructure weekly and still be quite accurate to workloads shifting minute by minute. It's the great trap, because if you don't know what infrastruc-

---

16. Adapted from Dana Gardner. "New HP products take aim at managing complexity in 'hybrid data center' era." HP BriefingsDirect, June 15, 2010. Available at http://h30501.www3.hp.com/t5/BriefingsDirect-by-Dana-Gardner/New-HP-products-take-aim-at-managing-complexity-in-hybrid-data/ba-p/2497 (accessed July 28, 2010).
17. https://h10078.www1.hp.com/cda/hpms/display/main/hpms_content.jsp?zn=bto&cp=1-11-15-25_4000_100.

ture your application is depending on from one minute to the next, you can't troubleshoot it when something goes wrong.

Source: *http://h30501.www3.hp.com/t5/BriefingsDirect-by-Dana-Gardner/New-HP-products-take-aim-at-managing-complexity-in-hybrid-data/ba-p/2497*

Other elements of BPM 9.0 include

■ *BAC Anywhere*, a service that lets organizations monitor external Web apps from anywhere, even outside the firewall, from a single integrated console.
■ *HP Operations Manager 9.0*, which promises to improve IT service performance by way of "smart plug-ins" that automatically discover application changes and updates them in the run-time service model.
■ *HP Network Management Center 9.0*, which aims to give companies better network visibility by connecting virtual services, physical networks and public cloud services together

12.3.6   HP's Test Data Management[18]

In competition with IBM's Smart Business Development and Test, HP announced software that aims to accelerate application testing while reducing the risks associated with new delivery models. Dubbed HP Test Data Management, HP also promises the new solution lowers costs associated with application testing and ensures sensitive data doesn't violate compliance regulations.

HP says the improvement helps simplify and accelerate testing data preparation, an important factor in making tests and quality more integral to applications development and deployment, again, across a variety of infrastructure models.

Along with HP Test Data Management, HP launched new integrations between HP Quality Center and the Collabnet TeamForge an integrated application lifecycle tool (http://www.collab.net/products/ctf/) with the

---

18.   Adapted from Dana Gardner. "New HP products take aim at managing complexity in 'hybrid data center' era." *HP BriefingsDirect*, June 15, 2010. Available at http://h30501.www3.hp.com/t5/BriefingsDirect-by-Dana-Gardner/New-HP-products-take-aim-at-managing-complexity-in-hybrid-data/ba-p/2497 (accessed July 28, 2010).

goal of improving communication and collaboration among business analysts, project managers, developers and quality assurance teams.

The integration with CollabNet, built largely on Apache Subversion,
will help further bind the "devops" process. Subversion is an open source
version control system.[19]

12.3.7   HP Partners with Enomaly[20]

HP, Intel, and cloud software maker Enomaly have partnered to offer a full
end-to-end IaaS platform for cloud service providers. Along with service
providers, the cloud platform is targeted at hosting firms and Internet data
center providers. The partnership gives service providers the ability to
deliver timely, comprehensive services to customers leveraging products
from each member, the companies said.

According to Enomaly, the offering is built with products including HP
ProLiant servers, HP StorageWorks storage systems; and ProCurve networking gear packed with Intel Xeon processors. The Intel-based server, storage
and network solutions are coupled with Enomaly software. Enomaly's Elastic Computing Platform (ECP) Service Provider Edition, which the company calls a "cloud in a box" solution, lets providers offer revenue-
generating IaaS cloud services with a customer self-service portal and integration with billing and provisioning systems, "essentially everything you
need to deploy a complete revenue focused cloud service," Enomaly said.

Reuven Cohen, founder and CTO of Toronto-based Enomaly, said,
"We've been working with HP to create an optimal cloud computing stack"
adding that by optimal he means a cloud stack that will help solution providers generate money and achieve swift ROI.

The joint cloud platform offering is available through HP's channel.

"This is the first time HP is going after the service provider segment [in
the cloud]," Cohen said, adding that previously the conversation was geared
toward enterprise internal and private cloud offerings and virtual data center approaches as opposed to public facing cloud offerings.

The combination of products gives service providers, whether they
offer shared hosting, dedicated hosting, virtual and cloud hosting, or managed services, the ability to offer new services to customers.

----

19.   http://subversion.apache.org.
20.   Adapted from Andrew R. Hickey, "Triple Threat: HP, Intel, Enomaly Team for Cloud Provider Plat-
         form." *UBM ChannelWeb*, June 4, 2010. Available at www.crn.com/software/225402005
         (accessed July 28, 2010).

12.3.8   HP's Alliance With Microsoft[21]

In January 2010, HP and Microsoft announced[22] a three-year agreement to invest $250 million to significantly simplify technology environments for businesses of all sizes. The companies plan to deliver new solutions that will:

- Be built on a next-generation infrastructure-to-application model
- Advance cloud computing by speeding application implementation
- Eliminate complexities of IT management and automate existing manual processes to lower the overall costs

Mark Hurd, then HP chairman and chief executive officer stated: "This collaboration will allow HP and Microsoft to offer our customers transformative technology that will reduce costs, generate business growth and accelerate innovation."

The new infrastructure-to-application model from HP and Microsoft will be delivered as integrated offerings for large, heterogeneous data center environments as well as through solutions designed for small and midsize businesses. Some solutions are available immediately, with new offerings being introduced throughout the next three years.

"This agreement, which spans hardware, software and services, will enable business customers to optimize performance with push-button simplicity at the lowest-possible total cost of ownership," said Steve Ballmer, chief executive officer, Microsoft. "Our extended partnership will transform the way large enterprises deliver services to their customers, and help smaller organizations adopt IT to grow their businesses. Microsoft and HP are betting on each other so our customers don't have to gamble on IT."

12.3.9   HP Resources

For more information about HP's cloud solutions:
- HP Software as a Service for HP Business Availability Center: https://h10078.www1.hp.com/cda/hpms/display/main/ hpms_content.jsp?zn=bto&cp=1-23^3171_4000_100__

---

21.   Adapted from HP and Microsoft, "HP and Microsoft Simplify Technology Environments With Solutions Built on New Infrastructure-to-Application Model" (press release). Available at http://www.microsoft.com/presspass/press/2010/jan10/01-13InfToAppPR.mspx (accessed July 28, 2010).
22.   www.hp.com/go/microsoft/infra2apps.

- HP Software as a Service for HP Performance Center: https://
  h10078.www1.hp.com/cda/hpms/display/main/
  hpms_content.jsp?zn=bto&cp=1-23^3183_4000_100__
- HP Software as a Service for HP Project and Portfolio Management Center: https://h10078.www1.hp.com/cda/hpms/display/
  main/hpms_content.jsp?zn=bto&cp=1-23^3206_4000_100__
- HP Software as a Service for HP Quality Center: https://
  h10078.www1.hp.com/cda/hpms/display/main/
  hpms_content.jsp?zn=bto&cp=1-23^3214_4000_100__)
- HP Software as a Service for HP SiteSeer: https://
  h10078.www1.hp.com/cda/hpms/display/main/
  hpms_content.jsp?zn=bto&cp=1-23^32666_4000_100__
- HP Software as a Service for Service Manager: https://
  h10078.www1.hp.com/cda/hpms/display/main/
  hpms_content.jsp?zn=bto&cp=1-23^12505_4000_100__

For more information about Enomaly's Elastic Computing Platform,
see www.enomaly.com.

12.4   Oracle (Sun)

Oracle is, as it's fond of saying, the world's largest enterprise software vendor, with about $24 billion in revenue. It made Larry Ellison the third rich-
est American.[23] In late 2009, Mr. Ellison was ranting at the "absurdity" of
the idea of cloud computing and the "nitwit" venture capitalists trying to
invent a new industry by simply coming up with a new term:

> *My objection is the absurdity--the absurdity!—it's not that I don't like
> the idea—it's this [he sneers] NONSENSE—I mean, the guys say,
> "Oh, it's in the CLOUD!" Well, what is that? And then [to inter-
> viewer] you say, "Are we dead?" Uh, yeah, we're dead—if there's no
> hardware or software in the cloud we are so [big sneer] screwed. . . But
> it's NOT water vapor! All it is is a computer attached to a NET-
> WORK—what are you TALKING about?? [crowd roars with laugh-
> ter] I mean, whadda you think Google RUNS on? Do they run on
> WATER VAPOR? I mean, cloud—it's DATABASES, and OPERAT-
> ING SYSTEMS, and MEMORY, and MICROPROCESSORS, and*

---

23.   http://blogs.forbes.com/billions/2010/01/27/ellison-to-ibm-make-our-day/.

THE INTERNET!! [big applause from crowd] And all of a sudden, "NO, IT'S NONE OF THAT—IT'S THE CLOUD!!" What are you TALKING ABOUT?? Now—and the VCs—I love the VCs: "We only fund—oh, is that cloud?" Whoa, whoa—Microsoft Word—change "Internet" to "cloud"—mass change—and give it back to these NIT-WITS on Sand Hill Road![24]

Strong words. But you can't grow a business to a $24 billion and ignore the fastest growing aspect of computing. By January, 2010, he was weaving the terms and concepts of cloud computing into this public comments, as he did later on a quarterly earnings call when he described his vision for the Oracle-Sun systems business:

And those clusters are now called private clouds—that's the more-fashionable term for clusters—and we're using our software, our operating system—both Solaris and Oracle Linux—and our virtualization—the ability to dynamically allocate and reallocate resources, which is essential for cloud computing—as well as integrated networking and integrated storage to deliver a complete private cloud to our customers.[25]

(These comments remind me of Chapter 3, in which we discussed vendors lacking a DBMS offering who tinkered slightly with their products and rechristened them a DBMS).

However, Oracle has been moving cautiously into the clouds nonetheless. Since about half of their total revenue is partner-generated or -influenced, and many of those partners sell equipment, they are careful not to poison the well. As a result, Oracle has focused primarily on "the Enterprise Private Cloud." Oracle sees cloud computing as SaaS, PaaS, and IaaS. In Oracle's view, the private cloud offers greater control, is easier to integrate, and has lower overall costs (capital expenditure and operating expense combined). They believe that the high efficiency, high availability, and elasticity that characterize cloud computing are approximately equal in public and private clouds. Oracle is not a provider of PaaS or IaaS. However, it is committed to providing customers the ability to deploy Oracle technologies in either private clouds or public IaaS clouds. Their objectives are to ensure that cloud computing is "fully enterprise grade" and that customers have a

---

24.   www.informationweek.com/news/global-cio/interviews/showArticle.jhtml?articleID=225200363&queryText=larry%20ellison%20embraces%20cloud.

25.   www.informationweek.com/news/global-cio/security/showArticle.jhtml?articleID=222002676.

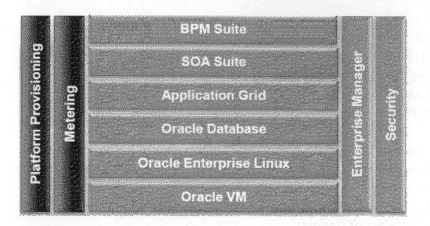

Figure 12.1   Oracle Fusion Middleware. (Courtesy Oracle, Inc.)

choice. Figure 12.1 shows the components of Oracle Fusion Middleware, the foundation of Oracle's Enterprise Private Cloud.

The Oracle Platform for SaaS includes Oracle Database, Oracle Fusion Middleware, Oracle Enterprise Manager, and Oracle VM, a comprehensive, open and integrated set of technologies that allow independent software vendors (ISVs) to build, deploy and manage SaaS and cloud-based applications.

The Oracle Platform for SaaS provides ISVs with a single, integrated platform for both on-premise and cloud-based deployments, allowing ISVs to offer their customers a choice in where to run their software. Additionally, the Oracle SaaS program provides business and technology support to ISVs, hosting service providers and system integrators.

Oracle customers can now use their existing Oracle licenses or acquire new licenses to deploy Oracle software on Amazon's EC2. Oracle has also announced its intention to license others as well. However, it views public cloud as appropriate for rapid experimentation. Oracle is also making available a set of pre-installed, preconfigured virtual machine images for Amazon EC2 environment—Amazon Machine Images (AMIs)—to allow users to easily provision a fully functional Oracle environment in a matter of minutes.

Amazon AWS can be used to back up Oracle databases. Using the newly introduced Oracle Secure Backup Cloud module, it is now possible to move database backups to the Amazon Simple Storage Service (S3) for offsite storage.

Oracle offers two SaaS applications:

- *Oracle CRM On Demand*, a subscription-based CRM for sales, service, marketing, and contact-center operations

■ *Oracle Argus Safety,* an advanced drug safety and risk management solution for life science companies

Oracle intends to make additional "Oracle on Demand" (Oracle's data centers providing outsourcing services) resources offerings (see www.oracle.com/us/products/ondemand/hosted-managed-applications-068564.html) available in an SaaS environment.

12.4.1   Oracle and Sun

Oracle outbid IBM to acquire Sun Microsystems. In January 2010, after a lengthy government review, Oracle completed its acquisition of Sun in a deal valued in excess of $7 billion. Sun was not only an equipment provider, but also developed and controlled key open source Internet technologies including MySQL and Java. It was an early proponent of cloud technologies based on OpenSolaris (see Figure 12.2).

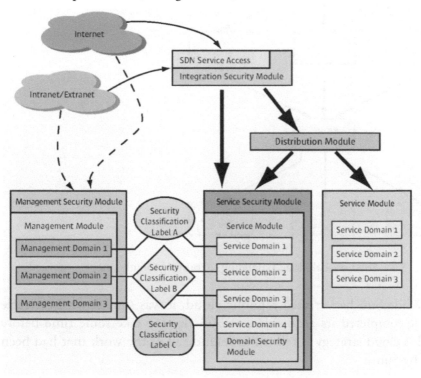

Figure 12.2   Oracle Fusion Middleware. (Courtesy Oracle, Inc.)

The VeriScale architecture is designed to optimize load balancing by implementing the networking logic locally in the service instance's containers and treating the networking logic as part of the application. This enhanced approach is shown in Figure 12.3.

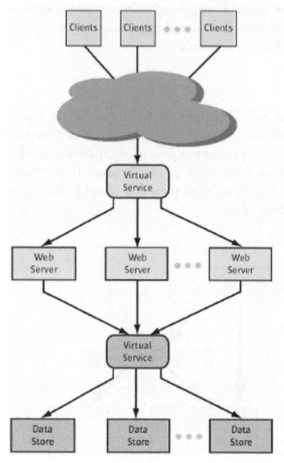

Figure 12.3   Sun Veriscale load balancing. (Courtesy Oracle, Inc.)

While Sun had created a public cloud, it was shut down by Oracle after it completed its acquisition of Sun. It may take some time before Oracle's cloud strategy is refined to include all of the work that had been done by Sun.

12.4.2   Oracle Resources

- Oracle Cloud Computing Center: www.oracle.com/technology/tech/cloud/index.html
- Oracle and AWS: http://aws.amazon.com/solutions/global-solution-providers/oracle/
- Oracle in the Cloud: www.oracle.com/technology/tech/cloud/pdf/oracle-in-the-cloud-datasheet.pdf
- Veriscale Architecture: www.oracle.com/dm/sun/44034_821-0248.pdf

12.5   CA Technologies

CA Technologies (CA) was formerly known as Computer Associates, Inc., and is now legally known as CA, Inc. CA was one of the first independent software vendors that sold software for IBM mainframes, creating an industry. Previously, there was no systems software industry, as IBM gave away its software and charged only for hardware. Founded in 1976, CA is still the world's leading independent information technology (IT) management software company.

In February 2010, CA announced a definitive agreement to acquire privately held 3Tera, Inc., a pioneer in cloud computing. 3Tera's AppLogic offers an innovative solution for building cloud services and deploying complex enterprise-class applications to public and private clouds using an intuitive graphical user interface (GUI). We discussed 3Tera in Chapter 4.

In May 2010, CA unveiled the CA Cloud-Connected Management Suite, which will enable customers to meet this emerging challenge with four key products:[26]

- **CA Cloud Insight** will enable organization to gain visibility into internal IT environments in terms of relative measures of service, such as quality, agility, risk, cost, capability, and security. Customers will be able to compare and contrast internal options with external ones to determine the best choice based on their current business situation.
- **CA Cloud Compose** will allow customers to abstract applications from their underlying infrastructure to make it easy to deploy, manage, and move composite infrastructure stacks to

---

26.   http://investor.ca.com/releasedetail.cfm?ReleaseID=470429.

internal or external cloud environments.

Using an extensible catalog of reusable software components, CA Cloud Compose customers will be able to leverage cloud computing capabilities to increase their quality of service while simultaneously reducing cost and time to market for new solutions. It's an organized way of dealing with code reuse, discussed in detail in Chapter 10. By providing both the cloud infrastructure and the service creation and deployment capabilities in one product, CA Cloud Compose will provide integrated high availability, metering, operations monitoring and management capabilities to help customers rapidly achieve their business goals through their IT supply chain.

- **CA Cloud Optimize** will help customers analyze alternatives across business measurement characteristics and present options to the user for how to improve IT service delivery and sourcing choices. Customers will be able to actively lower their operating costs and be much more agile in aligning with business requirements for capacity, performance and other service parameters. This will give customers the ability to be more proactive about getting increasing business value out of their IT budgets.
- **CA Cloud Orchestrate** will enable customers to manage the deployment of the suggestions that come from CA Cloud Optimize. This will build on a broad array of capabilities from the existing product portfolio, recently acquired companies, and new organic development within CA Technologies.

Following CA's long-time strategy, CA has entered the cloud arena by acquisition, and new solutions will build upon AppLogic, technology recently acquired from 3Tera that simplifies the design and deployment of composite applications as a single logical entity in the cloud. CA plans to develop new software organically, as well. By unifying application configuration, application deployment, and a virtual server fabric—functions that are otherwise typically performed in a fragmented manner—AppLogic helps reduce costs, improve productivity and increase service quality

CA also recently acquired:

- *Oblicore*, service level management for cloud vendor management and assurance of cloud service quality
- *Cassatt* software solutions and technologies for operating green data centers

■ *NetQoS*, which provides network performance management software and services that improve application delivery across complex networks

Supporting this new product family are two other important initiatives: The Service Measurement Index and Cloud Commons.

The Service Measurement Index (SMI) consortium, being led by Carnegie Mellon University (CMU), is an initiative to address the need for industry-wide, globally accepted measures for calculating the benefits and risks of cloud computing services. With the help of a planned consortium of educational institutions, end-user organizations, and technology providers, CMU expects to develop a set of business-centric performance indicators that will provide IT with a standardized method for comparing cloud services from internal or external providers.

Cloud Commons, sponsored by CA Technologies along with other organizations and participants and launched in 2010, provides a place for like-minded end users, partners, industry experts, and others to share experiences, best practices, and qualitative and quantitative information about the many types of cloud services available. Cloud Commons enables people to describe their experiences with cloud services and compare them with others' experiences. The site also facilitates collaboration through the ability to comment on news, best practices, and other insights, and to interact with others in the community.

Nimsoft Unified Monitoring Solutions (see Chapter 5), available either as an on-premise or on-demand (SaaS) application, provide complete visibility into the performance and availability of IT environments. The Nimsoft Unified Monitoring architecture eliminates the need to deploy a new monitoring solution for outsourced services, public or private clouds, or SaaS implementations with a single, highly scalable monitoring toolset.

In addition, CA is leveraging its own IT Management Software, which is now available using a Software as a Service delivery model (ITM SaaS) with offerings such as Clarity™ On Demand for project and portfolio management. It is also investing heavily in its partnership with Carnegie Mellon.

CA is also planning SaaS offerings for most of its IT management solutions, not unlike IBM's approach. CA also announced that CA Technologies designed an On Demand Self Service Portal, scheduled to be available in summer 2010 which will enable customers to easily buy, provision, and administer CA Technologies IT management solutions as a service through a common modern interface.

CA is focused on its traditional strengths in management and security. Businesses are increasingly consuming "composite services" that combine services from multiple sources, spanning virtual and physical resources both inside and outside the firewall. Without extending existing management disciplines and tools, this mash-up of services can create rapidly multiplying security gaps and monitoring blind spots. This can leave the business vulnerable to holes in security and disruptions in service availability and performance, while making it harder for IT to gain advanced warning of impending failures or to diagnose the root cause of a problem hiding in a virtual global haystack.

Greg Montjoie, general manager of Hosting Solutions at Internet Solutions, says[27] that CA aims to distinguish between cloud computing and computing in the cloud. While cloud computing allows maintenance, migration, and hardware optimization irrespective of geographic location, computing in the Cloud involves an individual accessing specific applications via the Internet to perform computing tasks.

12.5.1   Partnership with NetApp[28]

CA and NetApp have announced an extension of their existing partnership, integrating CA's virtualization, automation, and service assurance offerings with NetApp's storage management solutions. The integrated offerings are intended to help customers improve business agility, productivity and service quality, while also helping to lower costs and reduce risks that are associated with virtualization and cloud-based infrastructures, says Patrick Rogers, vice president of Solutions and Alliances for NetApp.

The companies' current efforts include integrating CA Spectrum Automation Manager with NetApp Provisioning Manager to enable customers to automate their cloud infrastructure end-to-end, streamline the provisioning process for faster deployment times, and support improved utilization of critical resources, as well as allow the storage to be automated alongside the server, network, and applications in an orchestrated fashion. Future plans include integrating CA Spectrum Service Assurance with the NetApp SANscreen suite to extend the CA solution's business service modeling capability

---

27.   Greg Montjoie. "Is Cloud Computing or computing in the cloud?" *Tech News Headquarters,* May 27,2010. Available at http://technewshq.com/computing/27-76/is-cloud-computing-or-computing-in-the-cloud.html. (accessed August 4, 2010).

28.   Adapted from Steve Wexler, "CA, NetApp Extend Collaboration To The Cloud." *ChannelInsider,* February 10, 2010. Available at www.channelinsider.com/c/a/Cloud-Computing/CA-NetApp-Extend-Collaboration-To-The-Cloud-296756/ (accessed July 28, 2010).

into the storage domain and provide users with new insight into how storage status impacts specific business services or puts them at risk.

12.5.2   CA Resources

- CA has organized its cloud resources to be accessible from its website at www.ca.com/us/cloud-solutions.aspx.
- Cloud Commons can be accessed at http://www.cloudcommons.com

12.6   Unisys

Unisys was formed in 1986 through the merger of two computer industry pioneers, Sperry and Burroughs. Its history goes back more than one hundred years.

Unisys' equipment line includes the the company's ClearPath family of mainframes, capable of running not only mainframe software, but both the Java platform and the JBoss or Java EE Application Server concurrently. ClearPath systems are available in either a Unisys OS 2200-based system (Sperry) or an MCP-based system (Burroughs). Those ClearPath models are named Dorado and Libra, respectively. The ES7000 server family uses Intel processors and Windows and/or open source Linux operating systems.

12.6.1   Unisys Stealth Security[29]

Unisys has a large base of customers in the public sector, and as we noted in Chapter 8, it places strong emphasis on security; this has carried over to its cloud offerings. Unisys Stealth security solution, an innovative, patent-pending data protection technology initially designed for government applications, is now available to commercial clients. The Unisys Stealth technology cloaks data through multiple levels of authentication and encryption, bit-splitting data into multiple packets so it moves invisibly across networks and protects data in the Unisys secure cloud. The Unisys Stealth technology enables encrypted "data in motion" to remain invisible as it traverses the infrastructure until it is reassembled upon delivery to authorized users.

---

29.   Adapted from Unisys. "Unisys Delivers Secure Cloud Solution, Expanding CIOs' Options for Moving Application Workloads to the Cloud" (press release, August 3, 2009). Available at www.unisys.com/unisys/news/detail.jsp?id=10020100016 (accessed July 28, 2010).

Unisys also announced that it is planning a Stealth solution for data security on storage area networks (SAN) by providing the same cloaking capability for "data at rest" in a virtualized storage environment.

Supporting its cloud computing strategy, Unisys announced three principal offerings:

12.6.2   Unisys Secure Cloud Solution

Unisys Secure Cloud Solution is a managed cloud service providing comprehensive data security for multi-tenant environments, in which clients share a common IT infrastructure. Because the solution uses Stealth technology, Unisys says enterprise clients can move existing business applications—including those with secure or sensitive data, such as human resources, financial, and healthcare information—into a managed, shared cloud service, without needing to rewrite or alter applications.

As a managed public cloud service, Unisys Secure Cloud Solution enables global delivery of multiple new services: Secure Infrastructure as a Service (IaaS); Secure Platform as a Service (PaaS); My Secure Application as a Service (AaaS); three Secure Software as a Service (SaaS) offerings: Secure Unified Communication as a Service, Secure Virtual Office as a Service and Secure Document Delivery Service; and Secure Disaster Recovery as a Service (DRaaS).

Based on the Information Technology Infrastructure Library (ITIL) standard for service management, the Unisys Secure Cloud Solution uses the automation and virtualization capabilities of Unisys real-time infrastructure solutions, which enable the IT infrastructure to respond automatically to changes in the business environment.

The Secure Cloud Solution also provides a self-service portal that enables organizations to scale IT resources in real time. The Unisys Converged Remote Infrastructure Management Suite solution provides a unified view of the entire IT infrastructure and enables end-to-end management of the Secure Cloud Solution.

As client needs or data security requirements dictate, the Unisys Secure Cloud Solution can balance workloads across a global network of Unisys data centers, which are certified to key international standards such as ISO/IEC 27001:2005 for security, ISO/IEC 20000 for service management, and the SAS 70 Type II auditing standard.

12.6.3   Unisys Secure Private Cloud Solution

The Unisys Secure Private Cloud Solution is designed to help organizations realize the operational and economic benefits of cloud computing in their internal data centers. This solution leverages the technology and expertise behind Unisys Secure Cloud Solution. Unisys says that it enables clients to reduce IT costs through server and storage virtualization; remove IT bottlenecks through automated operations and immediate, as-needed self-service provisioning of resources; and align the supply of IT resources to fluctuating business demand. Clients can typically run existing Microsoft Windows applications without alteration, reducing migration costs and realizing the business benefits of cloud deployment more quickly.

Clients using the Secure Private Cloud Solution can either monitor the infrastructure themselves or have Unisys do it through the Unisys Converged Remote Infrastructure Management Suite solution. They can also optionally choose to implement *Unisys Stealth* for additional data protection.

12.6.4   Unisys ClearPath Cloud Solutions

Unisys ClearPath Cloud Solutions allow Unisys mainframe clients to subscribe to and access Unisys-owned computing facilities incrementally to run, modernize, or develop ClearPath applications. Unisys says this helps clients avoid unscheduled capital equipment expenditures and make more efficient use of their own ClearPath systems.

In July 2010, Unisys announced availability of the first solution in the series: the ClearPath Cloud Development and Test Solution, offered as "platform as a service" (PaaS). This solution provides access to Unisys-hosted virtual resources, when needed, for creation, modernization, and functional testing of specific applications.

The ClearPath Cloud Development and Test Solution also draws on the infrastructure behind Unisys Secure Cloud Solution for provisioning and resource management—including Unisys Converged Remote Infrastructure Management Suite.

Unisys plans additional ClearPath Cloud Solutions, including a full cloud-based production environment for smaller applications; data replication and disaster recovery to preserve critical business information; and managed, industry-specific "software as a service" (SaaS) application solutions to complement existing solutions such as the Unisys Logistics Management System for air cargo management.

12.6.5   Unisys Cloud Transformation Services

In addition, Unisys Cloud Transformation Services are available to clients of all three Unisys cloud computing solutions. These advisory, assessment, and migration services allow clients to plan and migrate to the type of cloud environment that best meets their business goals. Unisys service professionals help clients assess what application workloads can be moved to the cloud, how that can be done, and the technological, financial, and security implications of their choices.

12.6.6   Unisys Resources

- The Perfect Storm for Enterprise-Class Clouds: www.unisys.com/ unisys/common/download.jsp?d_id=10018700002&backurl=/ unisys/ri/wp/detail.jsp&id=10018700002
- Hosting Unmodified Applications in the Unisys Secure Cloud: www.unisys.com/unisys/common/down- load.jsp?d_id=1120000970001710129&backurl=/unisys/ri/wp/ detail.jsp&id=1120000970001710129
- A New Era in IT: Cloud Computing Takes Center Stage: www.unisys.com/unisys/common/down- load.jsp?d_id=1120000970000310199&backurl=/unisys/ri/pub/ pov/detail.jsp&id=1120000970000310199

12.6.7   Unisys Partnerships

For Unisys Secure Cloud Solution and Secure Private Cloud Solution, Unisys has partnered with VMware on the software side. On the hardware side, Unisys has partnered with Intel to develop the computing architecture Unisys has collaborated with EMC, drawing on that partner's storage technology to create the information infrastructure that enables fast storage and delivery of information securely in the cloud. Software from partners Scalent Systems and iWave Software enables repurposing and orchestration of IT resources to meet the service levels required for clients' business. Software from BMC (see Chapter 13)helps power the Converged Remote Infrastructure Management Suite, which provides unified operational control of the cloud solutions.

12.7 Cloud Research

In October 2007, Google and IBM announced a collaboration with major universities[30] the University of Washington (UW), Carnegie-Mellon University, the Massachusetts Institute of Technology, Stanford University, the University of California at Berkeley, and the University of Maryland to further the development of cloud computing technology. More recently, IBM announced that Italy's University of Bari is working to improve supply management of local businesses, including fisherman, winemakers, and trucking companies by helping them determine product demand, shipping preparations, and other actions on handheld devices. The university is creating real-time scenarios using end-user devices, sensors, analytics software, and power from a mainframe.

Also, IBM announced a research partnership with the University of Missouri. The University is a recipient of a Shared University Research (SUR) Award from IBM, consisting of high performance computing technologies to advance the school's bioinformative research with the goal of developing a first-of-a-kind cloud computing environment for genomics research collaboration at a regional level. Joining the genomic cloud could make possible large-scale sharing and collaborative scientific discovery in a wide range of fields.

Not to be outdone, HP, Intel, and Yahoo jumped on the bandwagon and are teaming up with some lesser ranked groups, the most prominent of whom are the Infocomm Development Authority of Singapore (IDA), the University of Illinois at Urbana-Champaign, and the Karlsruhe Institute of Technology (KIT) in Germany.

Summary

IBM and Unisys are actively hosting cloud applications on their own servers. They, as well as Sun, also provide complete solutions for private clouds. HP and CA are making certain applications available on their own servers with SaaS delivery, and are also selling software for use by cloud vendors and enterprises. Oracle is making some its solutions on the Amazon cloud and intends to offer the solutions to other cloud service providers. They are actively marketing their solutions for deployment on private clouds. IBM has made a series of announcements around development and testing of applications that feature its WebSphere software, SuSE Linux, KVM and

---

30.   http://www.eweek.com/c/a/IT-Infrastructure/Google-IBM-Plant-Distributed-Computing-Seeds.

Java, but seems focused on testing, building clouds for the client, or offering a hosted private service behind the firewall.

Oracle—who bought Java steward Sun Microsystems in early 2010 just as Sun was trying to fluff its own Java cloud strategy—has ruled out providing its own cloud for Java applications. Instead, Oracle is content to sell its database, Java middleware, and hardware to cloud providers.

Chapter 13

Cloud Service Providers

Overview

In Chapter 6, we looked at Amazon's AWS. Chapter 7 examined virtualization and VMware; Chapter 10 reviewed Microsoft Azure. Chapter 11 looked at Google's cloud offerings and Chapter 12 reviewed offerings from enterprise cloud vendors. In this chapter, we look at what other cloud service providers are offering.

We are not aiming for completeness, an impossible goal in an environment that is growing at warp speed, and where new offerings appear daily, particularly in the SaaS space. Jeremy Geelan wrote about "The Top 250 Players in the Cloud Computing Ecosystem,"[1] and he struggled to constrain the list to that size.

Throughout the book we have referenced monitoring, planning and other software tools; we don't repeat ourselves here.

It's a rapidly growing field. I keep up with the latest developments in cloud computing on my Web site, Eyeonthecloud.com. You will also find links on the Eyeonthecloud.com site to other useful Web sites.

13.1   Comprehensive Cloud Service Providers

Joyent

Joyent is the only Cloud provider company to deliver all the three layers of the Cloud Stack (i.e., IaaS, PaaS, and SaaS). It has partnered with Dell to provide more than $3 million worth of hosting services to Facebook developers without charge. It offers a public cloud competing with Amazon EC2, as well as private clouds in partnership with Dell. It also offers professional services, while Amazon relies on a network of approved partners.

Web site: www.joyent.com

---

1.   http://linux.sys-con.com/node/1386896 (accessed June 25, 2010).

13.2   IaaS Providers

13.2.1   Rackspace

More than 99,000 customers—including more than 80,000 cloud computing customers—and 2,900 employees, make Rackspace a leading cloud hosting service. They offer Rackspace Cloud, providing Cloud Sites, scalable, virtualized servers, Cloud Servers for hosting scalable Web sites, and Cloud Files, storage service in the cloud. They are also behind OpenStack, which we discussed in Chapter 7.

Web site: www.rackspacecloud.com/cloud_hosting_products

13.2.2   GoGrid

GoGrid offers a wide variety of ready-to-go Windows and Linux Cloud Servers, either as on-demand, self-service hosting, or as dedicated hosting of scalable networks in a hybrid environment. It has the most generous SLA in industry: 24/7 support and one hundred percent uptime.

13.2.3   ElasticHosts

ElasticHosts provides virtual servers based on Linux KVM, running on their own server farms, located in three fully independent data centers across two continents. ElasticHosts monitor, service, and upgrade the underlying infrastructure, providing customers with high performance, availability and scalability.

The company states that its virtual servers offer the power and control of a traditional hosted server, with the following benefits:

- Instant flexibility: to scale your machine up or down using any web browser
- Peace of mind: of running on professionally managed infrastructure, with automatic failover
- Cost efficiency: of buying exactly the capacity you need on an infrastructure built to scale, and growing only when you need to
  Source: www.elastichosts.com/cloud-hosting/infrastructure
  Web site: www.elastichosts.com

13.2.4   SymetriQ

SymetriQ is a provider of cloud computing Infrastructure-as-a-Service (IaaS). SymetriQ offers virtual server hosting on a UK-based infrastructure, which the client can deploy in minutes to create a virtual data center. The company says:

> *Specifically we provide you with the following services via our virtual servers and all are available on a pay-as-you-go basis, like utility billing:*
> - *Processing power*
> - *Memory*
> - *Storage*
> - *Bandwidth*
> - *Operating Systems (Windows, Solaris, Linux)*

Source: *www.symetriq.com/what-we-offer*

Building a custom virtual image is accomplished through drag and drop, as shown below:

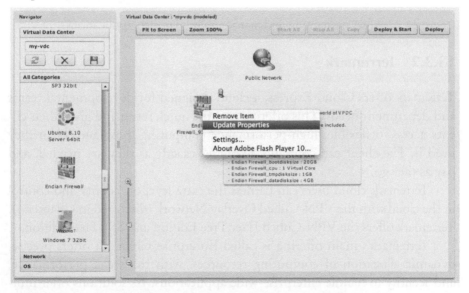

Figure 13.1   Building a custom virtual image with SymetriQ.

Web site: www.symetriq.com

13.3 PaaS Providers

13.3.1 AT&T

AT&T Enterprise Hosting Services support business applications with a range of monitoring and management options. Their customer portal, BusinessDirect®, allows customers personalized, secure online access to detailed information about hosted infrastructure and applications.

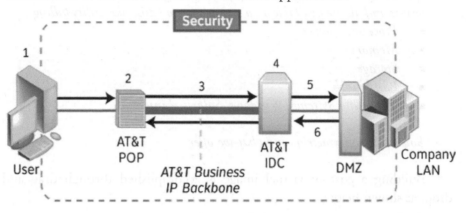

Figure 13.2   AT&T monitoring and management of hosted applications.

13.3.2 Terremark

Terremark offers Cloud Express, a cloud designed for developmental teams and department needs. This offering permits quick setup and gives their clients access to flexible, high-performance computing, how and when they need it. The client can configure resources exactly as they are needed, and pay as they go.

Terremark cloud users can harness the extra level of security and control in the cloud with the VPN-Cubed Overlay Network (discussed in Chapter 4). Terremark offers the VPN-Cubed IPsec Free Edition and SSL Free Edition.

Terremark's main offering is called Enterprise Cloud. It offers precise, dynamic allocation of computing resources, with the scale, performance, and security to handle enterprise-wide applications. Its solutions offer multiuser capacity, dedicated resource pool architecture, and a role-based security model, as well as private network connectivity and physical device integration.

The Enterprise Cloud combines the power and flexibility of IaaS with the expertise, security, and availability that large organizations with mission-critical computing needs demand of their infrastructure. It provides An easy-to-use Web-based management interface that gives its clients command and control over a cloud-based resource pool of compute, storage, and network, built on a fully clustered enterprise-class computing architecture featuring virtualization technology from VMware.

Terremark's charges are based on resources rather than on large and inflexible server units, allowing for more precise and dynamic allocation of computing resources when and where they're needed.

The Enterprise Cloud supports more than 450 operating system configurations, including Windows Server 2003 and 2008, Red Hat Enterprise Linux, CentOS, FreeBSD, Solaris, SUSE Linux, and Ubuntu. If you have pre-existing ISOs or custom OS needs, you have the freedom to upload and install on blank virtual machines.

The Enterprise Cloud can be combined with your dedicated servers and managed from the same Web-based interface. Exposing this server in The Enterprise Cloud takes only a few minutes; once a LAN-LAN connection is established, you have complete control over these dedicated resources. This provides the best of both worlds—the elasticity of the cloud combined with the security and compliance of dedicated hardware.

Web site: www.terremark.com

13.3.3   EngineYard

Engine Yard AppCloud is an hosting alternative for a wide range of Rails applications, from smaller-scale Web applications that run within a single compute instance to production applications that require the elasticity, scalability, and reliability of a Rails Application Cloud. Engine Yard offers automated load balancing and full spectrum monitoring, along with essential infrastructure services such as persistent storage, Web-based gem installs, data backup/restore, and system monitoring—all backed by Engine Yard Rails support and the battle-tested Engine Yard Ruby on Rails stack, a standardized Ruby on Rails Web application framework stack, designed and optimized for business-critical Ruby on Rails application development. The stack has been refined over the past three years by expert cluster engineers and seasoned DBAs for Web server performance, database efficiency and long-term scalability.

Web site: www.engineyard.com

13.4   SaaS Providers

13.4.1   NetSuite

Netsuite's SuiteCloud Platform is a comprehensive offering of on-demand products and development tools. It is also a leading provider of Web-based business software suites for CRM, ERP tools, accounting and e-commerce.

Web site: www.netsuite.com/portal/home.shtml

13.4.2   Intuit

Founded in 1983, Intuit makes the well-known QuickBooks software; its annual revenue exceeds $3 billion. The Intuit Partner Platform allows customers to:

- Rapidly build and deploy rich Software as a Service (SaaS) apps capable of seamless integration with QuickBooks data
- Reach a potential market of nearly 25 million users within the 4 million small businesses using QuickBooks

Web site: https://ipp.developer.intuit.com/ipp/native

13.4.3   Intacct

Intacct is a leading provider of cloud financial management and accounting applications for companies of all sizes. The Intacct cloud financial management system provides comprehensive functionality, is easy to use and configure to match your business processes, and is designed to integrate easily with your other key business systems.

- Fully auditable and Sarbanes-Oxley compliant; prevents fraud with strict permissions, separation of duties and financial controls.
- Supports distributed and global businesses, making it easy and quick to consolidate financials from multiple business units who may also transact in multiple currencies.
- Automates key business processes, freeing you from time-consuming and manual work.
- Works well with other key business applications, including Salesforce CRM, ADP, Avalara, Avectra, BNA Software, Boomi, Callidus, CCH, Compupay, expensecloud, Pervasive, SmartTurn,

and SpringCM, eliminating islands of information and wasted time, errors and duplication from re-keying.

■ Provides a Web-based interface, enabling you to access your financials from anywhere, at anytime as long as you have an Internet connection.

Intacct runs on the Oracle dbms and uses SunGard for disaster recovery. The AICPA and its subsidiary CPA2Biz have named Intacct their preferred provider of financial applications, and CPA2Biz is now the exclusive distributor of Intacct to the CPA profession.

Web site: http://us.intacct.com/products/index.php

13.4.4   FinancialForce.com

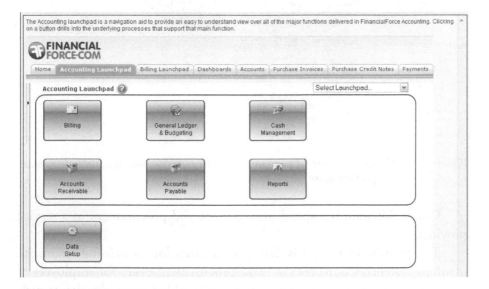

Figure 13.3   FinancialForce.com launch screen.

FinancialForce.com, developed on Force.com, delivers comprehensive accounting and is pre-integrated with Salesforce.com's CRM.

Web site: www.financialforce.com

13.4.5   Coupa Software

Figure 13.4   Coupa platform of procurement and expense management. (Courtesy Coupa Software)

Coupa Software is a spend management and procurement as a service provider.

The promise of Coupa is that it is an extension of existing enterprise planning systems. Coupa tries to make procurement easier for employees of all stripes within an enterprise. Coupa recently added enterprise clients such as Michaels, Diagnostic Health Corp., and PGi. Salesforce.com and Taleo are also customers.

Coupa is looking to solve the buyside problem and apply to a broader audience of enterprise workers. "You get into any company and any person sitting in a cubicle and they ask 'how do you buy something?'" said Coupa CEO Rob Bernshteyn. "We're looking at wider use cases."[2]

---

2.   Larry Digman. "Five Questions with Coupa Software CEO Rob Bernshteyn." ZDNet.com, June 18, 2010. Available at http://www.zdnet.com/blog/btl/five-questions-with-coupa-software-ceo-rob-bernshteyn/35997 (accessed July 29, 2010).

Coupa now competes with Ariba, somewhat, as Ariba launched its Commerce Cloud, a Web-based platform for buying and selling between corporations. Ariba is more similar to eBay, with an on-premise software focus compared to Coupa, a cloud procurement option built on Amazon Web Services infrastructure.

Bernshteyn says that Coupa is designed to be a strategic extension of SAP and Oracle.

13.4.6   AT&T

AT&T TopLineISV^{SM} enables independent software vendors (ISVs) to launch a software-as-a-service (SaaS) business. AT&T now allows ISVs to tap into AT&T's infrastructure, methodologies, expertise, and reputation to avoid newcomers' missteps and immediately seize a competitive advantage.

Web site: http://www.business.att.com/enterprise/Family/application-hosting-enterprise/software-as-a-service-enablement-enterprise

13.5   Specialized Cloud Software Providers

13.5.1   Appistry

Appistry delivers Cloud IT infrastructure to the enterprise, for intelligence and defense organizations, and to ISVs and SaaS providers.

As shown in Figure 13.5, Appistry supports public, private, and hybrid clouds. Appistry serves large enterprise customers, including FedEx, Sprint, and the U.S. government.

Web site: www.appistry.com

13.5.2   BMC Software

BMC Software is a venerable software vendor dating from the early mainframe days. The new BMC product, dubbed Cloud Lifecycle Management, primarily addressed towards management of private clouds, also supports hybrid configuration. It provides self-service management, provisioning, and unified management. It includes:

- *A Service Catalog, purpose-built for cloud offerings*
- *A Self-Service Portal, allowing service owners to perform basic administrative activities on their own services (and only on their own services), and to request new services with . . .*

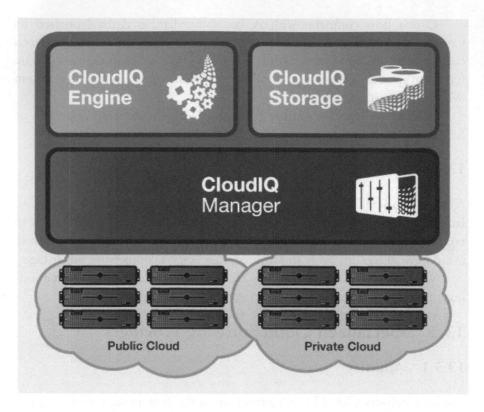

Figure 13.5   Appistry CloudIQ architecture.

- *A Service Request Wizard, permitting customized, on-demand provisioning of services, within constraints defined and controlled by the catalog designer, service retirement and resource reclamation.*
- *Pre-built workflows that integrate with existing IT management systems, allowing organizations to introduce Cloud while continuing to leverage existing policies, processes, people, and tools*
- *Automated full-stack layered provisioning across heterogeneous platforms*

Source: http://communities.bmc.com/communities/community/ bsm_initiatives/cloud/blog/2010/05/25/introducing-cloud-lifecycle- management

BMC states that the new product was created in conjunction with several (unnamed) strategic design partners—both enterprise and service providers in the United States as well as in EMEA and APAC countries—and further validated by an additional 25 customers. Working closely with such a broad set of customers during the design and implementation has helped BMC ensure that the resulting product meets clear and compelling customer needs and delivers immediate real-world value.

Web sites:

- http://documents.bmc.com/products/documents/18/26/141826/141826.pdf
- www.bmc.com/Cloud
- http://documents.bmc.com/products/documents/32/99/133299/133299.pdf

13.5.3   Nasuni

Nasuni is an intereresting offering for cloud data storage. Nasuni has partnered with four cloud providers (Amazon AWS, Iron Mountain Digital, Nirvanix, and Rackspace) to provide encrypted, *portable* file storage. Data is encrypted by the Nasuni Filer on the client premises, using OpenPGP with AES-256, and remains encrypted in the cloud. This guarantees end-to-end data protection, as the data is never visible to anyone at Nasuni or the cloud.

Customers can escrow their encryption keys with Nasuni or a trusted third party, or they can generate and store their own keys. The Nasuni Filer also functions like a traditional NAS, retaining such NAS functionality as Windows Shares and Active Directory. Shares are created and access control is managed in a familiar way. You can also consolidate any number of NAS boxes into one Nasuni Filer.

Nasuni's charges vary by the cloud provider. Monthly storage costs are $0.15 on AWS and on Rackspace per GB, $0.48 per GB for Nirvanix, and $0.65/GB for Iron Mountain. The last two provide various value-added services, which justify their higher charges. For example, Nirvanix's standard service utilizes RAID 6, striping files to three separate discs to ensure data integrity. Customers have the option of replicating data on multiple nodes where each node utilizes RAID 6. This process is automated using Nirvanix's policy-based Checksum operations on data uploads, along with frequent internal integrity checks to preserve the integrity of data in transit and at rest. Moreover, every file copy or transfer within the Storage Delivery Network is validated against a stored MD5 hash to verify that the additional copy has not been corrupted in transit.

The ability to move data easily among its providers and the customer's facilities helps prevent lock-in.

Web site: www.nasuni.com

Summary

Beyond the largest vendors whose offerings are described in earlier chapters, this chapter presents additional large cloud service providers, such as Rackspace, GoGrid, and Joyent (a newer entry); robust cloud offerings from some you might not have expected, like AT&T; specialized vendors like EngineYard for Ruby on Rails; interesting SaaS vendors like NetSuite, Intuit, and Intacct; as well as cross-platform vendors like Appistry, BMC, and Nasuni. (Other software products are referenced throughout this book.)

Keep up to date on new offerings and cloud news at eyeonthecloud.com, a free Web site.

Chapter 14

Practice Fusion Case Study

14.1 Overview

This chapter describes a case study demonstrating an effective, cloud-based applications that would be impossible or prohibitively expensive to offer in a non-cloud (conventional) environment.

14.2 Practice Fusion

Founded in 2005, Practice Fusion is an electronic health record (EHR) application for healthcare providers. Over 40,000 physicians and practice managers in 50 states currently use Practice Fusion's Electronic Health Record.

Practice Fusion employs the "freeconomics" business model[1] via its free, Web-based electronic health information system (some optional modules, such as electronic claim billing and submission are fee-based). Practice Fusion is a user-friendly electronic health record (EHR) system that can be activated in less than five minutes. It includes scheduling, medical history, charting, billing (including electronic claims submission), laboratory interfaces, and e-prescribing (Practice Fusion's e-prescribing technology allows doctors to submit electronic prescriptions to more than 50,000 pharmacies in the United States at no cost). Amazingly, e-mail and telephone support are also offered without charge.

It is this essentially free business model that made it interesting for us as a case study.

---

1.   *Free*, by Chris Anderson (Hyperion, 2009).

Practice Fusion derives revenue from sources similar to Google: it embeds advertisements in a banner at the bottom of its electronic medical record system and it sells de-identified patient and doctor data from its system to third parties, maintaining full HIPAA compliance along the way. Practice Fusion also gives physicians the option to operate an ad-free electronic medical record system for $100 per month, which is still substantially less than the competition charges. However, as expected, most physicians choose to run the advertisement-based model, according to Matthew Douglass, Practice Fusion's Vice President of Engineering, who was kind enough to walk me through a "behind the scenes tour."

Despite the revenue from advertising and the sale of de-identified data, for the business to work, costs must be kept low. Matthew says that he accomplishes this three ways: widely accepted internet standards, cloud computing, and a secure database management system.

- As we emphasize in Chapter 9, Scale and Reuse, Practice Fusion not only reuses code from others, it exposes certain modules via the Practice Fusion platform, which allows authorized developers to build their own add-ons/modules.
- Cloud computing and virtualization are provided by a large, low-cost provider. (Due primarily to HIPAA compliance concerns, Practice Fusion operates as a private cloud.)
- For security and stability, Practice Fusion is built on a Microsoft .Net platform and uses Microsoft SQL Server as its database management system.

14.3   Non-Trivial, Maybe Life-Saving

Comprehensive electronic history, charting, scheduling, billing and reporting are complex applications.

Practice Fusion's EHR includes a single-screen function for uploading, viewing, downloading, and signing documents. All paper documents can be imported, including labs, X-rays, and insurance cards. A document can be digitally marked-up or annotated before associating the file with a patient's record.

Capturing, recording, and tracking medical information electronically has been shown to reduce preventable drug errors; it supports patient-physician interactions, making them more efficient, and improves patient care and diagnostic processes by allowing physicians to tap into computer tools, protocols, resources, and checks—flags that indicate adverse drug interactions, for instance—that could enhance medical decision making.

Current vendor software products are prohibitively expensive,[2] and this financial barrier represents the primary limiting factor for widespread adoption of electronic medical record systems by physicians.

> *The electronic medical record (EMR) is possibly one of the most costly information technology system upgrades that any health care provider can undertake. The cost of implementing a basic EMR can run from the tens of thousands to several million dollars, depending on the size of the organization and the scope of implementation. The high capital cost of such an investment is reason alone for numerous health care organizations to shy away from EMR implementations.*[3]

The Figures 14.1, 14.2, and 14.3 offer a glimpse into some of the elements of the comprehensive, Web-based application that is Practice Fusion.

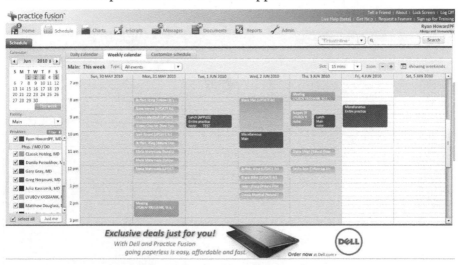

Figure 14.1   Practice Fusion view of schedule.

2.   Anderson, Chris. "Free! Why $0.00 is the future of business." Wired Magazine: 16.03. February 25, 2008. Available at www.wired.com/techbiz/it/magazine/16-03/ff_free?currentPage=all (accessed June 6, 2010).

3.   Richard Lyman et al. "Legal implications for electronic medical records." 2008 Health Law and Compliance Update. Ed. John Steiner. Chicago: Aspen Publishers + Wolters Kluwer, 2008. 9-1-9-30. Via www.wellsphere.com/healthcare-industry-policy-article/practice-fusion-and-quot-free-conomics-quot/413514.

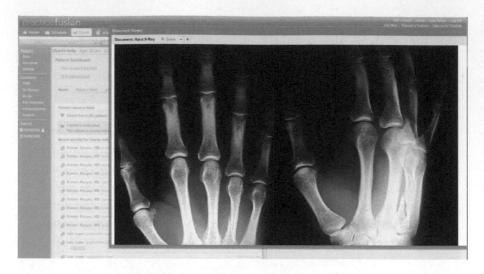

Figure 14.2   Practice Fusion online view of X-ray.

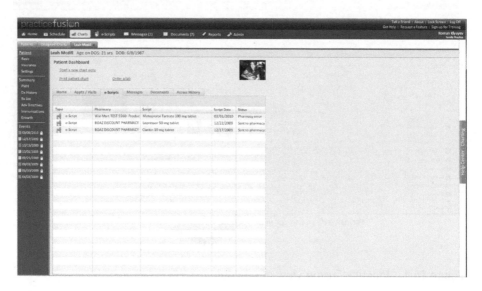

Figure 14.3   PracticeFusion e-prescription summary.

14.4   Typical User[4]

A typical user is Lynn McCallum, MD, a family practice physician in Redding, California. She became a Practice Fusion user in February 2009.

Dr. McCallum's practice is a full-service family practice office in Northern California, with one physician, one nurse practitioner, two back office personnel, a front desk receptionist and a biller. She sees all ages of patients and she does low risk obstetrics, pediatrics with immunizations, well female and well male exams, general family practice visits and in-office procedures including vasectomy, skin biopsies, circumcisions, lacerations, and so forth. Dr. McCallum describes how she Interacts with Practice Fusion:

> We use the Practice Fusion scheduler as it is convenient for both our office and our patients to have the system generate the email reminders for appointments. We have received a lot of positive feedback on that feature.
>
> I have a laptop on a small desk on rollers in each exam room. I review meds and chart on the patient as I sit in front of them. This way I can chart on my laptop and still maintain eye contact with my patient. If a referral for a consultation with a specialist is required, or a referral for an imaging study, I send a message to the MA on Practice Fusion, right in front of the patient. Often the entire note is completed before we leave the room. This minimizes my charting time at the end of the day.
>
> We use the templates provided by Practice Fusion but we also have created a variety of custom templates for our practice, which really speeds up the charting, yet also ensures a complete and thorough chart note.
>
> I have pulled up a patient file on Practice Fusion on the computer at the hospital to assist me in completing an H&P for an admission, and since Practice Fusion is web based, I can access it anywhere! I have used Practice Fusion from home when I get an after-hours patient call and I can instantly access their med list and their visit history etc to help me help them. I also chart that note right at the time they are on the phone with me; no more sticky notes and random pieces of paper that get lost!
>
> I love that the pediatric growth charts are automatically graphed when you input the vitals. I love that the Past Medical/Surgical history is completed once, then just added on to as time goes on, rather than the redundant way we had been charting in the past. We also have a cur-

---

4.   Adapted from PracticeFusion, "Case Study: Medical Office Software in Action." Available at www.practicefusion.com/pages/lynn_mccallum.html (accessed July 28, 2010).

rent medication list that we can print for the patients if needed and can easily review for completeness. I could go on . . .

Source: *www.practicefusion.com/pages/lynn_mccallum.html*

14.5   Practice Fusion Resources

- Web site: www.practicefusion.com
- White Papers:
  - Data and System Security Whitepaper: www.practicefusion.com/Whitepapers/SecurityWhitepaper.pdf
  - "Freeconomics" in Health Care: www.practicefusion.com/Whitepapers/FreeconomicsinHealthcare.pdf

14.6   Summary

Practice Fusion has demonstrated that cloud computing enables it to offer sophisticated applications to a wide audience, at extremely low cost, while respecting HIPAA privacy and security mandates. Physicians are armed with good and complete data at the point of care; this is a significant paradigm shift from traditional paper-centric processes. A cloud-based environment prepares providers by focusing on the condition rather than asking repeated questions around past medical history of the patient because they couldn't find it in a traditional paper chart or non-interoperable environment.

Chapter 15

Support and Reference Materials

Overview

This chapter begins with the full-text of the Definition of Cloud Computing adopted by the National Institute of Standards and Technology's (NIST). We then quickly review the basic definitions of cloud computing as well as its characteristics, delivery models, and deployment models. We enumerate the commonly cited benefits, articulate the main concerns, and identify pathways for mitigating the risks. We also specifically articulate security concerns and pathways for mitigating security risks. We then provide a handy series of questions to ask providers to understand common issues and questions regarding:

- Workload migration to the cloud
- Avoiding cloud lock-in
- Service Level Agreements
- Security
- Costs

Finally, we provide detailed work programs for implementing the capacity planning concepts described in Chapter 5. This chapter provides summaries and reference materials that are meant to be used together with the rest of the book.

The NIST Definition of Cloud Computing

Authors: Peter Mell and Tim Grance

Version 15, 10-7-09

National Institute of Standards and Technology, Information Technology Laboratory

Note 1: Cloud computing is still an evolving paradigm. Its definitions, use cases, underlying technologies, issues, risks, and benefits will be refined in a spirited debate by the public and private sectors. These definitions, attributes, and characteristics will evolve and change over time.

Note 2: The cloud computing industry represents a large ecosystem of many models, vendors, and market niches. This definition attempts to encompass all of the various cloud approaches.

Definition of Cloud Computing:
Cloud computing is a model for enabling convenient, on-demand network access to a shared pool of configurable computing resources (e.g., networks, servers, storage, applications, and services) that can be rapidly provisioned and released with minimal management effort or service provider interaction. This cloud model promotes availability and is composed of five essential characteristics, three service models, and four deployment models.
Essential Characteristics:

- *On-demand self-service. A consumer can unilaterally provision computing capabilities, such as server time and network storage, as needed automatically without requiring human interaction with each service's provider*
- *Broad network access. Capabilities are available over the network and accessed through standard mechanisms that promote use by heterogeneous thin or thick client platforms (e.g., mobile phones, laptops, and PDAs)*
- *Resource pooling. The provider's computing resources are pooled to serve multiple consumers using a multi-tenant model, with different physical and virtual resources dynamically assigned and reassigned according to consumer demand. There is a sense of location independence in that the customer generally has no control or knowledge over the exact location of the provided resources but may be able to specify location at a higher level of abstraction (e.g., country, state, or datacenter). Examples of resources include storage, processing, memory, network bandwidth, and virtual machines*

- *Rapid elasticity. Capabilities can be rapidly and elastically provisioned, in some cases automatically, to quickly scale out and rapidly released to quickly scale in. To the consumer, the capabilities available for provisioning often appear to be unlimited and can be purchased in any quantity at any time*
- *Measured Service. Cloud systems automatically control and optimize resource use by leveraging a metering capability at some level of abstraction appropriate to the type of service (e.g., storage, processing, bandwidth, and active user accounts). Resource usage can be monitored, controlled, and reported providing transparency for both the provider and consumer of the utilized service*

Service Models:

- *Cloud Software as a Service (SaaS). The capability provided to the consumer is to use the provider's applications running on a cloud infrastructure. The applications are accessible from various client devices through a thin client interface such as a web browser (e.g., web-based email). The consumer does not manage or control the underlying cloud infrastructure including network, servers, operating systems, storage, or even individual application capabilities, with the possible exception of limited user-specific application configuration settings*
- *Cloud Platform as a Service (PaaS). The capability provided to the consumer is to deploy onto the cloud infrastructure consumer-created or acquired applications created using programming languages and tools supported by the provider. The consumer does not manage or control the underlying cloud infrastructure including network, servers, operating systems, or storage, but has control over the deployed applications and possibly application hosting environment configurations*
- *Cloud Infrastructure as a Service (IaaS). The capability provided to the consumer is to provision processing, storage, networks, and other fundamental computing resources where the consumer is able to deploy and run arbitrary software, which can include operating systems and applications. The consumer does not manage or control the underlying cloud infrastructure but has control over operating systems, storage, deployed applications, and possibly limited control of select networking components (e.g., host firewalls)*

Deployment Models:

- *Private cloud. The cloud infrastructure is operated solely for an organization. It may be managed by the organization or a third party and may exist on premise or off premise*
- *Community cloud. The cloud infrastructure is shared by several organizations and supports a specific community that has shared concerns (e.g., mission, security requirements, policy, and compliance considerations). It may be managed by the organizations or a third party and may exist on premise or off premise*
- *Public cloud. The cloud infrastructure is made available to the general public or a large industry group and is owned by an organization selling cloud services*
- *Hybrid cloud. The cloud infrastructure is a composition of two or more clouds (private, community, or public) that remain unique entities but are bound together by standardized or proprietary technology that enables data and application portability (e.g., cloud bursting for load-balancing between clouds)*

Note: Cloud software takes full advantage of the cloud paradigm by being service oriented with a focus on statelessness, low coupling, modularity, and semantic interoperability.

The NIST Definition of Cloud Computing is public domain, although attribution to NIST is requested. It may be freely duplicated and translated. NIST is an Agency of the U.S. Department of Commerce.

15.1   Characteristics of Cloud Computing

- On-demand self-service
- Ubiquitous network access through standard Internet-enabled devices
- Pay as you go (pay only for resources you consume)
- Rapid elasticity (consumers can increase or decrease capacity on demand

15.2   Commonly Cited Benefits of Cloud Computing

- Agility (increased speed of deployment; faster to market)
- Eliminates capital expenditures (pay only for what you use)

- Reduced in-house IT staffing (reduced maintenance costs)
- Lower monthly costs
- Enables adoption of latest technology
- Encourages standardization
- Simplifies sharing
- Reduces unused (wasted) computing capacity
- Easy on-ramp to experiment with newer technologies

15.3 Most Cited Risks of Cloud Computing

- Increased delegation to third parties
- Increased data security risks
- Reduced ability to limit physical access
- Reduced control over compliance (HIPPA, GLBA, Sarbannes-Oxley, ISO 17799, other privacy and regulatory laws, export restrictions)
- Reduced control over disaster recovery control in event of a pandemic
- Fear of increased overall costs
- Fear of reduced control over performance
- Fear of reduced availability
- Heightened integration concerns with in-house legacy systems
- Risk of vendor business failure
- Risk of vendor lock-in and lack of portability

15.4   Coping Strategies for Perceived Risks Associated with Cloud Computing

Risk	Coping Strategies
Delegation	Delegation of privileges and authorization management must be explicitly set by policy and enforced by software[*]; maintain accountability even as operational responsibility is delegated.
Data Security	Ensure cloud provider has demonstrated SAS-70 attestation and ISO 27001 compliance; automatic offsite backup, SysTrust compliant.
Physical Access Control	Ensure cloud provider has demonstrated SAS-70 Type II Service Auditor's Report and ISO 27001 compliance.
Regulatory Compliance	SAS 70.[†]
Disaster Recovery Management	SAS 70[‡]-compliant data center. redundant service providers delivering high data rate connectivity (10GBbps) or greater. Use secure facility with high availability via UPS and diesel generator failover power. Maintain backups are maintained online and accessible during the entire retention period and retrievable in accordance with SLA.
Cost Control	Enforce maximum usage limits at each level of delegation for best cost effectiveness.
Performance Management	Ensure adequate measurement of usage and business activity and adequate projection of requirements.[**]
Availability	Ensure adequate SLA agreements for all aspects of the application, not just an instance Verify the cloud provider's ability, resources and processes to ensure the adherence to the SLAs.
Legacy Integration	Use IP Sec and VPN to connect cloud applications to legacy applications.
Vendor Business Failure	Ensure portability; review SAS 70 Report for "Going Concern" reservation.
Vendor Lock-in	Use software such as Eucalyptus, which promotes usability on multiple cloud providers and ensure portability.[††]

[*]   See "Securing Privilege Delegation in Public and Private Cloud Computing Infrastructure," www.beyondtrust.com/WhitePapers/PDFS/wp043_Cloud_Computing.pdf (accessed June 29, 2010).

†   *"Each entity needs to determine its own risk in the event of an emergency that would result in a loss of operations. A contingency plan may involve highly complex processes in one processing site, or simple manual processes in another. The contents of any given contingency plan will depend upon the nature and configuration of the entity devising it."* The Department of Health and Human Services, 45 CFR Parts 160, 162, and 164, Health Insurance Reform: Security Standards; For Final Rule, see: www.cms.hhs.gov/SecurityStandard/Downloads/securityfinalrule.pdf

‡   AppAssure's Cloud Recovery Service gives organizations of all sizes the ability to easily and affordably ensure continuous data protection and business continuity in the face of any outage from a single server failure to a total catastrophe. (www.appassure.com/)

**   See discussion in Chapter 5.

††   See detailed discussion in Chapter 4

15.5   Threats to Security in the Cloud

Threats to security include:

- *Failures in Provider Security*
  Cloud providers control the hardware and the hypervisors on which data is stored and applications are run. Failures can threaten customers
- *Attacks by Other Customers*
  In the cloud, the entire infrastructure is shared among multiple customers. If proper isolation is not maintained, and the barriers between customers break down, one customer can potentially access another customer's data or interfere with another customer's applications. If one customer's environment is breached due to an outside attack, the effects of that attack must be contained within that customer's environment
- *Availability and Reliability Issues*
  Cloud data centers like enterprise data centers are usually safe and secure. However, outages do occur. Also, the cloud is only usable through the Internet, so reliability and availability of the Internet and access to it are essential
- *Legal and Regulatory Issues*
  The virtual, international nature of cloud computing raises many legal and regulatory issues. Few of them are being sorted at the time this book is written
- *Perimeter Security Model Broken*
  Many organizations use a perimeter security model with strong security at the perimeter of the enterprise network. This model has been weakening over the years with outsourcing and a highly mobile workforce. Cloud computing strikes its death knell. The

cloud is certainly outside the perimeter of enterprise control, but it will now store critical data and applications

- *Integrating Provider and Customer Security Systems*
A unified directory and other components of security architecture such as automated provisioning, incident detection and response, are required. Does the cloud provider integrate with these or rely on manual provisioning and uncoordinated responses?

15.6   Reasons for Capacity Planning

Capacity planning provides decision support data for IT:

1.   Prepare initial and ongoing budgets and cost controls.

2.   Size the application to the service provider's various available machine configurations so the least cost is achieved.

3.   Determine points when capacity should be added. If added capacity is managed autonomically, ensure there are constraints so that runaway additions are prevented.

4.   Ensure that costs per business unit of work stay within the boundaries set by profitability.

5.   Prevent unplanned expenses.

6.   Determine the practical capacity— for each offered real or virtual system configuration, and instance type, where "practical capacity" is defined as the range within which the SLAs are met.

7.   Determine application scalability and when and where bottle-necks may emerge as demand increases.

8.   Determine how much capacity is available for vertical scaling within each offered configuration before another instance must be added for horizontal scaling.

15.7   Step-by-Step Work Plan for Capacity Planning with Amazon EC2

Capacity planning in the cloud exists on two levels, physical and virtual. Physical involves selecting the appropriate instance type, with appropriate resources (e.g., number of processors, processor type, memory, disk capacity and power, etc.). Virtual instances with the selected characteristics can be provisioned and deprovisioned. In the public cloud, the cloud PaaS vendor is generally responsible for preventing thrashing (excessive paging) by limiting the number of virtual instances running simultaneously. In a private cloud, that's usually your job.

EC2-specific steps are shown in italics; the concepts are applicable generally to cloud computing.

For each step of the work plan, we provide samples of the required information and sample results of analysis. Prices mentioned were based on prices obtained from http://aws.amazon.com/ec2/ in effect on August 9, 2010; it's a competitive market and price improvements are likely over time.

The work plan follows.

1. Obtain and document business activity requirements and the Service Level Agreements (SLA) they necessitate.

   The only SLA commitment Amazon now makes is 99.95% availability per EC2 region. At the time of this writing, there are four geographically dispersed Amazon EC2 regions in the U.S. Higher availability can be obtained by spreading the acquired instances across multiple regions and spreading the work among the regions.

   We recommend that customers seek at least the following additional SLA categories from cloud computing vendors:

   a. Deployment latency by instance type

   b. Request response time

   c. Number of network connections that can be provided

   d. Speed of network connections

   Businesses always have additional service level requirements, beyond simple platform availability, which are typically defined and driven by the type of business activity.

The following is a simple example of activity types for a business and their typically associated service level needs. The capacity planner's job is to ensure that the procured EC2 instance quantities and capacities provide the service levels required by the business.

Activity	Peak Hour Rate	Required Service Level
Log In or Out	1,800	<5 sec./request
Shop	50,000	<1 sec./request
Check order status	500	<5 sec./request
"Hot" business reports	0.25	<4 hrs./report
Business reports	20/day	<24 hrs./report

2. From periods of actual critical business activity levels or the forecasts of such peaks, develop one or more snapshots (measurements) of baseline business activity and the related IT utilization levels.

    The baseline snapshots of activity levels are used to determine which EC2 instance features the enterprise requires.

3. Incorporate results as needed from application development, change management, load tests, and performance engineering.

    Where data from an existing application is unavailable, then the performance and capacity sizing metrics may be obtained from the other areas listed above in this step.

4. Obtain business activity forecasts and derive from them a summary by function required for supporting them.

    For example:

Activity	Peak Hour Rate in Jan. 2012	Peak Hour Rate in Sep. 2012
Log In or Out	2,700	3,600
Shop	75,000	100,000
Check order status	750	1,000
"Hot" business reports	0.37	0.50
Business reports	25/day	30/day

5. Determine the competing cloud computing vendors' system configuration options and associated prices, and compare to prices of do-it-yourself alternatives if this is an option.

    Amazon EC2 offers three types of instances, on-demand, reserved, and spot, with eight levels of prices based on the compute capacity of the instance. On August 9, 2010, prices of the three types of *instances from http://aws.amazon.com/ec2/ ranged from a low of $0.031/hour for a Linux/UNIX small spot instance, to a high of $1.16/hour for an extra large high-CPU on-demand Windows instance. The processor capacity is provided in EC2 Compute Units (ECU) from one ECU up to twenty-six ECU maximum. One ECU provides the equivalent CPU capacity of a 1.0–1.2 GHz 2007 Opteron or 2007 Xeon processor. The additional options of the configurations include: (a) the number of virtual processor cores, from one to eight, (b) memory, from 1.7 to 68.4 GB, (c) local storage, from 160 to 1,690 GB, and (d) Linux, UNIX, and Windows operating systems. The last set of options is the most involved, because it involves the application- specific configuration. EC2 offers many predefined Amazon Machine Images (AMIs) for specific needs like databases, batch processing, Web hosting, application development, video streaming, and application servers.*

6. *Service level needs drive the compute capacity and the instance type. For example, the highest required service levels may only be guaranteed by procuring a sufficient number of reserved instances.*

Processing, which can be finished hours or even days later, can be satisfied at the lowest cost by procuring spot instances. On-demand instances of appropriate capacity can be employed to accommodate spikes in demand.

Perform capacity analysis and recommend the required mix of Amazon EC2 instances by type. Some of the ways the capacity analysis may be performed include spreadsheet-based custom-developed tools, analytic modeling, or simulation tools. Following are sample results from a capacity plan based on the configuration options offered by Amazon EC2.

Instance Type and Capacity	Instances Needed in Jan. 2012	Instances Needed in Sep. 2012
Reserved High-CPU Extra Large	2	2
Reserved High Memory Extra Large	20	28
Reserved Standard Large	60	80
On-demand Standard Large	180	240
Spot Extra Large	8	12

7. Monitor SLAs and instance utilization levels against forecasts, and manage the scaling up and down (provisioning and deprovisioning) of instances based on business workload demands and within defined constraints.

    Amazon EC2 offers three services for the monitoring and management of instances:

    a. Amazon CloudWatch aggregates and stores monitoring data such as CPU utilization, disks reads and writes, memory utilization, network traffic, request counts, and requests latency at a cost of $0.015 per instance hour.

    b. Auto Scaling adds instances during demand peaks and scales instances back when demand drops off. Auto Scaling can be enabled by CloudWatch at no additional cost above the CloudWatch cost per hour.

    c. *Elastic Load Balancing automatically distributes the incoming application traffic across the available instances, and costs $0.025 per Elastic Load Balancer hour, plus $0.008 per gigabyte of data processed by the Elastic Load Balancer.*

    These three Amazon services have competition from other vendors, and capacity planners may decide to develop their own approaches as well.

    Hyperic Inc. (www.hyperic.com), offers Hyperic HQ for EC2 for performance monitoring and management of a customer's Amazon EC2 instances.

    A number of vendors also offer traditional capacity-planning services as a SaaS product. The choice should be determined by the customer's requirements. As of this writing, the SaaS capacity-planning products all offer mathematical trending as the main approach for forecasting. If the customer has discreet forecasts for various business applications, then the capacity planners must ensure that the tools or services are capable of any type of "what if" analysis with such forecasts.

8. Report as needed to ensure SLAs are met and exceptions detected before they can cause business activity failure.

    The typical set of reports should include at least the following:

    ▪ Business activity actual rate versus forecasts

- Actual costs versus the budget and the forecast
- High level summary of all cloud computing components utilized
- *All* the measured SLA mandated service attributes

15.8   Cloud Capacity Planning and Classical Approach Compared

- The preceding capacity planning work plan for a cloud computing service offering is not different from classical analysis in any way, which may alter how the activity has to be performed
- Capacity planning for cloud computing is easier because all the available options are clearly listed and priced by the providers. Since the tasks required to perform the analysis are the same, an experienced capacity planner does not confront any learning curve
- While new tools may emerge claiming cloud-computing-specific awareness, we do not believe that a tool requires such "awareness." The IT Service Management (ITSM) critical success factors all remain the same

15.9   SLA Failures and Potential Solutions

SLA failures occur when an application performs poorly and fails one or more SLAs, or when the application hangs at various stages within the business unit of work. The causes and potential remedies are the same for both.

Typical Causes, Manifestations and Remedies for SLA Failures

Resource	SLA Failure Manifestations and Remedies
Processor (CPU)	Manifestations: long CPU queue and service times, high utilization, excessive application response time.
	Remedies: (1) reduce CPU requirements, (2) redistribute or reschedule work, (3) buy more CPUs, (4) buy faster CPUs
	Manifestation: the mix of contracted instance types does not scale up fast enough to prevent SLA failures, or scale down at a rate which most cuts costs.
	Remedy: Perform analysis of all the contracted instance types and determine if a change in the mix of types is required, or the vendor must improve the time required for an instance to be brought online and made available to run production work.

Memory (RAM)	Manifestations: paging and task swapping are elongating all service times. Remedies: (1) reduce memory requirements, and/or (2) increase memory
Disks	Manifestations: read/write (R/W) input/output (I/O) operations are numerous and/or take a long time. Remedies: (1) eliminate/minimize I/O operations via data in memory techniques such as use of memcache, a free, open source, high-performance, distributed memory object caching system, intended for use in speeding up dynamic Web applications by alleviating database load. (2) buy faster disk subsystems, (3) buy more disks, (4) isolate and protect performance of key files.
Network	Manifestations: data transmission times are often the largest component of total service time. Remedies: (1) buy faster connectivity, (2) buy more connections, (3) review and redesign applications to reduce "chattiness" and data received/sent so total load on network is reduced, and (4) add data compression for network traffic.

15.10 Coping Strategies for Security Threats

Threat	Coping Strategies
Failures in Provider Security	People are the greatest threat. Countermeasures include screening, training, and monitoring of provider personnel. Physical and network security for cloud data centers are also essential.
Attacks by Other Customers	Virtualization (using a hypervisor) and network separation (via firewalls, VLANs, and/or encryption).
Physical Access Control	Demonstrated SAS-70 Type II Service Auditor's Report and ISO 27001 compliance
Legal and Regulatory Compliance	Use of Self Encrypting Drive (SED) eliminates concern about loss or theft of a hard drive or backup media. Software encryption provides similar protection, but with higher complexity, lower performance due to higher processor needs, and less security.
Breakage of Perimeter Security	Eliminate perimeter-based security model and rely on alternate approaches. Security must be integrated with your existing enterprise security model and your internal monitoring systems.

Security Can't Be Verified	The cloud provider's (CP's) customers must be able to:
	Verify integrity of the CP's machines.
	Verify identity of machines as well as users, administrators, and cloud customers.
	Verify kinds of network security measures being used.

15.11 General Questions to Ask When Migrating to the Cloud

- Does the vendor support the operating system(s) and programming languages that you require?
- Which database management systems are required? Is there a vendor-maintained "image" that supports your DBMS?
- How much memory and processing power is required? Does the vendor provide sufficiently powerful machines, and is there room to grow?
- Do you choose a private, public, or hybrid cloud? What impels your decision?
- Do the management tools you have in place support management in the cloud? Are there upgrades available? If not, you need to select one or more of the tools described in this book
- How rapidly do your needs change, and can your vendor provision and de-provision fast enough?
- Does the vendor's SLA meet your needs?
- Is your auditor satisfied with the vendor's documentation of its compliance with SAS 70 and ISO 27001? Is SysTrust Certification available?

Questions for Avoiding Lock-In[1]

- *Application*—Do you own the application that manages your data, or do you need another tool to move your data or application?
- *Web services*—Does your application make use of third-party Web services that you would have to find or for which you would need to build alternatives?
- *Development and run-time environment*—Does your application run in a proprietary runtime environment and/or is it coded in a

---

1.   Adapted from RightScale. "Avoiding Lock-In." Available at www.rightscale.com/products/advantages/avoiding-lock-in.php (accessed July 29, 2010).

proprietary development environment? Would you need to retrain programmers and rewrite your application to move to a different cloud?

- *Programming language*—Does your application make use of a proprietary language, or language version? Would you need to look for new programmers to rewrite your application to move?

- *Data model*—Is your data stored in a proprietary or hard-to-reproduce data model or storage system? Can you continue to use the same type of database or data storage organization if you moved, or do you need to transform all your data (and perhaps the applications accessing it)?

- *Data*—Can you actually bring your data with you, and if so, in what form? Can you get everything exported raw, or only in certain slices or views?

- *Log files and analytics*—Do you own your history and/or metrics and can you move it to a new cloud, or do you need to start from scratch?

- *Operating system and system software*—Do your system administrators control the operating system platform, the versions of libraries, and tools, so you can move the know-how and operational procedures from one cloud to another?

15.12 Vendor Questions About Security for Cloud Providers (CP)[2]

15.12.1 Data Security (At Rest)

- *How does the CP secure data at rest (on storage devices)?* The best practice for securing data at rest is cryptographic encryption on storage devices and assurance that data is destroyed when no longer needed by deleting the encryption key

15.12.2 Data Security (In Transit)

- *How does the CP secure data in transit (within the cloud and on its way to and from the cloud)?*
  Data in transit should always be encrypted, authenticated, and

---

2. Adapted from Steve Hanna and Jesus Molina, "Cloud Security Questions?" Cloud Computing Journal, March 24, 2010. Available at http://cloudcomputing.sys-con.com/node/1330353 (accessed July 29, 2010).

integrity protected. Reliable standard protocols (e.g., TLS and IPsec) and algorithms (e.g., AES) should be used to ensure security and interoperability

15.12.3   Authentication

- *How does the CP authenticate users?*
  Passwords and stronger forms of authentication such as certificates and tokens should be employed, as well as standards such as LDAP and SAML

15.12.4   Separation Between the Customers

- *How are one customer's data and applications separated from other customers (who may be hackers or competitors)?*
  Each customer should use a separate virtual machine (VM) and virtual network. A hypervisor enforces separation between VMs and therefore between customers. Virtual networks are implemented using standard techniques such as VLANs (Virtual Local Area Networks), VPLS (Virtual Private LAN Service), or VPNs (Virtual Private Networks)
  Lumping all customers' programs and data in one big application instance and using custom-built code to prevent customers from seeing each other's data is a fragile and ill-advised approach

15.12.5   Cloud Legal and Regulatory Issues

- *How does the CP address legal and regulatory issues related to CC?*
  Laws and regulations vary from one jurisdiction to another. The CP must provide strong policies and practices that address legal and regulatory issues such as data security and export, compliance, auditing, data retention and destruction, and legal discovery (especially considering that one physical server may contain several customers' data). Each customer must have its legal and regulatory experts inspect CP policies and practices to make sure that they are adequate for the customer's needs

15.12.6   Incident Response

- *How does the CP respond to incidents and how are customers involved?*

CPs must have a well-documented incident response process that includes responding to affected customers. CPs must demonstrate the ability to detect trends which may cause outages, detect incidents, minimize their effects, and promptly inform customers of status. The attributes of incident response process are also essential elements of SLAs with the service providers

- *How will the customer and the vendor respond to incidents in the cloud?*
  Some responses may be automated with defined constraints of the range and scope of actions. Other will require immediate involvement of people from the CP and customer

- *Who is charged with responding for each type of incident?*
  Incidents by type must be mapped to who will respond and even when and how to escalate if the incident remains unexplained

- *Can you conduct forensic investigations to determine what caused an incident?*
  For each type of incident, ensure that enough of the data is preserved with long enough retention periods that the forensic investigation can review it at a later time

15.12.7   Data Export Restrictions

- Is export of data out of a jurisdiction restricted?
- If multiple jurisdictions are present, which jurisdiction's rules apply in case of conflict with data export?
- Who is liable for losses due to errors such as security breaches?

15.12.8   Questions to Ask Potential Cloud Providers About Costs

- What processor, disk storage and memory is provided in the base system? What other instances are available?
- How are IP addresses allocated? Is allocation elastic? What are the charges?
- What are the costs are for uploading data into the vendor's cloud?
- What are costs for downloading the data from the vendor's cloud?
- What are costs for data transfer between instances in different geographical regions of the cloud service provider?
- What are the costs for maintaining image and database persistence?

- How quickly can system resources be requisitioned, and how quickly can resources be released to avoid additional charges?
- Are high-memory and high-CPU instances available without charges for other, potentially unnecessary resources?
- Are reserved instances available at reduced rates in return for a longer-term commitment?
- Can instances be allocated in various geographical regions (for improved availability) and still be controlled centrally?
- Are nonguaranteed (spot) resources available at discounted prices? If yes, what do they cost?
- Are there automated mechanisms to limit charges?
- Can load balancing be performed dynamically and automatically without human intervention?
- What is the cost for load-balancing?
- What monitoring is available and what are the related costs?
- What are the charges for instances requiring specific licensing (e.g., Windows, Oracle)?
- What consulting services are available, and what are their prices?
- What support services are available?
- What support services are offered as standard, and what level(s) of support are available as premium services?

Index

T - #0101 - 101024 - C0 - 234/156/19 [21] - CB - 9781439830826 - Gloss Lamination